State Politics and the Affordable Care Act

AF695285

After a great deal of discussion and debate across all levels of government, President Obama signed the Affordable Care Act (ACA) into law in March 2010. Since President Trump's election into office, the ACA has stayed in the headlines. Trump has continued to call for the replacement and repeal of the ACA, and several efforts have spawned in both the House and the Senate to accomplish this goal. Unlike welfare reform, which was generally embraced by all states, the ACA has proved very divisive in some states, with some states actively seeking to block implementation. Alternative solutions continue to prove elusive.

To better understand the major factors driving decision-making process and state-level dynamics influencing state support or opposition of the ACA, this book examines the initial implementation through established support and opposition factors across four states: Alabama, Michigan, California, and New Hampshire. The choices made by states are a direct consequence of long-term forces and the choices made at the national level.

State Politics and the Affordable Care Act will be of interest to scholars researching in public administration, policy formulation and implementation, and policy analysis.

John C. Morris is Professor of Public Administration in the School of Public Service, and Professor of Political Science at Old Dominion University. He holds a PhD from Auburn University and has studied collaboration and public–private partnerships for more than 20 years. Dr. Morris has published widely in public administration and public policy.

Martin K. Mayer received his PhD from the School of Public Service at Old Dominion University in the fall of 2016. Martin's research interests include healthcare policy, local government innovation, and environmental policy. His work has been published in *Social Science Quarterly*, *Politics and Policy*, *The Social Science Journal*, and *Politics and the Life Sciences*.

Robert C. Kenter holds an MPA from Troy University, Alabama, and a PhD from the School of Public Service, Old Dominion University, Norfolk Virginia. His research interest includes collaboration, privatization, and southern politics. His work has appeared in several journals and edited books.

Luisa M. Lucero graduated with a PhD from the School of Public Service at Old Dominion University in 2017. Her dissertation focused on state-level health policy design, and she is currently working on additional research projects examining health policy.

Routledge Research in Public Administration and Public Policy

Community Development and Public Administration Theory
Promoting Democratic Principles to Improve Communities
Edited by Ashley E. Nickels and Jason D. Rivera

Contextualizing Compliance in the Public Sector
Individual Motivations, Social Processes, and Institutional Design
Saba Siddiki, Salvador Espinosa, and Tanya Heikkila

The Politics of Fracking
Regulatory Policy and Local Community Responses to Environmental Concerns
Sarmistha R. Majumdar

The Data Economy
Implications from Singapore
Sree Kumar, Warren B. Chik, See-Kiong Ng and Sin Gee Teo

Corruption Prevention and Governance in Hong Kong
Ian Scott and Ting Gong

Judicializing the Administrative State
The Rise of the Independent Regulatory Commissions in the United States, 1883–1937
Hiroshi Okayama

State Politics and the Affordable Care Act
Choices and Decisions
John C. Morris, Martin K. Mayer, Robert C. Kenter and Luisa M. Lucero

For more information about this series, please visit: www.routledge.com/Routledge-Research-in-Public-Administration-and-Public-Policy/book-series/RRPAPP

State Politics and the Affordable Care Act

Choices and Decisions

John C. Morris, Martin K. Mayer, Robert C. Kenter and Luisa M. Lucero

Routledge
Taylor & Francis Group
NEW YORK AND LONDON

First published 2020
by Routledge
52 Vanderbilt Avenue, New York, NY 10017

and by Routledge
2 Park Square, Milton Park, Abingdon, Oxon, OX14 4RN

Routledge is an imprint of the Taylor & Francis Group, an informa business

First issued in paperback 2021

© 2020 Taylor & Francis

The right of John C. Morris, Martin K. Mayer, Robert C. Kenter and Luisa M. Lucero to be identified as authors of this work has been asserted by them in accordance with sections 77 and 78 of the Copyright, Designs and Patents Act 1988.

All rights reserved. No part of this book may be reprinted or reproduced or utilised in any form or by any electronic, mechanical, or other means, now known or hereafter invented, including photocopying and recording, or in any information storage or retrieval system, without permission in writing from the publishers.

Trademark notice: Product or corporate names may be trademarks or registered trademarks, and are used only for identification and explanation without intent to infringe.

Library of Congress Cataloging-in-Publication Data
A catalog record for this book has been requested

ISBN: 978-1-138-62409-2 (hbk)
ISBN: 978-1-03-209196-9 (pbk)
ISBN: 978-0-429-46103-3 (ebk)

Typeset in Times New Roman
by Apex CoVantage, LLC

This book is dedicated to Molly, Addison, Elizabeth, Brady, and Sebastian—the next generation.

Contents

Tables

Abbreviations

ACA	Affordable Care Act
ADOI	Alabama Department of Insurance
BCBSAL	Blue Cross/Blue Shield of Alabama
CBO	Congressional Budget Office
CHIP	Children's Health Insurance Program
CHRT	Center for Healthcare Research and Transformation
CMS	Centers for Medicare and Medicaid Services
FMAP	Federal medical assistance percentages
FPL	Federal poverty level
GDP	Gross domestic product
HHS	U.S. Department of Health and Human Services
MCPP	Mackinac Center for Public Policy
NFIB	National Federation of Independent Business
NHHP	New Hampshire Health Plan
NHID	New Hampshire Insurance Department
PPACA	Patient Protection and Affordable Care Act
SBM-FP	State-based marketplace federal platform
SCOTUS	Supreme Court of the United States
SPM	State–Partnership Marketplace
UAW	United Automobile Workers

Acknowledgments

This project began as a series of conference papers and journal articles that sought to explain state implementation of the Affordable Care Act (ACA). We began to explore this topic in 2015; at that time, the initial implementation of the ACA was in full swing, yet there was much uncertainty about the future of the ACA. Nonetheless, we believed there was an interesting story to be told, and we worked to produce manuscripts that analyzed the policy activity associated with the act. Some of that work was published, and other versions were abandoned in favor of new approaches. This early work was subject to the scrutiny of panel discussants, audience participants, anonymous journal reviewers, and journal editors, and we thank them all for their collective contributions to this project. We also wish to acknowledge the contributions of Lien Nguyen, PhD candidate at Old Dominion University, for her assistance with the final production of this manuscript. We are also indebted to our editor at Routledge, Natalja Mortensen, the Editorial Assistant for Politics at Routledge, Charlie Baker, and our copyeditor, Wendy Jo Dymond, without whom this manuscript would be a much less perfect product. Finally, we wish to thank our families for their love and support during this project.

1 Why Do States Matter? Contemporary State Policy Choice

Perhaps no single piece of legislation in modern American history has been more contentious, and more polarizing, than the Patient Protection and Affordable Care Act of 2010. More commonly known as the Affordable Care Act (ACA), it is also widely known as Obamacare. The ACA was the signature piece of legislation of President Barack Obama's first term, and fulfilled a campaign promise made during the 2008 presidential election cycle. As we will see later in this volume, health care reform was not a new policy demand, nor was it a partisan demand—health care reform had been on the national policy agenda for many years, and policymakers of all persuasions, ideologies, and parties had sought solutions to a range of identified "problems" with the health care system.

The contentiousness did not end with successful passage in 2010; indeed, the legislation became a rallying cry, particularly for Republicans at the national level, as they mounted a vigorous campaign against the ACA. The ACA was a major campaign issue in the 2012 elections; although Obama was reelected by a fairly comfortable margin, the Democratic Party lost control of both the U.S. House of Representatives and the U.S. Senate. Many of the ads berated incumbent Democrats for supporting the ACA. After the election the House lost no time in voting on legislation that would repeal the ACA, an action they would repeat more than thirty times over the next four years. However, President Obama regularly threatened to veto any attempt to repeal the ACA, and without a veto-proof majority, such votes were largely symbolic in nature. Attempts to repeal the ACA were reborn after the election of President Trump in 2016; one of the first actions of the new Congress in 2017 was to attempt again to repeal the ACA. The measure passed easily in the House along a party-line vote. However, the measure failed in the Senate by one vote when Senator John McCain (R-AZ) shocked his party (and many others) by voting against repeal, thus defeating the attempt. Even so, it is notable that his vote was not so much a vote in favor of the ACA but, rather, a combination of the lack of a suitable replacement bill and his disdain for congressional "bullies" (Huetteman, 2018). Although legislative attention has moved on to other issues, most observers do not believe the effort to repeal the ACA is yet settled; efforts to repeal, defund, and challenge in court continue.

As many policy instruments tend to be in the U.S. context, the ACA was ultimately an incremental change from an existing health care system. In spite of early debate centered around the option of a single-payer system, the ACA simply built on the existing combination of private insurance, Medicaid, and Medicare to deliver and pay for health care services. Still, the ACA did include some new and different policy tools, including the use of an individual mandate for citizens to purchase health insurance. The net result was a boisterous, contentious, and, at times, nasty debate over the ACA; moreover, the national debate was very much centered around party and ideological divides. Even some eight years after its passage, the ACA elicits visceral reactions among many, and it continues to serve as a touchstone for partisan politics.

Because the ACA is incremental in nature, it did not appear out of thin air. It is both ironic and a sign of our ideological divide that the policy model upon which the ACA is based is drawn from a program implemented in Massachusetts several years before the passage of the ACA, at a time when the governor of Massachusetts was a Republican named Mitt Romney. Romney would go to great lengths to criticize in successive presidential campaigns the very model he championed as governor of Massachusetts. Moreover, observers on both sides of the ideological divide generally agree that the Massachusetts program has been a success.

Another important feature of the ACA was that the legislation gave states the authority to make several important decisions regarding the implementation of the ACA. In a nutshell, the purpose of this book is to look more closely at the decisions made by states. Some states wholeheartedly embraced the ACA and moved swiftly to implement the legislation. Other states moved just as swiftly to oppose or block implementation, and still other states seemed to dither and avoid making firm decisions. Previous research into this question (Jacobs & Callaghan, 2013; Mayer, Kenter, & Morris, 2015) has approached the topic from a 50-state perspective, seeking patterns that can explain overall state choice, and to identify the most important factors in state decisions. Indeed, the results of that research are not, at first glance, surprising—it's politics, stupid! Variables representing party control, political ideology, and partisanship at the state level tend to be the most important factors in these 50-state models, and they explain the bulk of the variation across states. But, just as important, these variables fail to explain a not insignificant fraction of the variance in the 50-state models. If this is the case, there must be other factors, not otherwise accounted for, that help us better understand these state decisions. So, why did states make the choices they did? This is the question that drives the research presented in this volume.

THE ACA AGAINST THE BACKDROP OF FEDERALISM

The choices provided to states under the ACA are not accidental; they are very much the product of existing norms and definitions of federalism in the U.S. Our current understanding of federalism is a product of the presidency of Ronald Reagan and what is often termed "Reagan federalism" (see Grant, 1995; Conlan, 1988; Nathan & Doolittle, 1984). When he was elected in 1980, Reagan promised a new approach to the relationship between the national government and the states. Based loosely in a redefinition of states' rights, Reagan federalism includes a reduction in federal requirements placed on states, the elimination of unfunded mandates, and an overarching belief that the national government is too big and too powerful. The goal is to reduce the size and cost of the national government by giving more authority to states and reducing the presence and reach of the national government across a wide range of policy arenas. As a former governor of California, Reagan had been an early and vocal critic of Nixon's revenue sharing program (California was a net loser in the program), and Reagan ultimately terminated the program during his first term.

Although several pieces of legislation enacted during the Reagan years can serve as examples of this modified relationship between the national governments and the states, two programs, in particular, help set the stage for the structure of state choice in the ACA. While these two programs are in very different policy areas, the structure of each in terms of state choice provides for a firm foundation of comparison. A brief glance at their common characteristics helps place the structure of the ACA in context and provides a framework through which policy activity in the ACA might be viewed.

The Water Quality Act of 1987

The Water Quality Act (WQA) of 1987 is the name given to the act that reauthorized the original Clean Water Act, passed in 1972. The Clean Water Act (CWA) was, in many respects, a landmark piece of legislation. It became the second major mandate for the then-new Environmental Protection Agency (after the Clean Air act of 1970), and fundamentally changed the ways in which the nation addressed wastewater. The CWA set national standards for clean water and allowed for the possibility that states could become responsible for enforcement of those standards (see Crotty, 1987). Moreover, the CWA provided funding through the Construction Grants program to provide funds directly to communities to help offset the costs of compliance with the national standards.

To the Reagan administration, the CWA was a prime example of overreach by the national government. Under the CWA, Congress chose which communities would receive federal funding, thus removing state governments from the decision process. In the years leading up to the passage of the WQA in 1987, the Reagan philosophy of minimal federal involvement meant that the replacement for the original CWA would have to take a different approach to both funding and enforcement. The result was an act that provides seed money to states to create and operate revolving fund programs, thus placing decisions about the distribution of public funds firmly in the hands of states. Under the WQA, states have the authority not only to make loans as they see fit but also to structure and operate the state program as they see fit. States can choose to leverage funds to increase the corpus of the fund, they can choose the loan recipients, they can operate the program as a standalone program or commingle the program with other like programs (state infrastructure banks, the Drinking Water State Revolving Fund [SRF] program, etc.), and they can set the interest rate and other loan terms charged to loan recipients. Previous research reports that states have taken full advantage of these choices.

The Personal Responsibility and Work Opportunity Reconciliation Act of 1996

More commonly referred to as Temporary Assistance for Needy Families (TANF), the Personal Responsibility and Work Opportunity Reconciliation Act (PRWORA) serves as another, more recent, example of policy models that fit the Reagan federalism model. Prior to the passage of TANF, the national welfare program was the Aid for Families with Dependent Children (AFDC), a federal entitlement program enacted as Title IV of the Social Security Act of 1935. Originally called just Aid for Dependent Children (ADC), it was renamed in 1962 and became AFDC. The original program allowed states the choice to participate, although in the roughly 60 years between the creation of the ADC and TANF, most states participated in some manner. A provision approved in 1962 allowed states to seek waivers from the secretary of health, education, and welfare (later Health and Human Services [HHS]) to operate state programs that differed from the national program. While both the Reagan and Bush administrations approved waivers, it is notable that the Clinton administration approved waiver requests from forty states in the period from 1993 to mid-1996 (HHS, n.d., p. 8). By the 1990s, Reagan federalism had firmly taken hold at both the national and state levels.

The TANF legislation replaced the federal program with a block grant program that gave states annual grants based on a funding formula. States were then free to create a program within fairly broad bounds within the law (Soss, Schram, Vartanian, & O'Brien, 2001), including the length of time recipients could receive program benefits, the amount of money paid in benefits, and several other choices. In many respects, the model of TANF is perhaps an appropriate model for the ACA, enacted some 14 years later. In both programs, the national government provides funding and states create and operate state programs based on a range of choices available in the program. States are not required to participate in all aspects of both programs, but both programs contain incentives to encourage state participation.

These are but two examples of what was, in many ways, a fundamental redefinition of the relationship between the national and state governments. Like any other defined relationship, Reagan federalism contains tradeoffs. While Reagan federalism provides much greater state choice, it does so at the expense of national policy leadership. The national government can incent desired behaviors, but states are free to ignore those incentives as they see fit. Indeed, states can make policy choices on the basis of whatever set of factors they choose. This is probably most apparent in terms of programs that are designed to meet certain needs: One might think that states would structure their programs to meet identified program needs, yet it often appears that explanations of state need provide little explanatory power in the quest to understand state choice—such is the case in health care reform, for example. In many senses, Reagan federalism has given testament to Yehezkel Dror's (1968) observation that states are policy laboratories. Under Reagan federalism, states are truly free to explore, design, implement, and administer unique programs under a larger umbrella of minimal federal guidance. This leads us directly back to our question: Why do states make the choices they do?

WHY STUDY STATE CHOICE?

The federalism issues described earlier draw our attention directly to the choices made by states in the context of federalism. While some national policy initiatives provide little discretion to states in terms of implementation, even the most restrictive national policies generally require states to make implementation choices. As state discretion grows, so does the potential range of state action. Grant programs are illustrative of this point: categorical grants provide little state discretion; block grants allow a great deal of discretion; revenue sharing (no longer used in the U.S.) provides almost unlimited state discretion.

In many ways, this study is as much about state decision-making and state discretion as it is about health care. The contentious nature of the health care debate has served to place state choice directly in the crosshairs of both public and scholarly attention, and states have not disappointed in their responses. The debate in states over the ACA serves as a vehicle, in a sense, to talk about state choice. If Dror (1968) is correct, we must move beyond generalized, deductive analyses and seek specific, nuanced, and relevant explanations of state choice. The state choices present in the ACA process provide a rich opportunity to study these differences between states and to examine the factors within states that led states to certain choices and outcomes. Understanding these factors and conditions can not only aid our understanding of past decision but provide insight into future decision-making as well.

Furthermore, the specific mix of constraints and opportunities within a state is not entirely static. Some elements, such as political history or political culture, only change over periods best measured in decades or centuries. Economically poor states can improve their economic well-being, but rapid change in this regard is, at best, rare. On the other hand, other factors that serve to constrain or broaden state choice may appear unexpectedly, even as states cope with known factors. An unexpected budget windfall, for instance, can create new opportunities for program expenditures, while a budget shortfall has the opposite effect. These conditions are difficult to predict but nonetheless alter the choices available to state decision-makers.

Finally, state policymakers live in a virtual "space" in which trade-offs are an inevitable element of the task. When considering whether to spend scarce state dollars on Medicaid expansion, for example, state policymakers must balance this choice against policy demands for school funding, new roads, law enforcement, environmental protection, welfare-to-work programs, and a host of equally pressing and reasonable demands. Against a backdrop of public opinion that eschews tax increases for public programs, state policymakers are faced with increasing demands for increasingly scarce revenues. A state with a billion-dollar shortfall in its current Medicaid program is unlikely to consider an expansion of the program that might encumber even more scarce state funds in the future.[1] Likewise, a state faced with crumbling bridges may decide that public safety in the transportation system is a higher priority than health care. Conversely, a state that finds itself with higher-than-expected revenues could decide to make investments not possible with fewer dollars available. Policymakers must balance these priorities against needs and demands, all within a context of party politics, citizen preferences, political culture, and state history.

These trade-offs are inevitable, and the specific mix of tradeoffs in a given state is almost impossible to predict. To this end, we proceed from the assumption that *all* states face trade-offs of some description. Even so, that assumption leads us back to the same starting point: states make policy decisions based on a set of factors largely unique to that state (and completely unique in terms of the specific mix of factors at that point in time and the history and culture of the state over time). Our task in this book is to examine state choice within this framework and to employ the ACA as the vehicle to better understand these constraints and opportunities.

HOW CAN WE STUDY STATE CHOICE?

If all states were largely the same, we might hypothesize that there would be little variation in state choice, and legions of state comparativists would need to find gainful employment examining different questions. But, to the delight of those same state comparativists, the states continue to provide a seemingly endless array of choices to be analyzed, typed, and reported. There are many ways in which states can be classified differently: population, land area, wealth, political culture, level of industrialization, and so on. In fact, many of the state characteristics that are important in the 21st century are the same state characteristics that became apparent during the Constitutional Convention in Philadelphia in 1789. There is no doubt that patterns can be found, but what is missed in the process?

The debate comes down, ultimately, to two competing methodologies and their respective strengths and weaknesses. Paradigmatic questions aside,[2] the two methodological approaches in widespread use for state comparative studies are 50-state quantitative modeling and case studies. Quantitative modeling has several important advantages. First, it allows direct comparison of all 50 states, and if the unit of analysis is "state," then it is often possible to have data from the full population of states. This allows researchers working in this methodology to be very confident of the relationships found; data do not need to be estimated from other cases. This obviates the problem of generalizability. Second, data costs are relatively low, as many data are collected and reported in the normal course of governance. Both the national government and state governments regularly collect and publish volumes of data on nearly all facets of public programs. In addition, generations of scholars over the decades have developed a wide variety of indicators, measures, and indices to further allow comparison across states. Third, the statistical techniques applied are generally agreed on in the literature, and those techniques are also widely taught in graduate schools. Thus, students are trained, generally early in their degree programs, to both evaluate and conduct work using these tools. Finally, because of the "cases-variables" problem (see Goggin, 1986), simplifying assumptions can be made that often serve to streamline theory-building. As variables are added to the equation, degrees of freedom disappear, so the onus on the researcher is to keep the number of variables (and thus the complexity of the theory) to a minimum.

On the other side of the ledger, qualitative, case study–based research also offers important benefits. Where quantitative modeling effectively requires a limit on the number of important variables that can be included, there is no upper limit to the number of variables that can be considered in a case study. An in-depth case study design can unpack events relevant to the case at hand and seek a much deeper understanding of the phenomenon under study. Case studies can also take into account nuances of context and can tie events and outcomes to those contextual nuances. In short, case studies allow a much deeper "dive" into the case than is possible in a quantitative model, allowing a significantly greater level of understanding about the case.

As mentioned earlier, however, trade-offs abound. While the data costs for quantitative research are relatively low, data costs for qualitative data are exceptionally high. Qualitative data collection and analysis are time-intensive and require much thought and discussion to ensure the relationships that emerge are not spurious. If the qualitative researcher is conducting in-person interviews, high travel costs and scheduling conflicts can become the order of the day. Because quantitative models can only employ a limited number of variables, they are vulnerable to underspecification and may leave large amount of unexplained variance. On the other hand, the high costs of data collection and analysis mean that 50-state qualitative studies are exceptionally rare. Qualitative studies are thus typically limited to a few states, which makes generalization largely impossible. However, for most qualitative work, generalization is not the goal.

Veritable generations of social scientists have been trained in qualitative methods following the guidance of Robert Yin (1994); indeed, the two generations of scholars represented by the authors of this book were trained in this manner. Yin provides justification for different choices of cases, depending on the goals of the research. To this end, we employ Yin's guidance by choosing cases most representative of the different phenomena under study. Guided by our previous quantitative work (Mayer et al., 2015; Travis, Morris, Mayer, Kenter, & Breaux, 2016) that develops an index of state choice under the ACA, we choose cases that fall at the extreme ends of our scale, as well as two cases that represent the middle of the scale. The cases are also chosen, in part, based on the availability of a clear and accessible record of state decision processes.

In short, the choice of qualitative or quantitative methods for state comparative study comes down to the purpose of the study at hand. In the present case, we are interested in going beyond the underspecified quantitative models (some of which we have published previously), and taking a deeper look into circumstances in states that cannot be captured in a few variables. To this end, we have chosen four states that represent different paths of state choice under the ACA: Alabama, which appears to be solidly opposed to the ACA; California, which appears to be solidly in favor of the ACA; and New Hampshire and Michigan, which have drifted a bit in between the extremes represented by Alabama and California. Are things really as they appear? Are these state choices really the result of partisan politics, or are there other forces in play in the states that influence the choices made by states? These are the questions best addressed through a case study methodology.

State Choice Under the ACA

Under the ACA, states could make a series of choices related to the delivery of health care in the state. The first choice states could make is whether to create a state health insurance exchange to allow health insurance companies to sell health insurance statewide. The state exchange would be administered and regulated by the state. States that failed to create state exchanges would automatically default to a federal exchange, created and administered by the federal government. Second, some states required legislation to emplace market reforms to allow the state exchange to function as envisioned. This legislation typically would allow greater competition within the state by removing regional barriers. Other states also required additional regulatory changes to administer a state exchange. Third, states could choose to expand Medicaid coverage. A choice to expand would mean that the income level for eligible recipients would be raised, bringing more citizens into Medicaid coverage. The idea was to close the affordability gap in private insurance and to cover those who were not covered by employer-provided insurance but whose annual income was too low to buy private insurance. The additional costs would be covered by the federal government at first, slowly ramping down the federal contribution to 90 percent over a period of years. Initially, the ACA effectively required states to expand Medicaid by tying current Medicaid payments to a state's willingness to accept the expanded Medicaid program. However, this provision was struck down in *National Federation of Independent Business (NFIB) v. Sebelius*, 567 U.S., 132 S. Ct. 2566 (2012). The result of the *Sebelius* decision was not to remove the state choice but to change the terms of the choice.

States could also choose to take action to block implementation of the ACA. For example, several states filed lawsuits in federal courts hours after passage of the legislation, with the goal of denying implementation by challenging the constitutionality of different parts of the law (including the Medicaid requirement, as mentioned in the preceding). A state decision to block implementation through legal challenges indicates a willful effort to defy the national government. Some states introduced and passed legislation that specifically prohibited states, state agencies, citizens, or other policy participants from adopting ACA-specific requirements. In other cases, states used the opportunity of the ACA to pass state legislation to add "poison pills" to ACA acceptance. For example, in an effort to discourage Democratic legislators from supporting the ACA, the Alabama legislature passed a bill that forbade any plan sold in the state's exchange to pay for women's reproductive services.

Taken together, state acceptance or denial of the ACA can be captured through the choices made across these dimensions. A state that defaulted to the federal exchange, failed to pass market reform legislation, did not expand Medicaid, and attempted to block implementation through other means (court action, state law forbidding compliance with the ACA) is considered as strongly opposed to the ACA. Likewise, a state that took all positive steps (and no negative steps) to embrace the ACA are considered strongly supportive. States that fall in the middle—that perhaps took some steps to accept or oppose—form the remainder of the continuum.

The four states represented in our case studies differ as to the choices they made. While partisan politics can explain some state action, it cannot explain all state actions. States with Democratic governors or Democratically controlled legislatures resisted ACA requirements, and states with Republican governors or Republican-controlled legislatures embraced elements of the legislation. More important, even states that ended up clearly in favor or opposed to the ACA (not to mention states in the middle of the spectrum of action) did not necessarily start at that place, nor was the path they took clear and unambiguous. These are nuances that simply cannot be captured in quantitative models, but they are appropriate fodder for a case study approach.

Themes of the Book

There are several themes present in this work. These themes serve to focus the larger issues revealed in this book and to place our cases in a broader context of scholarly work. With the goal of understanding the specifics of state choice in mind, we offer three specific themes present in all four case studies that also serve to tie those cases together in meaningful ways.

States Are Different

At its most basic level, this theme is both self-evident and pedestrian in nature. To say that the 50 states are different is equivalent to the observation that no two trees in the forest are identical. However, like trees in the forest, those differences are as important as the similarities. Fifty-state comparative analyses are conducted to detect and quantify patterns of sameness between states; in other words, the goal is to explain patterns through common factors. The variance left unaccounted for in many of these models is attributed to some combination of random error (measurement error or statistical error) and underspecified models. If the variance unaccounted for is large in magnitude, as it frequently is in comparative state studies, it begs the question: Are states more different than alike?

Clearly, states share many common elements. Daniel Elazar's work on political culture (1984) bears testament to this; political culture varies widely across states. Even so, states that share significant elements of the same political culture type—Mississippi and Alabama are both strong "traditionalistic" states (Elazar, 1984, p. 125), for example—states can also be quite different in terms of the policy choices they make. As we will see, even California and New Hampshire, which both share a dominant "moralistic-individualistic" political culture (Elazar, 1984, p. 136), approached the ACA in very different ways and arrived at two very different places. It is the unique conditions, experiences, cast of "players," and other factors that make states unique in policy terms. Similarities aside, the differences matter!

States Are Policy Laboratories

Yehezkel Dror's (1968) observation that states are truly "policy laboratories" is perhaps so ubiquitous in the literature as to be cliché. However, like any good cliché, there is a large measure of truth in the statement, and in the case of state comparative policy studies, this statement can also serve as either a theme or an underlying assumption of the work. In our case, it serves as both. As the relationship between states and the national government continues to evolve, states make choices about how best to structure and implement federal programs at the state level. If states are, in fact, different, then it follows that the choices states make will also be different. More important, states will make choices for different reasons, with different goals, different resources, and different politics. These factors all contribute to different state outcomes under the auspices of the same national policy.

The implementation of the ACA is but a recent case in point. Soss et al. (2001) examined the implementation of the TANF program in the late 1990s and found tremendous state variation in the program choices made by states. The TANF legislation was written in such a manner as to give states choices across a range of factors, and states collectively took advantage of the full range of options. Likewise, the WQA of 1987 created the Clean Water State Revolving Loan Fund program. In this case, states were not only free to structure the program as they saw fit, but states were also given freedom to choose to provide loan assistance largely as they saw fit (see Morris, 1997; Travis, Morris, & Morris, 2004). Very different patterns of behavior developed across the states, and the implementation choices made by states varied widely—and with different outcomes as a result.

The ACA is no exception to this same observation. The manner in which states approached the ACA and its associated mandates is characterized by significant variation. While it is beyond the scope of this work to delve into the outcomes of the ACA and state implementation choices, the behavior exhibited by states in the early implementation of the ACA reinforces Dror's observation: Given the same mandate, states reacted differently and chose a wide range of paths in response to the mandate.

States Are Captive to Their History

Perhaps no theme emerges more strongly from our work than the observation that state policymakers are constrained, albeit subtly, by the unique history and political forces within their states. Because states are truly different, their state histories and politics are also different; these differences serve simultaneously to both inhibit and empower certain behaviors.

History constrains action in the sense that the current norms of political behavior are the result of the cumulative events of a state's unique history, a history that often predates statehood. In Alabama, as we will see, a combination of distrust of the national government, coupled with a long-standing rivalry between agricultural and industrial interests in the state, very much dominates the subtext of Alabama politics in the 21st century. These factors should not be underestimated; they are powerful enough that policy actors regularly set aside choices that would make their citizens (and perhaps themselves) better off in favor of political positions determined by decades- or centuries-old rivalries or distrust. Much like in Alabama, decision-making in Michigan is still very much influenced by a century of industrialization, manufacturing, and unionization, despite much of the manufacturing having moved on and union strength and influence a shell of what it once was.

Conclusion

These are factors that are difficult, if not impossible, to capture in quantitative studies of state policy choice. By taking a careful look at these complex situations within states, we can better understand the results of our quantitative studies and achieve a more nuanced understanding of state policy choice. In Michigan, rivalries between different constitutional officers, the governor and the attorney general, led to a series of actions and decisions by both executive and legislative actors. California's experience was dominated by the state's determination to be the country's model for ACA implementation and bipartisan efforts to strengthen California's health care infrastructure so it could handle an influx of new patients, while in New Hampshire the main factor was a fierce dedication to states' rights. In Alabama, the physician-governor was "for" the ACA before he was opposed to it; at the same time, an ideological battle over states' rights drove the debate concerning the creation of a state insurance exchange.

Our journey in this book takes us through the implementation decisions made by these four states. As mentioned in the preceding, each of the four states represents a state at a different place on our continuum of state choice in the ACA. Through this process, we hope to identify the important explanatory elements present in each state, and in the process, reach a level of understanding of ACA implementation that goes beyond the simplistic "it's party politics, stupid!" explanation of state choice. While party politics is certainly not unimportant, it is also unsatisfactory as "the" explanation of state choice. Reality is much more messy, and much more interesting, than simple explanations would have us believe.

Notes

1. We are indebted to Tony Keck for this line of argument. Mr. Keck served as the Medicaid administrator in two different states (neither are states a part of this study) and reports that the issue of existing program costs were a significant factor in those state's choices.
2. We acknowledge the paradigmatic requirements related to differing ontologies and epistemologies, and the methodologies that tend to follow from these choices. However, in an empirical sense, both primary methodological approaches can be found in the state comparative literature. Our focus here is on the relative tradeoffs related to methodological choice, and we make no claim regarding paradigmatic choice, requirement, or adherence.

2 Getting to Obamacare

A History of Health Care Reform in the U.S.

Perhaps one of the most hotly debated policy topics of the 20th and early 21st centuries is the role of the national government in the provision, production, and delivery of health care. This policy arena is marked by an exceptionally high level of partisan conflict coupled with strongly entrenched interests set against a backdrop of skyrocketing costs and increasing need. The result is a century of patchwork policy decisions (Oberlander, 2012) that have served to stymie real policy reform (Starr, 2013) as much as providing meaningful relief to generations of citizens.

The most recent iteration of this battle is the passage of the ACA, and current attempts to replace the ACA with a different policy solution. The development of the ACA attempts to derail the legislation following that passage, and current efforts to undo the ACA and replace the law with something else have been marked by unprecedented levels of partisan rancor, legal challenges, political messaging, and citizen confusion. While it is perhaps convenient to paint the current situation as a reflection of the moment, the seeds of the current political conflict were sown decades before.

Although much of the debate of the last 10 years would lead the casual observer to conclude that health care policy is a relatively new phenomenon, this debate has been part of the American political landscape for more than a century. Our history is filled with earnest attempts to broaden access to health care, and earnest attempts to prevent access. Well-meaning people have disagreed about the appropriate scope of health policy, the best mechanism through which to accomplish the policy goals, how to pay for proposed policies, and who should benefit from the proposals. All of this has taken place in a setting in which various special interests have attempted to determine outcomes, in which party politics have been both a help and a hindrance, in which even nonpolitical experts disagree about both the scope of the problem and the methods to address the problem, and in which the average citizen is often overwhelmed by partisan and ideological rhetoric (and, in most cases, without the knowledge to develop an informed judgment). Indeed, while the battle over the ACA and its implementation represents all these issues, none of the issues are new to the health policy arena.

The ACA was enacted in 2010 in an environment of divisiveness rarely seen in American politics. From the halls of Congress, to state capitols, to dinner tables across the nation, differences of opinion about the ACA raged almost unchecked. News outlets paraded steady streams of pundits across American television screens, each predicting either the dawn of a new age of American enlightenment and prosperity or economic disaster and the ignominious end of the great American experiment in democracy. Somewhere in between these extremes were legions of administrators at the national and the state level with a constitutional duty to implement the ACA.

As we detail later in this book, an important feature of the ACA is the significant amount of discretion in policy design given to states in the implementation of the statute. A legacy of Reagan federalism (see Conlan, 1988; Morris, 1996; Nathan & Doolittle, 1984), the ACA was purposefully designed to be largely implemented by states; the federal government would only step in when states failed to act. In this way, the ACA could be tailored to meet the specific conditions of each state, rather than imposing a "one-size-fits-all" solution. In this sense, the ACA was much like the Personal Responsibility and Work Opportunity Act of 1996[1] (see Breaux, Duncan, Keller, & Morris, 2002; Soss et al., 2001)—both pieces of legislation created a framework under which states were free to make choices about program benefits and program implementation. As we discuss later, the ACA experience added an additional component in that several states took active measures above and beyond the law to try to block implementation of the law in its entirety.

In this maelstrom of political rancor and partisanship, states were thus faced with the task of implementing, or opposing, the legislation. Empirically speaking, there was a range of initial state responses to the ACA, ranging from immediate acceptance to attempts to seek court injunctions to prevent implementation. How and why states made the choices they did is the subject of this book. Are there discernable patterns of behavior among states that can explain their decisions? How much of a role did partisan politics play in state decision-making? Did economics, needs of citizens, or ideology matter?

However, 50-state models are limited in their explanatory power. While they are very helpful in spotting national trends, they necessarily overlook the fine distinctions between states and, more important, within states. Our initial research on this topic indicated that while we could explain variance in state behavior at a macro level with a fairly high degree of precision, one did not have to look too deeply into a state to realize that the debates, arguments, processes, and decisions within each state varied significantly. While some states were clearly on one side of the policy "fence" or the other, other states seemed to waver in their acceptance or opposition to the ACA. To this end, we focus our attention on the factors within states that can better help us understand the processes that ultimately led to specific state choices.

The purpose of this book is to more fully understand the responses of states to the requirements and options of the ACA. To grasp the current political landscape requires an appreciation of the past century of health care policy at both the national and state levels. To that end, this chapter seeks to explore this history, up to the passage of the ACA in 2010. Through this process we will be better able to understand both the state responses to the ACA, as well as prospects for future reform efforts.

The Early Years: From Progressivism to the New Deal

In his comprehensive history of health care policy reform, sociologist and historian Paul Starr (2013) identifies 1915 as the beginning of the debate over health care policy in the U.S. Although Germany had adopted a form of national health insurance coverage in the 40 years prior to this benchmark, efforts of a similar nature in the U.S. did not gain traction until Great Britain enacted a national health insurance program for workers in 1911. Other European countries created similar programs in the period between 1883 and 1911. A significant difference between the U.S. and the European nations was the relative popularity and political strength of the socialist movement in Europe and the relative obscurity of that movement in the U.S. (Starr, 2013). Although both socialism and communism had fervent followers in the U.S., these movements were largely kept outside the political establishment and were never a significant part of the policy conversation (Hoffman, 2008).

Early proposals in the U.S. were driven not by special interests but, rather, by the belief that comprehensive health care was a feature of a modern, progressive, enlightened society. The Progressive Party included a form of health coverage for workers on their 1912 platform, although the idea never gained much traction. The Progressive Era tension between centralized administration and states' rights was still a central feature of the American political discussion and left Progressives in a position limited by this tension. Bolstered by support from labor interests, the movement lost relevance with the entry of the U.S. into the growing war in Europe (Birn, Brown, Fee, & Lear, 2003). Moreover, opponents of the proposals were able to capitalize on strong anti-German sentiment in the U.S. (Oberlander, 2012); by equating government-sponsored health care with the German model of health care coverage, the ability of supporters in the U.S. to move their proposals forward was effectively stymied (Starr, 2013). New York State came close to success in 1919 before the effort was blocked by the Republican leadership in the State Assembly. Similar efforts in other states over the next 10 years were also unsuccessful.

The collapse of the stock market in 1929 and the ensuing Great Depression of the 1930s provided a set of political, social, and economic conditions uniquely suited to the development and acceptance of national health coverage. At the heart of this opportunity was a redefinition of the role of the national government and the widespread realization that many problems were beyond the capabilities of the individual states to address effectively. Unlike previous efforts that had focused almost exclusively on the working class, the conversation in the 1930s shifted to include the middle class as well. Likewise, the problem definition shifted from one of wage replacement, maternity benefits, and funeral cost coverage to one of sharply rising medical costs. The increase in costs affected not only lower class workers but, increasingly, the middle class. Furthermore, as unemployment grew, fewer people were able to afford to pay for medical care. The early part of the efforts at this time witnessed the creation of group health insurance plans offered by hospital associations. These plans, which became the basis for the Blue Cross system (Starr, 2013), were constructed on a nonprofit model and covered few people. The plans were offered to employees and were intended to cover hospital costs. However, these plans did little to address the growing demand for health coverage, particularly in a time of increasing economic instability.

This same period also saw a profound change in the structure of the health care industry, all of which conspired to raise the costs associated with health care. Beginning in the late 19th century, many states began to enact licensing requirement for doctors, which, in turn, led to a formalization of medical education and a significant reduction in the number of schools offering medical degrees. The net effect of these actions was to reduce the number of doctors, which, in turn, made the services of licensed physicians more economically valuable. Hospitals, which until this point had operated largely as charitable institutions, began to find the charitable model unsustainable as costs rose (including physician fees).

From the perspective of the Roosevelt administration, health coverage also proved a difficult issue to be balanced against other priorities in a context of political feasibility (Brill, 2015). Unemployment and economic security became higher priorities to the Roosevelt administration while health care reform became less significant from the administration's viewpoint (Kaiser Family Foundation, 2009). While no state to this point had created health coverage policy, several states had moved forward with forms of both unemployment insurance and pensions for the elderly. As these initiatives already had a "track record" in the public and political consciousness, they represented easier paths to success and were thus given priority over untested policy ideas. Moreover, the relatively recent history of opposition to health coverage, and the interests arrayed against health care policy, made clear to the administration where to expend their political capital. A grassroots movement to support the elderly (Starr, 2013) resulted in altered policy priorities.

Roosevelt formed a committee in 1934 composed of members of the administration. This committee was charged with developing policy proposals to address demands for unemployment insurance, old-age pensions, and health care. Although the committee discussed health care, concerns over opposition from the American Medical Association pushed health care from the forefront of the committee's work. The committee's initial proposal did contain some provisions for health care, but strong and immediate opposition from the American Medical Association (AMA), in an effort to preserve the status quo, caused the administration to drop health care from the proposal (Oberlander, 2012). When Congress passed the Social Security Act in 1935, health care did not play a significant role in the legislation.

The Roosevelt administration tried on two additional occasions to enact health care legislation. Bolstered by significant Democratic gains in the House and the Senate in the 1936 election, a second presidential commission developed a proposal that included universal health care for both the elderly and for citizens. Both programs were to be paid for through federal grants to states and would also include funds to include hospital construction, child health care, and special services for those with disabilities. However, once again the AMA announced its firm opposition of the bill, a move that led many in Congress to withdraw support for the legislation.

Roosevelt's last attempt came in 1944, shortly before his death in early 1945. As the Second World War was reaching its conclusion, Roosevelt perceived the need for a transition from wartime to peacetime. In his 1944 State of the Union speech, he called for legislation to protect the economic security of all Americans, including a right to medical care and protection from the economic costs of sickness. Development of this proposal began in the White House, but Roosevelt died before the proposal was complete.

Roosevelt's successor, Harry Truman, continued Roosevelt's agenda by calling for a national health care program to be administered by the federal government (Brill, 2015). Although Great Britain established its own National Health Service in 1947, in the U.S., Republicans regained control of Congress in the 1946 election, a move that virtually guaranteed the failure of any health care proposals at the national level (Roberts, 2012). Undaunted, Truman tried again in 1948 following his election to the presidency. Starr (2013) suggests that this attempt was as close as the U.S. has ever come to adopting national health care, yet the opposition remained both strong and well organized, and neither chamber of Congress formally considered legislation on this topic. However, Congress did pass legislation providing federal funding for new hospitals and investments in medical research. Moreover, in 1950 Congress passed a small pilot program to provide money for states for medical care for welfare recipients, a program that would later evolve into the Medicaid program.

Postwar to the Great Society

The 1950s and 1960s witnessed the solidification of the employer-based health care system present in the U.S. today. Building on the formation of group health plans that first appeared in the 1920s and 1930s, and that grew substantially in the 1940s, insurance companies began to offer plans to employees through specific companies. Although many companies initially doubted the viability of such plans and were fearful that only individuals with serious health issues would participate, the early experience of the Blue Cross plans demonstrated the economic feasibility of these plans (Starr, 1982). With the growth of the unionization movement in the postwar years, employer-based coverage increased substantially as unions won rights to these plans through collective-bargaining agreements (Oberlander, 2012).

In spite of the early popularity of these plans, several nagging questions remained, including questions regarding the tax implications of various types of plans. An Internal Revenue Service ruling in 1953 declared that financial contributions to individually purchased plans were taxable, while contributions to group plans were not. Faced with an apparent policy dilemma, the Eisenhower administration proposed to exclude all health plan contributions from taxable income and to provide an expanded deduction for medical expenses. However, as Starr (2013, p. 42) points out, this solution favored wealthier citizens at the expense of middle- and working-class citizens, for three reasons. First, those with higher incomes were more likely to have health insurance; second, wealthier people were likely to have more generous benefits in their health plans; and, third, the deduction was more valuable to higher-income citizens, especially those in the highest marginal tax brackets. Those opposed to the concept of a national health program favored the Eisenhower proposal as a way to avoid a discussion of alternatives. Labor leaders also backed the plan, in spite of the obvious inequitable distribution of the benefits of the proposal.

As the insurance market grew, early plans that had covered all workers in a community were replaced with plans that sought younger, healthier populations. The insurance offered to these healthier groups came at a lower cost, and participants flocked to the lower-cost option—a practice that became known as "cream-skimming." However, this meant that Blue Cross, the largest established nonprofit program, was left trying to insure a more expensive population—the sick, elderly, and poor. Blue Cross was thus forced by the market to adjust its price strategy as well, charging lower rates to healthier groups and much higher rates to riskier groups. This had the net effect of shifting coverage even more in favor of wealthier citizens and away from lower-income groups.

The Advent of Medicaid and Medicare

During the 1960 presidential election, John Kennedy made hospital insurance coverage a key element of his campaign. That same year, a bill sponsored by Rep. Wilbur Mills (D-AR) and Senator Robert Kerr (D-OK) was proposed in Congress. A forerunner to Medicare, the program covered between 50 and 80 percent of state costs associated with impoverished senior citizens. The program was limited in its coverage but eventually paved the way for other legislation (Smith & Moore, 2008). Kennedy's initial proposals met with stiff opposition from a coalition of Republicans and southern Democrats, and never gained much legislative traction as a result.

Following Kennedy's death in 1963, President Lyndon Johnson pushed to advance hospital coverage as an element of his Great Society initiative. Although initial efforts in 1964 met with only limited success, the landslide political victories in the 1964 election assured that the programs would pass during the next congressional session. The result of this effort was an expanded medical coverage program for seniors that included both Democratic and Republican initiatives. Democrats had envisioned a purely public program to cover hospital costs, but in an effort to attract Republican support, they expanded the proposal to allow for additional voluntary private insurance to cover nonhospital physician expenses. This private insurance would be federally subsidized in order to make it more affordable for seniors. The net result was the Medicare program. Part A created the compulsory hospital insurance, and Part B became the voluntary subsidized private insurance program. Moreover, the legislation included an expansion of the Mills–Kerr program, which effectively created the Medicaid program.

Starr (2013, pp. 46–47) notes that the net effect of this effort was to create a program that was not particularly liberal in its approach, in that it created "separate and unequal programs for the elderly and the poor—one piggy-backed on the shoulders of Social Security, the other shackled to public assistance ('welfare')" and thus created two very different means of funding for health care. In addition, while Medicare was conceived as a national program (and one that conferred an entitlement to seniors) with equal benefits across all states, Medicare was left to the vagaries and whims of state politics, with a wide range of services and eligibilities scattered across states. States could even choose to forgo participation; Arizona did not participate in Medicaid until 1982. From the outset, liberal-leaning states tended to cover more citizens, cover more services, and compensate physicians at higher rates. This meant that citizens eligible in one state might not be eligible in another state. Low reimbursement rates led many physicians in those states to refuse to treat Medicaid patients.

Medicare and Medicaid differed in other important ways. For example, while Medicaid services were potentially more generous, Medicare benefits were less so. Although some in the Democratic Party sought coverage for prescription medications and for catastrophic illness, these proposals were successfully deflected by the party leadership. On the other hand, Congress failed to impose any form of cost control on Medicare expenditures; instead, the law specifically forbade the national government from setting reimbursement rates. The net effect of this was to create an incentive for hospitals, doctors, and other providers to charge ever higher rates for services, effectively building inflation into health care. Representative Mills (D-AR) also added language that allowed certain hospital-based medical specialists, such as anesthesiologists, radiologists, and pathologists, to be paid on a fee-for-service basis, rather than the more customary salary structure in place at the time. The net effect of these provisions was a significant increase in health care costs and budget projections for both Medicaid and Medicare that greatly exceeded expectations.

The debate over health care and universal coverage continued in much the same pattern for the next 15 years. There were proposals to expand coverage, but none of the major reforms garnered enough political support to become law. There were small, incremental changes—Medicare benefits were extended to cover some groups younger than 65—but major change proved elusive. Efforts by President Richard Nixon to create a universal health care system during his second term were overshadowed by the growing Watergate scandal, and the tenuous agreement between Nixon and liberal Democrats soured in the face of the scandal (Brill, 2015). A more serious effort co-sponsored by Senator Edward Kennedy (D-MA) and Wilbur Mills (D-AR) was designed to curb growing health care costs by creating a universal health care system. Key differences in the funding sources ultimately led to the demise of the proposal: While Kennedy and Mills favored a payroll tax to fund the system, Nixon wanted an employer mandate. Nixon felt this would allow him to claim that the plan would be paid for without imposing new taxes. However, Nixon's resignation in August 1974 effectively ended the effort. Although Gerald Ford indicated support for the proposal, a blocking move by southern Democrats and conservative Republicans threw the proposal into jeopardy, and it was ultimately pulled from the House calendar.

By the mid-1970s, the economic outlook in the nation had changed. Growth in gross domestic product (GDP) had slowed, and the political dialogue had shifted to a more conservative tone that portrayed government programs as ineffective, costly, and inefficient (Birn et al., 2003). President Jimmy Carter was at best a lukewarm supporter of health care reform; his primary focus in terms of health care was cost control (Oberlander, 2012), a position that put him at odds with the liberals in his party, as well as powerful union interests. Rifts within the Carter administration left the White House largely ineffective in policy discussions (Dawes, 2016), a state of affairs that helped bring Ronald Reagan to the White House in 1981.

The Reagan Revolution and Policy Reversal

The election of Ronald Reagan marked the beginning of a significant shift in political outlook and policy outcomes. Termed by Johnson and Heilman (1987) as a "metapolicy shift," the new approach was captured by Reagan in an oft-repeated phrase: "Government is not the solution to our problems; government *is* the problem." In spite of this rhetoric (and many of the policies that flowed from this shift), the history of health care took an unexpected path during this period. Rather than reducing Medicaid, the program was expanded under Reagan (Smith & Moore, 2008). In addition, the Reagan administration sought and received authority to begin to regulate reimbursement rates for Medicare. The impetus for this change was not a deep-seated ideological belief but, rather, a growing fear of ballooning deficits—control of Medicare costs was viewed as a means to reduce federal spending (Klemm, 2000). As Starr (2013) points out, Reagan had been a longtime critic of Medicare, claiming that the structure of the program would mean increased government control over health care. Even though the original program explicitly prohibited such control, it was the Reagan administration that sought exactly the government control he had criticized (Dawes, 2016). In a system designed around pilot programs adopted in several states in the 1970s, the new plan allowed hospitals to receive a flat fee for a service based on customary costs. If hospital costs were higher, the hospital would lose money, but if its cost came in lower, the difference would be realized as profit. Because these payments were indexed to historic rates, hospitals generally experienced a financial windfall. The new controls not only slowed costs but also created record profits for hospitals (Starr, 2013, p. 65). By the early 1990s, a similar requirement was applied to physician fees, with a fee schedule replacing the "customary costs" model from the original legislation.

The 1980s also saw the growth of employer-provided, self-funded health insurance plans. Legislation passed in the 1940s had allowed these plans to operate free of federal regulation; regulation was left to the states. While these plans generally enjoyed an unregulated business environment, in 1986 Congress imposed a requirement to allow employees who left employment to continue to buy insurance in the plan for up to eighteen months after leaving the company. The legislation did not include any subsidy or payment; the full cost of the insurance was the responsibility of the individual. That same year, Congress passed legislation requiring hospitals to provide emergency medical treatment to any individual who sought treatment. Although the requirement was tied to hospitals that received Medicare funds, the requirement effectively ensured that nearly all hospitals were covered under this requirement. A separate attempt to provide catastrophic health coverage under Medicare actually passed and was signed into law in 1988 only to be repealed the following year because of concerns over a combination of spiraling cost estimates and the ways costs and benefits would be distributed in society (Klemm, 2000).

The Rise and Fall of the Clinton Health Care Plan

Universal health care returned to the policy agenda in 1991 in the form of an issue in a special election for an open Senate seat in Pennsylvania. Lagging in the polls, the Democratic candidate, Harris Wofford, argued in favor of universal health care. At a time when the nation was deep in a recession, Wofford's argument struck a chord among Pennsylvania voters, and Wofford won the election. In the preceding decade, more and more people had lost health insurance (Starr, 2013), and health care costs had continued to outpace inflation. Sparked in part by Wofford's victory and the importance of the issue in that election, several efforts were undertaken in Congress to reintroduce the idea of universal health care. In fact, the idea of universal coverage had renewed support from many groups across the political spectrum. However, one critical element in the agenda-setting process was missing: a clear consensus about the underlying causes of the health care issue. In Kingdon's (1995) terms, the problem, political, and solution streams had collided, but the contents of both the problem stream and the solution stream were, at best, unclear.

The disagreements not only cut across party and ideological lines but also across intraparty lines as well. Liberal Democrats favored a single-payer system modeled on the Canadian health system, while more moderate and conservative Democrats favored market-oriented solutions. Liberal Republicans tended to favor market-based approaches, while more conservative Republicans tended to be opposed to the issue altogether. The result was little meaningful congressional action during 1991–92.

The 1992 presidential election offered an opportunity for a new policy entrepreneur (Kingdon, 1995) to take center stage. While health care was not necessarily the premier issue on Clinton's agenda (economic growth also played a prominent role in the discussion), candidate Clinton initially sided with the moderate/conservative wing of his party during the primaries but shifted in the general election to a stance for universal coverage that would be based on competing private plans. The incumbent, George H. W. Bush, talked about health care during the election cycle but was more focused on economic issues than on health care. Bush favored a program of tax credits aimed at low-income people to incent the purchase of private insurance, coupled with proposed state requirements to allow citizens to purchase a basic-level insurance plan with the tax credits they received. This plan reflected two principles favored by Republicans: market-based solutions and greater state choice and control over federal programs. However, Bush's lack of focus on health care meant his proposals received little public attention. Polls suggested that voters favored Clinton's plan over Bush's plan and trusted Democrats more than Republicans to address health care reform. Clinton was elected in a relatively close election.

Shortly after Clinton formally took office, he announced the President's Task Force on Health Care Reform, to be chaired by his wife, Hillary Clinton. The group consisted of several trusted advisors, cabinet members, congressional staffers, state officials, and others but ultimately proved ineffective as a policy formulation group. The existence of the task force was met with legal challenges that questioned the role of the First Lady, and others that demanded that all meetings be open to the public. At one point there were more than 500 people—Democrat and Republican—spread across thirty working groups. Little was accomplished, and the group was dissolved in May 1993 without making any recommendations. As Starr (2013) points out, one of the great ironies of this approach was that, in an effort to include as many groups as possible in the process, a strong sense of exclusion developed among those not invited to the meetings. The task of formulating a health care reform policy then fell to an ad hoc group of advisors and analysts, often led by Clinton himself. The group met sporadically into September 1993. Although the initial goal was to provide a plan that could be included in the 1993 budget reconciliation process (requiring only a simple majority in the Senate, rather than the supermajority needed for a vote of cloture), the opposition of Senator Robert Byrd (D-WV) meant that the White House had no option but to delay the process.

The multitude of positions and ideas offered by members of the pared-down ad hoc group proved to be a harbinger of the larger public debate to follow. Some in the ad hoc group favored generous, comprehensive plans, while others favored more basic coverage. Others favored a program modeled on the Medicare model, in which some Americans could purchase supplemental private insurance to enhance the basic coverage offered. Others favored a managed competition plan, while still others argued for price controls. The consensus proposal called for a benefit plan that would provide a level of coverage slightly above the existing median level of coverage for health plans; the proposal also included a proposed plan for prescription drug coverage for Medicare recipients. Still other questions revolved around how to pay for the plan. Some members, including Clinton, favored a new payroll tax that would guarantee a basic level of coverage. Business interests tended to favor a capped premium model that would protect businesses from increased costs. The final proposal proposed to cap employer contributions at 80 percent of the cost, determined by total payroll costs and the size of the firm.

An additional element of the discussion revolved around the ability of consumers to choose the level of their plan coverage. While employers would pay 80 percent of the cost of the basic plan, consumers could opt to purchase enhanced coverage and assume all costs above the required employer contribution. This provision would lead to the formation of purchasing alliances, in which consumers (or employers) could "shop" for plans from a variety of insurers, which, in turn, would generate competition among health insurance companies to lower prices to attract new subscribers. These purchasing alliances could also be spread beyond employers to communities, thus changing significantly the composition of the risk pool. However, the policy group was concerned that the cost scoring system of the Congressional Budget Office (CBO) would undervalue the benefits of potential competition, so the final proposal included a more top-down regulatory framework and less emphasis on market competition.

The Clinton plan was presented before a special joint session of Congress held on September 22, 1993, although the details of much of the plan had been leaked to the press prior to the formal announcement. The president's speech highlighted the principles that undergirded the plan, and the speech was delivered with earnestness and passion that marked much of Clinton's public speaking. Initial public reaction was strongly positive, and early polls showed strong support for the proposal (Starr, 2013). While few details of the plan were included in the speech, both the plan and the idea of reform captured much of the public and political attention. However, moving from a powerful speech to public policy would prove an impossible task.

Clinton's focus on health care reform was a signature element of his first term and its ultimate failure is due to a variety of factors. Although Clinton sustained pressure on Congress to pass health care legislation, the reasons for its failure are myriad. While many observers at the beginning of the process believed that success was inevitable, a closer examination reveals a story of political ineptitude, divisiveness within the Democratic Party, and concerted efforts by Republicans to ensure the reform effort failed. And, while medical costs were indeed rising, there was no compelling economic reason to reform health care.

The Democratic Party was split internally, with different factions favoring different plans and approaches. While the House Democrats tended to favor a single-payer system, Senate Democrats tended to favor more modest approaches. Moreover, the opposition of Senator Byrd meant that the Senate would likely require 60 votes to pass a bill; with only 56 Democrats in the chamber, Democrats would have to compromise with enough moderate Republicans to reach 60 votes. To make matters in the Senate more tenuous, not all Democratic senators were in favor of the president's proposal. In the House, the Democrats were split between two major factions: one faction favored universal health care coverage while the other faction proposed a managed-care system without universal coverage. Meanwhile, in the face of the looming midterm elections, Republicans in both chambers began to band together in opposition to any legislation and resisted attempts to be engaged in negotiations and compromise efforts by both factions of the Democratic caucus. Outside of Congress, conservatives began concerted efforts to discredit the need for health care reform and concocted a plan to deny both the existence of need and to employ scare tactics to turn public opinion against the plan, including claims of loss of choice, degraded quality of care, and higher cost (Starr, 2013). Moreover, while Clinton and his advisors had expected enthusiastic support from groups representing affected interests, these groups tended to withhold their support from all proposals, perhaps reading the political "tea leaves." Chief among the opponents was the Health Insurance Association of America.

As the process wore on and passage became less certain, Clinton began to turn his policy attention to other issues, including gun control legislation, new tax increases, and the North American Free Trade Agreement. Layered over this was efforts by political opponents to embroil the Clintons personally in what became known as the "Whitewater" scandal,[1] which had the effect of further eroding the president's attention (and influence) in this policy arena. When the congressional session ended in late 1994 without legislation in place, the issue was effectively dead (Hacker, 1996; Johnson & Broder, 1997; Skocpol, 1996).

Incremental Policy Changes, 1994–2008

In the latter part of the 1990s as the population aged and more citizens became eligible for Medicaid and Medicare, health care reform made its way back to the agenda. An aging population and an increasing population eligible for Medicare led some to question whether these programs could be sustained in the long term. Republicans pushed hard to modify both programs, though largely without success. Finally, a deal was struck in 1996 in which Clinton accepted major reforms to welfare in return for the continued safety of Medicare and Medicaid.

Other proposals related to health care reform continued to receive congressional attention. In 1996 the Health Insurance Portability and Accountability Act (HIPAA) was enacted, which allowed people who left a job to keep their health care coverage, at their own expense, for up to 18 months. The act also prohibited insurers from refusing coverage for preexisting conditions. The act also addressed the issue of medical records, both in terms of medical records privacy, but also facilitated the use of electronic medical records. Working with moderate Republicans, Democrats crafted and passed the State Children's Health Insurance Plan (SCHIP), a block grant program that states could use to provide health care coverage to children in low- and moderate-income families. The SCHIP legislation also provided increased flexibility to states to operate their Medicaid programs under an increasingly broad waiver program.

By 1998, thanks to a growing economy, the federal budget moved from a deficit to a surplus. The possibility of surplus funds opened the door to additional policy proposals. In 2000 Clinton proposed an expansion of Medicare, the lowering of the eligibility age from 65 to 55, and the offer of coverage for prescription medications. Although little was accomplished in the last years of the Clinton presidency, the growing surplus suggested a new window of opportunity following the 2000 presidential election. Both candidates in the election offered health care–related proposals; Al Gore favored an expansion of the SCHIP program, prescription drug coverage for Medicare recipients, and an expansion of Medicare eligibility. George W. Bush was less willing to discuss health care but did eventually back a plan for prescription drug coverage for Medicare recipients. Bush also favored a plan to convert Medicare into a system of competing private insurance plans.

Following the election, the Senate was able to craft a bill that would allow Medicare recipients the choice to stay in the current Medicare system with the inclusion of a drug plan offered by a private insurer or to opt into a private managed-care plan. The House process proved more divisive, with conservatives pressing for the inclusion of a provision for the inclusion of medical savings accounts. Ultimately, the resulting legislation—the Medicare Prescription Drug, Improvement, and Modernization Act of 2003—contained three programs: coverage for prescription drugs for Medicare recipients, tax incentives for the creation of individual Health Savings Accounts, and new opportunities for private insurers in the Medicare market. Against a backdrop of the terror attacks of September 11, 2001; war in Afghanistan; and the evaporation of the budget surplus, it is somewhat surprising that Congress and the president were willing to enact health care legislation whose costs could exceed $400 billion (Holtz-Eakin, 2004, p. 2).

Overall, the period between 2003 and 2008 was largely devoid of any serious efforts to enact, much less discuss, health care, but larger economic forces were creating a new level of imperative. While the SCHIP program had succeeded in covering millions of children, the number of workers with access to health insurance decreased. Although economic growth continued through 2007, the real gains in wealth were concentrated in the highest income categories, yet health insurance premiums continued to increase at rates above the rate of inflation. It was thus inevitable that health care would again dominate a presidential election cycle and create a policy window that would finally allow successful health care reform after a century of failed policy attempts.

2008 to the Present: Promises versus Realities

In 2003, an Illinois state senator campaigning for the U.S. Senate voiced his support of a single-payer universal health care plan while recalling his mother's struggle to pay medical bills as she was dying of cancer. The Senator, Barack Obama, would not take steps to make health care reform a policy priority, however, until he was campaigning for president in 2008. His health care reform platform was ambitious and proposed establishing a publicly run program similar to Congress's health care plan, the Federal Employees Health Benefits Program (FEHBP; Cohen, 2010; Amadeo, 2016). The plan would be portable and allow people to keep their insurance if they lost or changed jobs and would no longer allow insurance companies to deny coverage to people with preexisting conditions. In an attempt to gather support from individuals who already had insurance, Obama's plan gave people a choice to stay with their existing plan or enroll in the publicly funded program. Low-income individuals with salaries too high to qualify for Medicaid would also benefit from the health care reform as Obama proposed to increase federal funding to Medicaid and broaden eligibility requirements to allow more people to enroll in the federally funded program. Although well intentioned, the Medicaid component of Obama's proposed plan was the most contentious piece as opponents argued it was the first step in creating a system of socialized medicine (Amadeo, 2016).

On January 20, 2009, Obama was inaugurated as president of the U.S., and he wasted no time making his mark on American policy as he introduced one of the most radical ideological agendas since the New Deal (Hulse, 2009). The agenda included making significant changes to three pillars of American society: health care, education, and energy (Krauthammer, 2010). Of the three, Obama's most recognized focus was health care reform and increasing the affordability and accessibility of health care for Americans. In a joint session to Congress on February 24, 2009, Obama said, "So let there be no doubt: Healthcare reform cannot wait, it must not wait, and it will not wait another year" (Smith, 2012). Despite Obama's determination, his health care agenda did not receive the warm reception that he had been expecting, and despite giving 29 speeches on health care he was unable to convince policymakers to support health care reform. The popularity boost he received from the presidential campaign faded. The decline in his approval poll numbers to 46 percent reflected many Americans' discomfort with a policy agenda they felt threatened the status quo (Krauthammer, 2010). Fighting accusations that he was a "do-nothing" president, Obama was desperate to pass a significant piece of legislation. Attempting to gain political support, Obama lobbied Hispanic members of Congress, referring to the health care bill as critical to both his legacy as president and the success of Democrats in the upcoming midterm election (MacAskill, 2010).

Although eager to gather support for his health care reform bill, the Obama administration had to tread carefully and learn from the health care policy missteps of the past, specifically the Clinton administration's failed attempt at health reform in 1993 and 1994. Keeping the Clinton administration's struggles in mind, President Obama focused on incorporating all key actors in the health reform process, which included having doctors, insurers, hospitals, pharmaceutical companies, and labor unions at the negotiating table (Stolberg, 2009). Obama was able to gain support for health care reform using this method, but the public option plan had become a problem, as it was an issue of contention for Democrats in Congress. The public option plan would create a public insurance plan that would compete directly with private insurance companies with the goal of reducing insurance premiums and health care costs. In the Senate, Charles Schumer (D-NY) and Jay Rockefeller (D-WV) were unable successfully to add the proposed public option amendments to the health care reform legislation in any stage of the policy process (Halpin & Harbage, 2010). Joseph Lieberman, an Independent senator from Connecticut, and a key health care vote, threatened to filibuster any bill that included a public option. Although President Obama had publicly supported a public option he was more concerned with passing the legislation and trusted Senate Majority Leader, Harry Reid (D-NV), who argued that removing the public option was the best opportunity to get the 60 votes needed to pass the health care reform bill (Cohen, 2010).

The ability to get 60 votes was a critical part of the health care reform success equation because it was the number of Senate votes needed to break a Republican filibuster (Cohen, 2010). Democrats could pursue a second option called budget reconciliation if they were unable to secure 60 votes. This process allowed the Senate to pass a bill with only 51 votes and without threat of a Republican filibuster. The process of budget reconciliation was created by the Congressional Budget Act of 1974 and is used to advance legislation that makes changes to spending, revenues, and the federal debt limit (Reich & Kogan, 2016). Budget reconciliation was a last-case scenario, as many moderate Democratic senators felt that the process was too partisan and should be avoided at all costs (Halpin & Harbage, 2010). Keeping the worst-case scenario in mind, the Obama administration wrote the health reform legislation using language that would allow the bill to be passed by budget reconciliation if Reid was unable to obtain 60 Senate votes. Despite having a plan in place, Obama continued to face an uphill battle as his administration struggled to get his bill through the Senate Finance Committee. The committee was worried about the cost of reforming America's health care system after the CBO estimated that Obama's plan could cause a deficit of more than $200 billion. In September 2009, President Obama announced in a speech that he would be able to reform health care for $900 billion over 10 years, which was enough to persuade the Finance Committee to accept the bill (Cohen, 2010).

Concessions were made as Democrats tried to secure the necessary votes in both houses. In the House of Representatives, Speaker of the House Nancy Pelosi (D-CA) needed 218 votes to pass the legislation. To reach this number, Pelosi had to compromise with Bart Stupak, a Democrat from Michigan, who refused to support the bill unless it banned insurance coverage for abortion procedures. Ultimately, Pelosi was forced to indulge Stupak but was successful in safeguarding 220 votes after the exclusion of the abortion language led to Stupak's support as well as that of Republican Ahn "Joseph" Cao of Louisiana (Cohen, 2010). In the Senate, Democrats were relying on Joseph Lieberman's support of the health care reform bill after the death of Ted Kennedy on August 25, 2009, left the party with only 59 votes. After the public option was permanently removed from consideration, Lieberman gave the Democrats his vote and on December 24, 2009, the Senate passed the health reform legislation. The fight was not over for the Democrats, however, as the bill still needed to be reconciled between the two chambers due to different approaches regarding how coverage would be provided to Americans and how the coverage would be paid for. Reconciliation would end up being nearly as difficult as passing the bill itself as Minority Leader Mitch McConnell (R-KY) promised, "This fight is not over. This fight is long from over. My colleagues and I will work to stop this bill from becoming law" (Murray & Montgomery, 2009).

After the legislation was passed, many Democrats expected to cut their winter break short to finalize the legislation, but President Obama insisted on waiting until January to reconvene Congress, which ended up putting the legislation further at risk (Cohen, 2010). In 2010, Democrats lost their filibuster-proof majority when Republican Scott Brown defeated Democrat Martha Coakley for Ted Kennedy's Senate seat in Massachusetts. Without enough votes to pass the reconciled bill, Pelosi, Reid, and the White House decided to pass the bill through budget reconciliation because it only required 51 Senators. Over the next few weeks the Democrats in the House and the Senate worked to merge their versions of the legislation and ensure the language met the requirements to be passed as a reconciliation bill (Cohen, 2010). On March 21, 2010, the Senate passed the Patient Protection and Affordable Care Act (PPACA) while the House passed additional related policies, both without Republican support. Following seven previous attempts and failures by presidents to reform health care, President Barack Obama became the first president to successfully pass a comprehensive health care reform bill into law when he signed the ACA legislation on March 23, 2010 (Smith, 2012; Murray & Montgomery, 2009).

Conclusion

The story of health care reform in the U.S. is one of incremental change over a long time. In many senses, the policy solutions discussed over that time have not changed substantially—the proposals considered in the 1930s are not markedly different from proposals introduced during the debate over the ACA some 80 years later. In a nutshell, the pattern of health care policy that has developed in the U.S. is one that favors market-based solutions for the provisions of health services, as well as the provision of coverage for health care through a private insurance market. The ACA builds on these fundamental patterns and decisions, resulting in a policy that, for all the rhetoric surrounding its passage, is not much different at its core from previous health care policies.

Of course, opponents of the ACA find plenty in the new law with which to disagree, that, in turn, gives rise to the battles in the states over how to respond to the law. Indeed, much of the disagreement revolves around issues in the ACA that are not found in previous national health care policies, such as the individual mandate. Still, the ACA is not, in policy terms, so very different from previous policy decisions.

Note

1. The Whitewater investigation was triggered by concern into a land-purchase arrangements in which the Clintons had been investors. Although the project ultimately went bankrupt, an investigation found banking improprieties, and several people connected with the project were convicted. The special investigator in the case never brought charges against the Clintons, but the investigation was a distraction from more pressing policy issues. Indeed, the distraction of Whitewater was eventually replaced by a scandal involving the president and a White House intern.

3 The "Nuts and Bolts" of the ACA

The final version of the PPACA (more commonly known as the ACA) offered a bundle of several initiatives that addressed a variety of health care–related issues built around controlling costs and mandating efficiencies. To ensure that all individuals had access to affordable insurance, the health reform legislation revolved around five major goals: sharing responsibility for universal coverage between the government, citizens, and employees; making health care a more equitable system by improving its affordability and quality; improving the efficiency of care to reduce wasteful health care spending while embracing diversity and inclusivity; improving access to primary and preventative health care services; and demonstrating an investment in American health by increasing accessibility to more clinics focusing on preventative and community health. The rigorous legislative effort that policymakers put into creating the ACA reflected these goals, but the complexity of the legislation and the unprecedented nature of health care reform in the U.S. resulted in lingering questions regarding whether or not the implementation of the ACA would be successful (Rosenbaum, 2011).

To overcome the barriers and policy uncertainties tied to implementing health care reform for the first time in American history, the Obama administration and the ACA policy designers chose to maintain the structure of the U.S.'s existing health care system to improve the chances that universal health care would be both manageable and successful. For this reason, employer-sponsored coverage, Medicare, and Medicaid were featured as three key components of the ACA (Hacker, 2011; Jost, 2014; Starr, 2013; Tuohy, 2011). Focusing on the two major themes of affordability and accessibility, the Obama administration also challenged health care professionals to be innovative and find ways to improve medical care delivery while lowering costs. Obama felt strongly that a health care insurance program could be affordable and meet the needs of citizens. Pointing to the Mayo Clinic in Minnesota, President Obama said, "We should learn from their successes and promote the best practices, not the most expensive ones. That's how we'll achieve reform that fixes what doesn't work and builds on what does. We must attack the root causes of skyrocketing health costs" (Stolberg, 2009). In order to successfully reduce health care costs while expanding accessibility, the ACA was designed around five primary provisions: change the way that the insurance markets operate, subsidize and provide health care coverage through federal and state Health Benefit Exchanges, use federal funding to expand Medicaid eligibility, and provide increased federal financial support to states that implement health care programs and services (Johnson & Metzker, 2017).

Health Care Reforms

The requirements of the new legislation primarily impacted health insurance markets serving small groups and individuals. One of the most significant changes protected individuals with preexisting conditions by including a clause that insurance companies could no longer deny individuals with preexisting conditions health insurance or charge them a higher fee than their peers without a preexisting condition. Insurance companies were forced to standardize their rates with variation in cost only allowed for age, tobacco use, or differences in geographical location. Additionally, insurance companies could not cap the amount that an individual could receive in health care coverage during his or her lifetime, with an exception for plans that had been grandfathered in. Insurance companies were also required to guarantee the availability of insurance, as well as the option to renew their insurance plan, provide an open enrollment period for those going through a qualifying life-changing event, and cover adults under their parents' plan until 26 years old (U.S. Department of Health & Human Services, 2017). In return for mandating insurance companies to cover all individuals for the same cost, regardless of preexisting condition or frequency of illness, the new law also required individuals without health insurance to enroll in an ACA approved health care program or pay a tax penalty. The tax penalty for adults in 2016 was $695 for adults, $347.50 for children under the age of 18, or 2.5 percent of one's household income, whichever was higher. Employers with 50 or more full-time employees also had to make changes to their insurance coverage and provide at least 95 percent of their full-time employees and their dependents health care coverage in order to meet the requirements of the ACA (Johnson & Metzker, 2017).

Health Care Exchanges

Online marketplaces were created to provide a place for individuals and small businesses with fewer than 50 employees to shop for health insurance coverage, receive a Medicaid coverage referral, or receive federal subsidies to help cover health insurance premiums. The health benefit exchanges were designed with only one open enrollment period, typically from November to January, to deter people from enrolling in an ACA-sponsored health plan only when they were facing a medical emergency. Individuals would be allowed to enroll midyear, however, if they were experiencing a qualifying life event such as the birth of a child. Additionally, all plans offered through the health benefit exchanges were required to provide essential health benefits. Despite this requirement, individuals did have options regarding the price and coverage of their insurance plan. All exchanges offered four tiers of coverage identified by naming them after precious metals. For example, health plans in the platinum tier had the highest premiums but lower copays and deductibles that covered 90 percent of the patient's medical costs.

Low-income citizens enrolling in health insurance through the health exchange with an income between 100 and 400 percent of the federal poverty level (FPL), without alternative options of health coverage, were provided with information pertaining to their federal tax credit and cost-sharing reductions while they applied for insurance so they would know the cost of their plan with the inclusion of the subsidy (Johnson & Metzker, 2017). Individuals living at 250 percent of the FPL would be eligible for lower out-of-pocket maximums and those living at 400 percent of the FPL would be given the option of subsidized premiums (Schoen, Doty, Robertson, & Collins, 2011).

Medicaid Expansion

In the initial ACA legislation signed by President Obama in March of 2010, Medicaid was expanded and all states were required to provide health coverage through Medicaid to children, parents, and childless adults living at or below the FPL. States that refused to comply with the expansion would be subject to having their Medicaid funds withheld by the secretary of the HHS. The Supreme Court of the U.S. (SCOTUS) later deemed this provision as unconstitutional in the case *NFIB v. Sebelius*, resulting in state choice on whether to expand Medicaid. Individuals receiving coverage due to their state's decision to expand Medicaid became known as the optional expansion population (Kaiser Family Foundation, 2012a; Johnson & Metzker, 2017). The federal government rewarded states choosing to expand their Medicaid program with a higher contribution to their federal medical assistance percentages (FMAP) to help manage the increased costs of covering the optional expansion population. FMAPs determine the amount of federal funds that will be given to a state to help offset payments made by the state for specific social services and state medical insurance expenditures, including enhanced federal contributions to the cost of Medicaid in each state (Office of Planning and Evaluation, 2015; Kaiser Family Foundation, 2012b; Johnson & Metzker, 2017). These percentages vary from state to state with some states receiving more than others based on a formula taking into account a state's average per capita income relative to the national average. For example, California received an FMAP low of 50 percent while Mississippi received an FMAP high of 75 percent. The lowest FMAP amount a state can receive is 50 percent (Kaiser Family Foundation, 2018a). In the first few years of ACA implementation, the federal government committed to pay 100 percent of FMAP to cover the optional expansion population. After 2016 states would have to start contributing, however, and in 2017 states would be responsible for 5 percent of the costs of covering the optional expansion population. In 2020, and the years following, the contribution would increase to 10 percent of Medicaid costs for this population (Johnson & Metzker, 2017).

Section 1115 Waivers

In an attempt to maximize the effectiveness of their Medicaid programs, some states applied for Section 1115 waivers. These waivers were originally intended to allow for innovative solutions to specific issues that the traditional Medicaid program was unable to address. Additionally, the waivers gave states more autonomy and the freedom to determine the best way to distribute benefits to their residents (Kaiser Family Foundation, 2011; Dewitt, 2018). Although many of the core components of the waivers stayed the same, after the implementation of the ACA states had the ability to alter the requirements affecting eligibility, benefits, cost sharing, and how providers are compensated (Kaiser Family Foundation, 2011). Elements of transparency were also added to the Section 1115 code by mandating that each waiver be formally evaluated to determine whether the waiver met its intended objectives. Initially the burden of evaluating effectiveness and determining waiver renewal fell on the secretary of HHS in an attempt to increase transparency, however, an increase in the use of Section 1115 waivers over the years has slowly shifted the burden of evaluation from HHS to the states (Kaiser Family Foundation, 2011).[1]

Additional Federal Funding

In addition to expanding Medicaid under the ACA, states would also receive a boost to their FMAP if they created and implemented new health care programs and services. Although some of the programs only qualified for a temporary increase in funds, other increases were permanent. Two significant programs that states had the option of enrolling in were the Children's Health Insurance Program (CHIP) and the Community First Choice Option (CFCO). CHIP is supported by both the state and federal government and provides health care to children and families that are considered low income but have incomes too high to qualify for Medicaid. Beginning in October 2015, states participating in CHIP would have between 88 percent and 100 percent of their costs to operate the program covered. Although the ACA authorized FMAP increases through federal fiscal year (FFY) 2018–2019, funding was only appropriated through 2017 (Johnson & Metzker, 2017). The CFCO program provided support to seniors and individuals with disabilities through home and community assistant services. States choosing to provide services through their CFCOs were given an FMAP enhancement of 6 percent beginning in October of 2012. In addition to these two major programs, the ACA also created funding for many smaller programs through the creation of the Prevention and Public Health Fund. The fund appropriated $7 billion in funding to all states through grants by various federal agencies to encourage prevention, public health, and healthy activities between FFY 2009/2010 through

FFY 2014/2015, with $2 billion allocated for years following this timeframe. Changes made by the Trump administration have led to cuts in the Prevention and Public Health Fund, however, and only $931 million is available annually moving forward (Johnson & Metzker, 2017).

ACA and Additional Revenue

The initial price tag of $900 billion for the ACA led to concerns about whether a universal health care model could be sustainable in the U.S. To help offset the costs, the ACA included plans to create new streams of federal revenue, primarily through new taxes. One of the new taxes added a 0.9 percent Medicare tax to individuals making over $200,000 a year and married couples making over $250,000. This same income group would also have an additional 3.8 percent surtax on their investments, which was projected to exceed $30 billion annually for FFY 2017/2018. The individual mandate tax penalty would also contribute $15 to $20 billion to the U.S. economy annually. Several of the new taxes created were directed at the health care industry. For example, the health insurance provider fee is an excise tax placed on health insurance providers, excluding self-employed employers, government organizations, and some nonprofit organizations (Gibson & Dominiak, 2013). The Congressional Budget Office (CBO) anticipated that the ACA would begin reducing the federal budget deficit and generate annual federal savings beginning in the 2018/2019 fiscal year (FY; Foster, 2009; Cohen, 2010). Moreover, the CBO projected that if all taxes were collected that revenues would add up to roughly $100 billion by FY 2017/2018. It was also projected that $20 billion in revenues would have amassed in that year alone (Miller, 2018; Johnson & Metzker, 2017). Not all taxes have been collected, however. In January 2018, a Republican-led Congress and the Trump administration delayed a 40 percent excise tax on high-cost employer-sponsored health plans until 2022 as part of an agreement to reestablish funding and end a partial government shutdown (Miller, 2018). In the same month, President Trump also signed an agreement that delayed a 2.3 percent excise tax on medical devices for two years (Mershon, 2018).

Legal Challenges to the ACA

On March 23, 2010, minutes after President Obama signed the ACA into law, the state of Florida filed a legal challenge to the constitutionality of the individual mandate and Medicaid expansion in federal district court (Kaiser Family Foundation, 2012a). Shortly thereafter, 25 more states,[2] as well as several other plaintiffs, including the NFIB, joined Florida in its lawsuit (Kaiser Family Foundation, 2012a). The state of Virginia chose to file separately due to State Attorney General Ken Cuccinelli's argument that the ACA conflicted with the state's law making it illegal to require Virginia residents to purchase insurance. The U.S. Court of Appeals for the 4th Circuit in Richmond ruled that Virginia lacked the standing to sue, resulting in Cuccinelli's threat to appeal their decision to SCOTUS. Lawsuits by several individuals and Liberty University, a private Christian University in Lynchburg, Virginia, were also dismissed by the 4th Circuit Court (Kumar & Aizenman, 2011). While many states were arguing against the ACA, 13 states[3] and the District of Columbia filed amicus briefs to support the individual mandate and Medicaid expansion (Kaiser Family Foundation, 2012a).

Although numerous lawsuits were filed challenging the constitutionality of the ACA, the Supreme Court decided they would only hear the decision from the U.S. Court of Appeals for the 11th Circuit in Atlanta. The 11th Circuit Court was the only judgment that struck down the mandate at the time, arguing that the mandate overstepped congressional authority and was not supported by Congress's constitutional power to regulate commerce or collect taxes (Liptak, 2011). By accepting this case, SCOTUS would determine the constitutionality of the individual mandate and Medicaid expansion. The court also agreed to consider two additional questions on the individual mandate portion of the ACA if they determined it was unconstitutional. First, if the individual mandate was deemed unconstitutional, the court would establish whether the mandate was severable, which would allow the remainder of the ACA to be put into effect. If the individual mandate was not severable, then the entire law would be overturned. Second, the court would determine if the Anti-Injunction Act required SCOTUS to wait on ruling on the constitutionality of the individual mandate until taxpayers were actually fined for refusing to comply with the mandate (White, 2012; Kaiser Family Foundation, 2012c). After hearing the case, Chief Justice Roberts joined Justices Breyer, Kagan, Ginsburg, and Sotomayor to form a majority and held that the individual mandate was an appropriate exercise of Congress's power to levy taxes. This decision was surprising because all the lower federal courts had found that the individual mandate was unconstitutional under Congress's taxing power. Moreover, due to the majority ruling for the constitutionality of the individual mandate, the decision to sever the individual mandate was moot (Kaiser Family Foundation, 2012a).

In their decision on Medicaid expansion, the court determined that Congress overstepped its spending clause power and that the guidelines for expanding Medicaid in the ACA were unconstitutional and coercive. The court ruled against the constitutionality of expansion because states did not have adequate notice to voluntarily consent and their inability to comply would enable the secretary of HHS to withhold state Medicaid funding. Although the court ruled 5–4, there were three different approaches to the decision. Chief Justice Roberts, Justice Breyer, and Justice Kagan called the Medicaid language in the ACA a "gun to the head" because states had only two options: to expand Medicaid or risk losing federal Medicaid financial support (Kaiser Family Foundation, 2012c). This ruling stated that Congress could offer states federal funds and apply conditions to the money, but they could not make a state's existing Medicaid funds contingent on their agreement to expand Medicaid. They also clarified that if the provision allowing the secretary of HHS to remove Medicaid funding from states if they did not comply with expansion was taken out of the ACA, then the constitutional violation would be resolved (Kaiser Family Foundation, 2012c).

Justices Scalia, Kennedy, Thomas, and Alito also found the Medicaid expansion provision unconstitutionally coercive, but they determined that Medicaid expansion is not severable from the rest of the ACA, and therefore the entire law should be invalidated. Lastly, Justices Ginsburg and Sotomayor ruled in favor of the constitutionality of the ACA. The three different findings resulted in no majority ruling, and therefore no clear process on how to deal with the unconstitutionality of Medicaid expansion (Rosenbaum & Westmoreland, 2012). For this reason, Justices Ginsburg and Sotomayor joined the Roberts, Breyer, and Kagan opinion, yielding a five-justice majority that Medicaid could only be expanded voluntarily and that the secretary of HHS could not coerce states to expand Medicaid. Although the constitutionality of the ACA was upheld, the difficulties were not over, as states took steps to implement state exchanges and expand health insurance to those without access to affordable care.

Political Opposition

The 111th Congress was the most productive in several years due to the legislative accomplishments made in the first two years of President Obama's presidency (Jacobson, 2011). Despite this success, however, the topic of universal health care divided Americans more than any other issue since the Vietnam War (MacAskill, 2010). Republicans began calling the health care reform legislation, "Obamacare." Representative Debbie Wasserman Shultz (D-FL) attempted to curb the negative connotation around health care reform by arguing it violated rules against critical comments about the president (Pecquet, 2011). Nonetheless, Republicans continued their attack on the legislation. Speaker of the House John Boehner (R-OH) was outspoken against the legislation, stating, "If we pass this bill there will be no turning back. In a democracy, you can only ignore the will of the people for so long and get away with it." President Obama had hoped that health care reform would be a bipartisan journey and encouraged Max Baucus, a Democrat from Montana, to gather Republican support. Baucus had one of the most conservative Democratic voting records, and the Obama administration hoped he would be able to attract Republican support for the bill, but all attempts to reach across the aisle failed (Cohen, 2010).

President Obama had reason to hope for Republican cooperation since many of the components of the ACA, such as reliance on private insurance, the individual mandate, consumer choice and competition, health insurance purchasing, and a significant role for states in the health care plans aligned with Republican values and had been included in previous Republican-supported health care plans (Quadagno, 2014). Democrats also hoped that the promise of federal dollars would persuade Republicans to focus on the law's conservative pieces or force them to accept that the issue of health reform was not going away, but all attempts to attract Republican support were futile. President Obama's adviser David Axelrod responded to the lack of Republican cooperation:

> We want to work with everyone who will work with us and we want to do it in the spirit of bipartisanship, but we can't defer reform and we want to move forward. Those who don't, they need to address those Americans struggling with higher premiums and losing their insurance.
>
> (Bipartisan Legislation, 2009)

Democrats only successfully passed health reform legislation because they had a majority in both houses of Congress: All Republicans voted no on the ACA (Murray & Montgomery, 2009). Despite their loss, Republicans used repeal of the ACA as a campaigning point for the upcoming midterm elections (Tumulty, 2010). This was bad news for Democrats running for reelection in difficult races, especially after a report from the CBO stated that the legislation would most likely lead to an increase in federal spending on health care, resulting in greater opposition to the ACA (Bipartisan Legislation, 2009).

The midterm elections led to a rise in partisan politics as debates over health policy continued, especially arguments focusing on the creation of health insurance exchanges and Medicaid expansion. Featured in many Grand Old Party–supported health care plans, state exchanges were largely supported by the public prior to the midterm elections (Jones, Bradley, & Oberlander, 2014). The midterm elections were detrimental to this support, however, as Republicans took over many seats that had been won by Democrats in both Congress and at the state level. The midterm election also resulted in a strong showing by the Tea Party and the loss of a Democratic majority led to growing opposition of state exchanges (Jost, 2014). The Obama administration attempted to change the narrative by renaming the state exchanges "marketplaces" but to no avail.

The growing public resentment towards state exchanges resulted in only seventeen states and the District of Columbia establishing their own health insurance exchanges prior to the ACA's inaugural 2013 enrollment period, leaving the federal government to operate exchanges across most of the country. Politics surrounding the exchanges were largely partisan, and of the thirty states with Republican governors, only four created exchanges, three of which had Democratic dominance of the state legislature[4] (Jones et al., 2014). In many respects, the ACA's emphasis on providing states a strong role in the implementation of health care reform added stress to the Obama administration as Republicans were given several avenues to resist the law as they addressed the new provisions of health care reform in their states. This issue was minimized, however, by the Republicans' refusal to create state exchanges, which gave the federal government control over many marketplaces and prevented significant damage to the ACA (Starr, 2013; Oberlander, 2016).

State Choices and Decisions

States had four choices when creating a state exchange: state-based marketplace, state-based marketplace federal platform, state-partnership marketplace, or federally facilitated marketplace (Kaiser Family Foundation, 2017). When making a decision states had four primary considerations prior to selecting a state-exchange option. First, states had to consider how much flexibility they would be given by the federal government if they decided to create a state exchange. Their second concern was how much control they wanted over their insurance markets and their ability to create plans that were specific to their insurance markets and populations. Third was the level of complexity in coordinating services with other state agencies and the federal government. Last, states had to take into consideration funding and resource limitations (Health Policy Brief, 2013). Although similar in many ways, each of the four plans varied and impacted individual states differently based on their response to the four considerations.

States selecting the state-based marketplace approach would be responsible for all parts of the health exchange marketplace for both individuals and the Small Business Health Options Program (SHOP). The state was also responsible for creating and maintaining a marketplace website and residents of states with these programs would apply and be enrolled in health care directly through the state's marketplace website (Kaiser Family Foundation, 2017). States deciding to use the state-based marketplace federal platform would use the federal marketplace information technology platform while performing all other responsibilities of the state-based marketplace. States selecting this type of marketplace would manage insurance for individuals and SHOP, but residents would apply and enroll in health insurance through the federal website, healthcare.gov. States establishing a state-partnership marketplace program relied on the HHS to perform all marketplace functions. Residents in these states and SHOP employers and employees would also apply and enroll in health insurance through healthcare.gov. In this system states typically have programs in place that allows them to conduct plan management and provide residents with in-person assistance if necessary. States selecting the federally facilitated marketplace approach depended on the HHS to perform all marketplace functions. All eligible residents, employers, and employees used healthcare.gov to apply and enroll in health coverage (Kaiser Family Foundation, 2017).

Regardless of their marketplace selection, states were expected to have their exchanges ready by October 1, 2013, when the first enrollment period would begin. States also had to have health care plans operational by January 1, 2014, when ACA coverage would begin for both individuals and small businesses (Health Policy Brief, 2013). Under the new law, the secretary of HHS had the authority to require states to offer coverage through the federally facilitated marketplace plan if they felt that the state exchange would not be ready by the January 1st deadline. The federal government did try to facilitate the creation of state exchanges by providing grants to states. Marketplace exchanges created by states without much federal input varied greatly from each other because although the ACA provided states with a framework and minimum standards, the states were given significant flexibility with the decisions they made regarding the structure of their exchanges (Health Policy Brief, 2013). By the time the ACA was set to begin in 2014, 12 states had chosen to implement state-based programs, 5 decided on state-based marketplace federal platforms, 6 selected state-partnership marketplaces, and 28 defaulted to the federally facilitated marketplace (Kaiser Family Foundation, 2017).

Minimizing Disruptions

The Obama administration was cognizant that one of the main reasons that the Clinton health plan failed to succeed was that many working-age individuals balked at the idea of being forced by the federal government to give up their existing insurance plan to join a regulated private plan, even if the insurance coverage would be an improvement (Cohen, 2010). Although controversial, the individual mandate had found success in some arenas. For example, Massachusetts implemented an individual mandate as part of their universal health coverage program in 2006 under Republican governor Mitt Romney. Much like the ACA, health insurance policy designers in Massachusetts recognized that sick people alone could not cover the cost of providing care to all in a universal health insurance system (McCluskey, 2017). Despite Romney's success in Massachusetts, Obama remained cautious and never formally advocated for an individual mandate maintaining that only children, not adults, would be required to purchase health insurance (Cohen, 2010). President Obama also stated publicly several times, "If you like your plan, you can keep your plan."

At first his emphasis on minimizing disruption for those with health insurance was not problematic because the 2009–2010 debate included little discussion over what would happen to people who were already enrolled in an individual insurance plan because it only pertained to five percent of Americans (Oberlander, 2016). As the ACA was being written it was initially expected that most Americans that had insurance policies would be able to remain enrolled in their existing policies and the uninsured and underinsured would be enrolled in Medicaid or private insurance plans. The creation of the health insurance exchanges had never been done before, however, and as the law came together it was determined that not all people would be able to keep their plans in order to provide a sufficiently balanced market pool (McCluskey, 2017; Oberlander, 2016). Although a grandfather clause was included in Section 1251 of the ACA, which would allow some individuals to keep their original insurance plan, the provisions were narrow, and many of the existing plans failed to meet the standards of the new law (Roy, 2013).

Ultimately, the ACA benefit and rating requirements placed on insurance companies led to the cancellation of millions of individual policies in the fall of 2013. In November 2013, President Obama said, "I am sorry that they are finding themselves in this situation based on assurances they got from me" (Salam, 2013). As a response to the political backlash to the individual mandate, the Obama administration gave states the option to allow their residents to remain enrolled in their existing plans until 2014, which was then extended until 2017. In fall of 2014, 40 states allowed their residents to remain enrolled in plans that were not compliant with the individual and small-group marketplace guidelines (Luca, Corlette, & Williams, 2014).

Summary

Despite the imperfections associated with the ACA and controversy surrounding the inability of people to keep their insurance plans, President Obama remains the only president to successfully pass substantial health care reform since health insurance became a politically charged topic in 1915. The story of health care reform in the U.S., however, remains one of crisis, opportunity, competing interests, political opportunism, agenda denial, and above all, incrementalism. As Lindblom (1959) has pointed out, incremental decisions are rarely perfect (or even coherent), but they almost always contain something for everyone to support. Health care policy illustrates this principle well, in that nearly all major reforms and programs were "satisficing" concoctions that represented what was possible within the prevailing political and economic conditions. Likewise, in times of strong partisanship (or even hyper-partisanship), agenda denial has proven to be a very effective tool to prevent policy change. The development of the ACA followed a very similar pattern. In some ways, the surprising thing about the ACA is not the form it took but the fact that it came to fruition at all.

Learning from the Clinton administration mistakes of the past, the Obama administration took several steps to overcome partisan agenda-denial barriers by including all health care stakeholders in the policy design process and creating a policy considerate of conservative values. The ACA is very "Republican" in its approach: It relies on private markets to provide coverage, it gives a great amount of discretion to states in terms of their ability to make decisions regarding implementation of the program, and it provides funding to reduce the impact of an otherwise unfunded mandate. Close examination of the ACA reveals that the legislation itself is an incremental solution that was designed to attract support from across the political spectrum. Despite the policy design compromises, Democrats still found themselves making compromises to gain support for their health reform bill. Unmoved by attempts at bipartisanship, Republicans fought the implementation of the ACA at every step but missed a key opportunity to undermine state market exchanges when many Republican governors defaulted to federally facilitated marketplaces.

Even after its passage, attempts to overturn the law have continued unabated. While other scholars have addressed the national political process that led to the creation of the ACA, our focus is squarely on the choices made by states in the implementation phase of the law. National politics most certainly played a role in determining state choice, but there were other important factors as well. Our goal for this research is to "unpack" those state decisions and thus better understand the nuances of the factors that drive state policy choices.

Notes

1. Currently there is no database of Section 1115 waivers and therefore no outlet for researchers to compare, contrast, and evaluate outcomes associated with waivers (Kaiser Family Foundation, 2011).
2. On March 23, 2010, Florida filed suit against the ACA in federal district court and was joined by 25 other states: Alabama, Alaska, Arizona, Colorado, Georgia, Idaho, Indiana, Iowa, Kansas, Louisiana, Maine, Michigan, Mississippi, Nebraska, Nevada, North Dakota, Ohio, Pennsylvania, South Carolina, South Dakota, Texas, Utah, Washington, Wisconsin, and Wyoming.
3. California, Connecticut, Delaware, Hawaii, Illinois, Iowa, Maryland, Massachusetts, New Mexico, New York, Oregon, Vermont, and Washington all filed amicus briefs demonstrating their support of the individual mandate and Medicaid expansion.
4. Republican governors in California, New Mexico, Nevada, and Idaho directed the creation of a state exchange. Of these states, California, New Mexico, and Nevada had Democratic majorities in their state legislatures. Idaho had unified Republican Control.

4 A National Look at ACA Implementation Choices

The state-level implementation of the ACA was one fraught with complexity and difficulties. Substantial differences between states along fiscal, health, and ideological lines further highlighted the divergent needs, approaches, and response by states to the federal reform efforts. Due in part to policy design, and to court case rulings, states had substantial autonomy in the decision-making process of how they would proceed with the implementation of health care reform. To understand the differences and complexities of the ACA implementation across state boundaries, this study examines implementation and innovation in four vastly different states.

Employing public record and popular media accounts, this work highlights the challenges and disagreements within and across states, even in instances where there was a consensus on implementation. Through a case study approach, this work builds on prior quantitative studies (see Mayer, Kenter, & Morris, 2016; Mayer et al., 2015; Travis et al., 2016) in an attempt to better understand state-level decision-making and the varying dynamics influencing state response to health care reform.

We examine state decision-making and measures of support and opposition during the three-year early implementation window from 2012 to 2014, in an effort to analyze state response to the initial ACA implementation. Utilizing a previously developed framework (Travis et al., 2016) assessing levels of statewide support and opposition and their impacts on decision-making, this research offers a detailed explanation of why selected states behaved in the manner they did, an explanation not possible in the prior quantitative studies.

The framework consists of a multicomponent dependent variable index, designed to measure state response across several factors in support and opposition of the ACA (Travis et al., 2016). The dependent variable index is unique in that it provides an additive measure of state support and opposition to the ACA. The index allows for the quantification of decision-making, a way in which to understand state support and opposition based on a number of actions and factors. In the initial analysis, all 50 states were scored over the three-year implementation window based on their level of support or opposition to several key policy directives: first, whether states adopted legislation in support of health care market reforms; second, whether they created their own insurance exchange; third, if they chose to accept Medicaid expansion funds; fourth, whether they participated in a lawsuit challenging the validity and constitutionality of the ACA; and, finally, whether they passed legislation impeding the implementation of the ACA within their state.

This variable allows for a more detailed instrument to measure support or opposition to the ACA. Mayer and Kenter (2014) and Barrilleaux and Rainey (2014) used whether or not a state expanded Medicaid as its gauge of ACA support and opposition. While these studies produced useful results, the results were limited in scope and only told a small portion of the ACA story. The index variable combines several well-thought-out decisions by the state and provides a more nuanced assessment of opposition or support than seen in much of the extant literature. By building on prior quantitative studies, we are able to more fully explore pertinent issues and developments raised in the research. However, we recognize some elements of the dependent variable may be solely viewed as a symbolic act of defiance to the ACA, while some decisions may be more representative of the actual capacity of the state to provide that portion of the act. Being unable to parse out the symbolic gestures from the pragmatic decisions, each decision was treated as equal and coded as such. This is an inherent limitation and one that is difficult to rectify, yet the results of treating decision-making factors equally allow for a baseline comparison across states and provide direction and structure to the analysis. This exercise revealed several fascinating trends and findings. In an effort to provide a thorough analysis and understanding of variation in state implementation, we ultimately settled on four states for examination. Alabama, Michigan, New Hampshire, and California were selected for study based on how they scored on support and opposition decision-making factors. Prior quantitative study revealed these states on varying points along the spectrum from outright opposition, uncertainty, indecision, and total support. The case study approach offers the ability to probe the decision-making process from state to state and to understand the complexity, action, and inaction that characterized state decision-making in a way that complements and extends the prior quantitative research.

These states were selected in order to illustrate the complexities and differences between states that were both in support of and opposition to the implementation of the ACA. Alabama was selected for inclusion as one of the staunchest state-level opponents of the ACA across the reviewed timeframe. Alabama had a Republican governor, a Republican-controlled state legislature, and a heavily skewed conservative population during the reviewed timeframe. This is important to note, because the early implementation of the ACA was characterized, and perhaps plagued, by partisan disagreements. Conservatives were mostly in opposition to the ACA, while liberal-leaning states were more supportive. Alabama is a prime example of why this is such an interesting subject of research. In a state that leaned heavily conservative and scored as one of the greatest opponents of the ACA reform, there was still documented early interest in exploring mechanisms of expansion and support from the highest levels of the Alabama state government. As the inclusion of Alabama shows, even in states where the decision-making process seemed like a foregone conclusion, the magnitude of the policy change led to several interesting and heated debates across the reviewed states.

In direct contrast to Alabama is the inclusion of California, a left-leaning, Democrat-controlled state, with the sixth-largest economy in the world. California scored as one of the most supportive states across the country related to health care reform, even taking several proactive measures to begin reforms before being mandated by law. Yet, much like in Alabama, while the majority favored one action and it ultimately won out, the decision-making process was more convoluted and influenced by several factors as the analysis will show.

With the conservative opposition and liberal supporting states represented, the third state selected fell solidly in between Alabama and California. Located in the upper Midwest, Michigan was selected for study as a state that remained neutral, with support and opposition measures canceling each other out over the initial three-year implementation. Despite the scoring, the inclusion of Michigan provides another fascinating review into state and local politics as they played out during the ACA decision-making process. Michigan, a union-dominated state, was bitterly divided on the issue. Disagreement could be found at all levels of government, with the attorney general and the governor facing off in a public and protracted legal squabble over who had the authority to move the state in either's chosen direction. The inclusion of Michigan also offers insight into the regional characteristics and culture found in the Midwest, which is contrasted with the inclusion of Alabama in the South, California in the West, and the last state analyzed, New Hampshire in the Northeast.

New Hampshire, the final state selected for study, exhibits the greatest movement from opposition to support during the early implementation window. The inclusion of New Hampshire illustrates how the conversation shifted within the state from one of opposition to one of support. Examining the culture and characteristics of the region and state, along with leadership and decision-making provides insight into the policy shift.

Collectively, the four states highlight the challenges and differences in the implementation of national policy at the state level. By coding each decision within the index as equal, we can further examine state policy variation and the factors, alike and different, from state to state. Each state had a vastly different response to the same broad policy framework and question posed when the ACA was signed into law. Examining these responses in the context of regional, political, and economic differences begins to shed light on the major factors driving state-level decision-making, why and how it differed with regard to the ACA from state to state, and the challenges in widespread policy implementation and adoption.

This book examines state-level decision-making and the political and socioeconomic factors that influenced the support and opposition of the ACA. Utilizing a case study approach and employing a previously developed framework (Travis et al., 2016) to guide the data collection and analysis; this work begins to highlight and explain the individual complexities influencing state-level decision-making related to the ACA. The framework, thoroughly discussed in the following sections, provides a map through which to catalog and analyze the varying sources of data. By examining written statements, press releases, legal transcripts, and other qualitative source material through the lens of the employed framework we can begin to better understand how political and socioeconomic factors influenced decision-making within the reviewed states.

The case study design allows for an in-depth examination of the decision-making processes within the reviewed states. The design further highlights the complexities, challenges, and contrasts that exist within and across each state and how those factors ultimately influenced state decision-making to support or oppose the legislation. While the case study approach offers results that are difficult to generalize, this concern is balanced out by the rich, in-depth, inquiry into the how and why the analyzed states behaved in the manner they did. By better understanding the contextual issues influencing state decision-making, we can also gain a more thorough knowledge of the intricacies involved in the decision-making process.

By examining decision-making at the state level, we are better able to understand the complexity of implementation and how contextual and divergent it may be from one state to the next. In addition, the state-level analysis highlights the challenges of national legislation being implemented across the states. How is the policy designed to fit the individual needs of the states, how much latitude and discretion do the states maintain during the implementation and enforcement, and how much choice do the states have in the matter? Examining each question in the context of the political climate and socioeconomic factors within the reviewed states provides evidence as to why states chose to support or oppose the ACA. By including states from different regions that had varying responses to the ACA, we further illustrate the impact and importance of contextual differences, regional culture, need, and politics, and how they coalesce to influence state decision-making.

Federalism and State Policy Variation

It is the American political system of federalism that provides the foundation for each individual state to shape policy that fits its particular ideology. Dating to the founding of our country, state power has been an issue of substantial debate. The Constitution is particularly vague and allows states significant latitude in developing and enforcing policy. The resulting fragmentation and state expansion have been the cause of considerable policy variation. While under the umbrella of federal policy, each state has great autonomy in its interpretation and implementation of public policy, often based on factors including party affiliation, political ideology, and political tradition. When policy decisions are pushed to the individual, state politics is often more important than the need of the citizens being affected by these policies (Soss et al., 2001; Mayer et al., 2015). However, Key (1949) argues that states with legislatures that share power or are closely split will tend to be more responsive to the needs of the marginalized and disadvantaged.

The ACA's main elements relied heavily on a system of shared governance in which the states were tasked with making several substantial decisions regarding vital portions of the act. While under a federal directive, ultimately the states were granted great discretion with how they chose to mold the ACA to their specific needs and desires. The success of this act relied heavily on the innovative tradition of policy implementation at the state level, and because of this, a single federal policy took on vastly different shapes from state to state. Due to these factors and many others, implementation is slow, uneven, and can vary widely from state to state (Haeder & Weimer, 2015).

Organizing Framework

Building from previously validated quantitative studies, this work employs a case study approach to add depth, context, and insight into state-level implementation of the ACA. Utilizing a previously developed framework (Travis et al., 2016) assessing levels of statewide support and opposition, this research offers an explanation to why selected states made the decisions they did.

The case studies are framed around the support and opposition index that was developed in prior study. This measure assesses state decision-making and rates states in their opposition and support of the ACA across several key decision points: first, whether states adopted legislation in support of health care market reforms; second, whether they created their own insurance exchange; third, if they chose to accept Medicaid expansion funds; fourth, whether they participated in a lawsuit challenging the validity and constitutionality of the ACA; and, finally, whether they passed legislation impeding the implementation of the ACA within their state. Several independent variable themes from the quantitative work are further explored in this research to provide additional insight into decision-making factors. These include party control of governor, party control of the legislature, citizen ideology, poverty, insurance, and state health.

Dependent Variable Deconstructed

As described earlier, the selection of the four states was driven primarily from the results of prior research that identified each as unique and interesting test cases for further research and analysis. This section discusses the creation and development of the five-component dependent variable index that was used to identify the four states in the analysis.

The five-component dependent variable index addresses the following state actions related to the ACA:

- Whether a state adopts legislation in support of health care market reforms
- Whether a state creates a health care insurance exchange. States were given the option to create an exchange or to allow citizens to enroll through a

federal exchange created and operated by the national government. Many states created a single exchange for both businesses and individual citizens, but Utah chose to create an exchange just for businesses (and not for individuals).

- Whether a state decides to accept funding for Medicaid expansion
- Whether a state is party to a lawsuit challenging the constitutionality of the ACA
- Whether a state has adopted legislation actively opposing the ACA

A primary mechanism of the ACA is the implementation of market reforms, such as access to coverage for young adults, a ban on the exclusion of those with preexisting conditions, and a minimum requirement of benefits, among other critical protections to consumers. These reforms provide federally mandated minimums with respect to critical portions of health care insurance intended to provide equal coverage for all participants. The market reforms, while established at the federal level, are the responsibility of the individual states to implement. We consider those states that have purposively taken regulatory or legislative action concerning these reforms as prescribed by the ACA to be in active support to the ACA.

A second vital mechanism of the ACA is the creation of health insurance exchanges or marketplaces. Exchanges were created to provide an affordable marketplace that allowed for a "one-stop shopping" experience, allowing participants to apply for federal subsidies, compare the cost and coverage of available plans, and subsequently purchase the plan in which they have chosen to enroll. The ACA allows each individual state the option of developing a separate state-based exchange or the option to take no action and, by default, opt into the federal exchange. Creating a state exchange allows significant flexibility in crafting the critical elements of the exchange to meet the individual needs of that particular state as long as they meet or exceed the minimum standards required by the ACA (Dash, Lucia, Keith, & Monahan, 2013). Those states that purposely create state exchanges as prescribed in the ACA are considered to be in support; those states that took no action therefore defaulted to the federal exchange are coded as in active opposition.

The acceptance or rejection of the third mechanism, increased federal funding for Medicaid expansion, can be viewed as either supportive or oppositional depending on the decision. The ACA is designed to pay 100 percent of the state Medicaid costs through 2017; after that, a declining percentage that reaches 90 percent in 2020 and goes no lower. By increasing the minimum level for Medicaid benefits to citizens at or above 138 percent of the poverty level, states have the ability to not only provide increased health care coverage to the working poor, but the law also provides an increase of federal funds designed to lower the amount of unreimbursed health care costs undertaken by that state's hospitals (Barrilleaux, 2013). Medicaid waivers are designed for states to experiment with alternative service deliveries options in an effort to still provide a level of care for those who qualify. While each state's waiver is different, there are certain minimum requirements states need to satisfy before a waiver is granted. These waiver states have made an affirmative effort to provide Medicaid benefits to their citizens. For the purposes of our analysis, states that accepted increased funding for Medicaid under waivers prior to the adoption of the ACA, and who did not reverse that decision under the ACA, are considered supportive of this mechanism.

The fourth component is whether states have become party to a lawsuit challenging the constitutionality of the ACA. There are several examples, and one of the most prominent is the *NFIB v. Sebelius* (2012) lawsuit. Joined by several states, the suit challenged several key provisions of the ACA and their constitutionality, in particular, the individual mandate and the scope of Medicaid expansion. While ultimately upheld, the ruling limited the scope of the legislation and gave states greater freedom in the acceptance and implementation of the provisions of the ACA. Several states were party to this and other lawsuits that challenged the constitutionality of the ACA. We consider these states to be in active opposition to the ACA and were coded as such (Kaiser Family Foundation, 2012c).

The final component of the framework measuring state support and opposition reviews whether states have proposed legislation related to the ACA. Several states have proposed legislation opposing the ACA using numerous strategies in an effort to limit, alter, and block state and federal efforts to implement the ACA. While the legal language may differ from state to state, the main goal remains the same: to oppose the ACA. Examples of this legislation include statutes that refuse to implement mandates or seek to nullify the ACA by restricting the amount of assistance the state will provide to those citizens seeking to enroll in the ACA. States have also passed nonbinding resolutions declaring their opposition (National Conference of State Legislatures, 2015). Those states that have enacted these forms of state legislation have been coded as being in opposition to the ACA.

Strengths

The primary strength of the case study approach is that it allows for a more thorough explanation of state policy choices than would otherwise be possible. This is not to discount the utility of a quantitative approach to the same question. In fact, we have authored several manuscripts in this vein and have utilized that research to drive this study. Where the case study methodology stands out is the researchers' ability to drill down on the identified trends and behaviors. In this case, decision-making, why did states make the choices they did with respect to supporting and opposing the ACA. The case study approach highlights subtle nuances, exposing internal divisions, even at policy extremes that illustrate the complexity of state decision-making.

The use of the framework allows for the comparison and analysis of divergent state needs, highlighting how starkly different similar concepts may be across state lines. This research shows how difficult achieving consensus may be, even on issues that seem cut and dried and enjoy a partisan majority. In quantitative research, there is often an assumption that states arrive at a clear consensus on a policy decision, factors driving the decision are considered equally important and thus treated equally across all states; our research illustrates the inherent limitation of such an assumption. This work illustrates the complexity of state decision-making and highlights where and why states diverge in their decision-making process.

Limitations

A primary limitation to qualitative work is a limited scope of analysis and the inability to generalize findings. While this research is no exception focusing on four states, it builds off several prior quantitative studies. This was done in a three-pronged effort to structure the analysis, to further explore the emergent themes from the literature, and to investigate decision-making with a certain degree of depth that was simply not possible in prior quantitative work. This study highlights the nuance and complexity of state decision-making; in doing so, it provides context for prior empirical work and emphasizes the depth and challenges faced by state lawmakers with regard to the ACA. While the results may not be generalizable, the findings certainly offer insight into the process and clarity on the nuances of state decision-making and the ACA.

Measuring State Implementation of the ACA

The support and opposition framework measures ACA support on a seven-point scale based on state responses to the above items. States adopting recommended legislation to reform their health care markets and those creating a state-run insurance exchange are given one point for each of these actions; 19 states took at least one step, with 17 taking both steps. The data for these actions are drawn from the Commonwealth Fund (Keith & Lucia, 2014).

We consider those states that have filed a lawsuit against the ACA or adopted legislation intended to impede the implementation of the ACA to be in active opposition and deduct one point for each of these actions. In total there are 32 states that took at least one of these steps to oppose the law. In addition, six states took action that can be coded as both in support of and in opposition to the ACA. Information on state legislation is drawn from the National Conference of State Legislatures (2015). Finally, a point is deducted for those states that refused to accept federal funding for Medicaid expansion, and one point added for those states that have accepted state funding to expand Medicaid. Therefore, a state that adopts all three positive reforms (market reform, insurance exchange, Medicaid expansion) would be scored a 3, indicating the highest level of support. States that have refused to expand Medicaid, adopted legislation designed to impede the ACA and participated in lawsuits to impede the ACA will be scored −3, indicating the least supportive states.

For example, California was scored with the highest possible support score of +3. California adopted regulations in support of health care reforms for +1, opted for a state health care exchange for +1, and expanded Medicaid for +1.

California chose not to take part in any litigation challenging the constitutionality of the ACA, that is, *Sebelius* or *King*, so a point was not deducted. And finally, California chose not to adopt any state laws actively opposing the ACA, which resulted in another point not being deducted. The resulting support/opposition score for California was +3, which indicates the highest level of support on the index. Alabama, a state that resulted in a score to be in greatest opposition to the ACA, received a score of −3 based on the following calculation: It did not adopt legislation in support of the recommended health care reforms; therefore, it was not given a point. Alabama refused to create a state exchange, therefore defaulting to the federal exchange; therefore, it was not given a point. The state opted not to expand Medicaid and was assigned −1 for that action. Alabama was party to the federal lawsuits challenging the constitutionality of the ACA and so was assigned −1 for those actions. And finally, Alabama enacted state legislation actively interfering with the implementation of the ACA. For that action, it was assigned −1. The resulting support/opposition score for Alabama was −3, which indicates that Alabama lawmakers are in greatest opposition to the ACA on the index.

Table 4.1 displays our final scores for the 50 states over the three-year early implementation period. Of the four analyzed states, Alabama scored a −3 in

Table 4.1 State Support

2012 State Scores for ACA Support

3	*2*	*1*	*0*	*−1*	*−2*	*−3*
CA, CT, MD, NY, OR, RI, VT	AR, HI, KY, MA, MN, NM WA	CO, DE, IL, NV, WV	IA, MI,	AZ, ME, NE, NJ, OH	AK, ID, IL, MS, MO, MT, NH, NC, PA, SD, TN, UT, WI	AL, FL, GA, KS, LA, ND, OK, SC, TX, VA, WY

2013 State Scores for ACA Support

3	*2*	*1*	*0*	*−1*	*−2*	*−3*
CA, CT, HI, MD, MA, MN, NM, NY, OR, RI, VT	AR, KY, WA	CO, DE, IL, NV, NJ, WV	IA, MI, NE,	AZ, ID, ME, ND, OH	AK, MS, MO, MT, NH, NC, PA, SD, TN, UT, WI	AL, FL, GA, IN, KS, LA, OK, SC, TX, VA, WY

2014 State Scores for ACA Support

3	*2*	*1*	*0*	*−1*	*−2*	*−3*
CA, CT, HI, MD, MA, MN, NM, NY, OR, RI, VT	IN, KY, WA	AR, CO, DE, IL, NV, NJ	IA, MI, NE, NH, PA, WV	AZ, ID, ME, ND, OH	AK, MS, MO, MT, NC, SD, TN, UT, WI	AL, FL, GA, KS, LA, OK SC, TX, VA WY

Source: Table created by the authors.

each reviewed year, indicating opposition on each measure; California scored a 3 each year, indicating support of each measure; Michigan remained neutral with a score of 0; and New Hampshire moved from a −2 score to a score of 0 or neutral in response to ACA support.

Political and Social Factors Influencing State Decision-Making

This book specifically explores the decision-making factors described earlier in measuring support and opposition across the four analyzed states. While these factors require and highlight decisions in each state, there are several other political and social factors that impact and influence state decision-making that will be discussed as appropriate in the analysis. This collection of variables has been used in several prior studies (Barrilleaux & Rainey, 2014; Haeder & Weimer, 2013; Travis et al., 2016) interested in and explaining state decision-making and the ACA. In prior modeling across several years, this collection of political and socioeconomic variables has routinely explained more than 75 percent of model variance (Mayer et al., 2015; Travis et al., 2016), making the inclusion both relevant and important in explaining why states chose the actions that they did with regard to the early implementation of the ACA.

Political Variables

Party Control of Governor

The governor's party affiliation has minimal effect on voting patterns in presidential elections (Erikson, Folke, & Snyder, 2012), the economic development of the state (Izraeli & Folland, 2007), the amount a state allocates for health care (Kousser, 2002), and the general voting patterns of legislators (Canfield-Davis, Jain, Wattam, McMurtry, & Johnson, 2010). This can change significantly, however, when a governor takes a direct interest in a policy outcome (Bernick, 1978). The ACA has had just such an impact as governors have given significant attention to the decision-making related to the implementation of the law due to the vast budgetary and political concerns associated with it (Callaghan & Jacobs, 2014). Recent scholarship has highlighted state executive control as a primary impediment to health care reform (Rigby, 2012) due to the "acute political, legal, and administrative dilemmas" it poses for Republican leadership (Jones et al., 2014, p. 99). Thus, we expect a governor's party affiliation to be significant in this particular context, taking into consideration the high-profile, contentious, and partisan views of the ACA.

Party Control of Legislature

The existing literature suggests the majority party dictates the legislative process at the state level by producing cohesive voting blocks and by controlling the political agenda (Coleman-Battista & Richman, 2011; Hayes-Clark, 2012;

Cox, Kousser, & McCubbins, 2010). Party control of the state legislature has also been found significant in determining the amount of funds allocated for Medicaid spending (Brown, 1995). Kousser (2002) argues "that state policy makers are not neutral" (p. 668); partisan politics plays a powerful role in policy outcomes, and "states with Democratic-controlled legislatures tend to fund their programs more generously than those with Republicans in charge." (p. 642). This is supported in recent studies examining state Medicaid expansion, where Republican legislatures have been found to have an even greater impact on state decision-making than Republican governors when it comes to deciding whether to expand Medicaid (Callaghan & Jacobs, 2014). Party control of the legislature can be tied closely to party control of the governor; it can further obstruct and confirm the actions of the chief executive. Party control, whether unified or divided, plays a critical role in advancing or opposing the governor's agenda.

Citizen Ideology

Citizen ideology independent of majority party control of the legislature can often be a predictor of state policy decisions (Kim, Powell Jr., & Fording, 2010; Breaux, Morris, & Travis, 2007; Soss et al., 2001; Grogan, 1994; Berry & Berry, 1992; Quaile-Hill, Leighley, & Hinton-Anderson, 1995). This measure is calculated based on voter and candidate preference of both winning and losing candidates in congressional elections and is measured on a liberal/conservative continuum. The score is calculated by assessing the district's incumbent ideology, the estimated ideology score for the challenger, and the results of the election. The scores were then computed using an unweighted average and placed on the continuum representing public opinion. The underlying premise is that state elected officials are, in fact, a collection of citizens; therefore, they will closely resemble the political ideology of their constituents (Berry, Ringquist, Fording, & Hanson, 1998). The result indicates that aggregate citizen perceptions can differ significantly between conservative and liberal states on similar issues, in turn, having an impact on state decision-making (Rigby & Haselswerdt, 2013). The higher the computed score, the more liberal the state ideology (Berry et al., 1998); assuming state representatives mirror their constituents, we would expect state ideology to correlate with party control of the legislature and have a substantial impact on state decision-making.

Socioeconomic Variables

Poverty

Poverty, an often debilitating cycle of interrelated issues, affects both individuals and communities in a way that frequently leads to social exclusion (Wilkinson & Marmot, 2003). The more social exclusion, the more at risk the individual and community are to quality-of-life concerns (Wilkinson & Marmot, 2003). The root of many of these concerns is a basic resource problem;

impoverished individuals typically lack the necessary resources, whether tangible or intangible, to address basic needs.

One of the primary goals of the ACA was to close the Medicaid coverage gap in which a number of individuals and families make too much money to receive the subsidy but not enough to afford the premiums (Holahan, Buettgens, Carroll, & Dorn, 2012; Holahan, Buettgens, & Dorn, 2013; Kaiser Family Foundation, 2013a). By standardizing Medicaid across the country and extending subsidies to families who earn up to 400 percent of the federal poverty line, it was thought that the ACA would address the coverage gap afflicting many currently uninsured individuals and families (Kaiser Family Foundation, 2013a). Instead, the increased subsidy program has fueled further confusion and criticism while contributing to a number of states choosing to opt out of the voluntary expansion (Haeder & Weimer, 2013). This development is further compounded by the already-restrictive Medicaid coverage standards of many of the states that have chosen to opt out or not expand coverage at this time (Kaiser Family Foundation, 2013b; Kaiser Family Foundation, 2013c).

State poverty rates provide insight into the resource problem and how it impacts low-income individual and family health (Gornick, 2002; Gornick, 2003). Measuring poverty has long been an issue of debate (Neff, 2013); using household rates allows for a standardized rate of poverty that is easily understood and interpreted. It is expected that states with greater poverty and need will also be the states to expand Medicaid at a greater rate (Richardson & Yilmazer, 2013). Due to the correlation between individual need and the poverty rate, we would presume this measure has an impact on state policymakers' decision to support the ACA.

Insurance

One of the primary stated goals of the ACA was to reduce the uninsured population, which had reached 47 million in 2012, by offering greater access to affordable health care (Holahan et al., 2012; Kaiser Family Foundation, 2013d). Through a series of mandates, subsidies, and penalties, the federal government is hoping to provide enough incentive while also greatly increasing access for the uninsured population in an effort to curb that number (Jeter, 2013).

Whether an individual or family has health insurance is rarely just an individual decision; cost, access, enrollment, and service delivery all play major roles (Eisenberg & Power, 2000). Furthermore, the actions of the state in providing access and information are critical to the success of the health care reform and lowering the uninsured population (Kaiser Family Foundation, 2013d). Failing to address these issues has a significant impact on the level of care available to individual citizens across each state (Eisenberg & Power, 2000).

With the importance of access established, there are also cost-saving factors to consider. Blavin, Buettgens, and Roth (2012) have estimated that by reducing the number of uninsured through health care reforms, it would also result in reduced uncompensated care, in turn saving states potentially significant amounts of money. Contrary to this seemingly straightforward revelation, recent research has indicated that states with the greatest need (largest uninsured populations) have been the last to act in creating state exchanges (Blavin et al., 2012). Furthermore, there has been some evidence of a correlation between states with high uninsured populations resisting Medicaid expansion (Rigby, 2012).

State Health

While the ACA is designed to standardize health care options across the states, great difficulty lies in establishing an appropriate standard and enforcing an appropriate standard across the states. Traditionally, health care has been viewed as a state issue, one that has varied a great deal from state to state with some states (such as California and Massachusetts) taking a more progressive approach than others (such as Mississippi and West Virginia). By allowing states to opt out of Medicaid expansion and design their own health care exchange programs, there is little doubt that health care reform will remain a state issue, albeit one that is now increasingly regulated by the federal government.

One of the primary impacts of health care reform as it relates to state health is the law's mandate that no longer can individuals in poor health or with preexisting conditions be excluded or dropped from insurance programs. This is of particular importance as it relates to health care access. Prior to the law, any number of conditions could impact health care coverage. Take obesity, for example: 35 of the 50 states had laws on the books permitting insurance companies to adjust the rates of those deemed obese; this had the potential to impact nearly 60 million Americans (Downey & Still, 2013). With the passage of the ACA, coverage is no longer in jeopardy for those at risk, and those previously deemed uninsurable now have options.

With such vast increases in service come a number of challenges; scheduling a routine medical visit may have to be done months in advance, and excessive wait lists have become common for low-income patients (Kardish, 2014). At the state level, cost, especially in states with large numbers of the population previously uninsured, can be exceedingly high; fortunately, much of the initial investment is being covered by the federal government. Thus, it is expected that states that are generally unhealthier and would require greater financial investment would be more likely to support the ACA while federal funds are available.

Data Collection

Data were collected for the initial quantitative study that structures the analysis from a variety of sources, including PoliData, the United Health Foundation, the American Community Survey, Berry et al. (1998), the Commonwealth Fund (Keith & Lucia, 2014), and the National Conference of State Legislatures (2015). The data are considered to be cross-sectional and were collected within the early implementation years of 2012, 2013, and 2014. The results of this exercise frame the qualitative inquiry through which data were collected through the review of public statements, including newspaper articles, the legislative record, press releases, state and national government reports, and other publicly available documentation. By utilizing open-source material from the public domain we are able to better triangulate data and sources than we may otherwise be able to by solely using traditional academic resources. Key stakeholders and interest groups were identified through their participation in public hearings and lobbying efforts, and their support and opposition were tracked and are presented herein. By tracing the efforts of key stakeholders both inside and outside of government in the reviewed states, we are able to begin understanding the dynamics influencing state-level decision-making toward the ACA and further examine the inherent complexity and variation across states.

Prior Empirical Research

For two primary reasons, 2012 was critical: It marked the reaffirmation of the ACA by SCOTUS, and it also kicked off the state implementation period

Table 4.2 Testing Determinants of Support

State-Level Determinants of Support for the ACA

	Market Reform	*State Exchange*	*Lawsuit*	*Medicaid*	*State Legislation*
Rep. Gub. Control	−1.19**	−2.00**	1.90***	−0.68	0.22
	(0.59)	(0.91)	(0.60)	(0.55)	(0.58)
Rep. Leg. Control	0.07	−3.20**	0.63	−0.88	1.11*
	(0.75)	(1.48)	(0.73)	(0.64)	(0.65)
Citizen Ideology	0.02	−0.03	−0.04	0.06*	−0.04*
	(0.02)	(0.03)	(0.03)	(0.03)	(0.02)
Poverty	.014	0.84**	−0.16	0.05	−0.14
	(0.15)	(0.37)	(0.19)	(0.16)	(0.16)
Uninsured Rates	.06	0.14	0.11	−0.08	0.09
	(0.08)	(0.13)	(0.10)	(0.08)	(0.07)
Health Levels	1.25	5.92***	0.51	−0.76	−0.33
	(0.78)	(2.25)	(1.21)	(1.00)	(0.90)
Constant	−3.96	−8.39	0.65	−1.23	1.09
	(2.37)	(4.58)	(2.52)	(2.40)	(2.31)
Pseudo R^2	.30	.68	.54	.44	.40
Log-Likelihood	−18.44	−10.20	−15.94	−19.48	−20.29

Source: Table created by authors.

Notes: Standard errors in parentheses.
Levels of statistical significance: *0.1, **0.05, ***0.01.
$N = 50$.

of the law. In prior work we examined political determinants of support and opposition for the ACA at the state level (Travis et al., 2016). In testing several model variations, the results were fairly consistent in every model during the early implementation period: Politics trumped need. Conservative governors and legislatures were more likely to oppose the ACA, while more liberal citizenships were more likely to support health reform. In the full model, only poverty remained a significant predictor among the socioeconomic variables of ACA support.

A primary challenge related to the use and implementation of the dependent variable index has been determining the impact of each component. For the sake of analysis we treat and score each decision equally, but in Mayer et al. (2016) we were able to shed light on the variations of each component and how they influence decision-making across several factors. Perhaps unsurprisingly, Republican governorship was again the most frequent predictor of opposition across a number of factors. Taken as a whole, the findings suggest that partisan politics supersede state need when it comes to supporting health care reform in the U.S. By further examining these factors through the case study analysis, we were able to further explore state decision-making related to the support and opposition of the ACA and to begin to speculate why some states have made the decisions they have regarding support of the ACA.

Table 4.3 Politics, Need, and Combined Models

State-Level Determinants of Support for the ACA			
	Model I	*Model II*	*Model III*
Rep. Gub. Control	−1.21**		−1.24**
	(0.47)		(0.46)
Rep. Leg. Control	−1.66***		−1.53***
	(0.53)		(0.53)
Citizen Ideology	0.04**		0.04**
	(0.02)		(0.02)
Poverty		0.36**	0.26**
		(0.17)	(0.11)
Uninsured Rates		−0.21**	−0.06
		(0.08)	(0.06)
Health Levels		2.22**	0.89
		(0.88)	(0.6)
Constant	−0.36	−1.44	−2.52
	(0.99)	(1.82)	(1.62)
Adj. R-squared	.65	.21	.67

Source: Table created by the authors.

Notes: Standard errors in parentheses.
Levels of statistical significance: *0.1, **0.05, ***0.01.
$N = 50$.

Conclusion

This chapter discusses the impetus of the project, how prior research led us in one direction, which was generally partisan, but begged for additional explanation of why states made the decisions they did with regard to the ACA. The limitations of our prior work and the challenge of explaining and detailing state decision-making spurred the desire to examine decision-making in greater detail that can only be done with a case study approach. Using the prior research to provide selection criteria and frame the analysis, this chapter further details the selection approach, why the variables studied matter, and how they will be approached in the forthcoming state case studies.

5 Opposing the ACA

An Alabama Case Study

The state of Alabama represents a state that seems to give voice to strong and consistent opposition to the ACA since the days of the legislation's nascent development in Congress. Against a backdrop of significant need, Alabama's rejection of the ACA is at once both puzzling and entirely understandable. Yet, a closer examination of the processes, debates, positions, and actions of the major actors in Alabama politics tell a different story: Instead of a united and unwavering opposition, the record is a mix of actions that span from cautious optimism regarding the ACA to an outright refutation of the legislation, and ultimately, a series of actions to attempt to block implementation, deny the federal role in health care, and challenge the constitutionality of the ACA. Ultimately, Alabama's strategy was to oppose implementation in any way possible, a strategy implemented with gusto.

As with the other states in this volume, to best understand state action it becomes necessary to look beyond the decisions themselves and to place those decisions in the broader context of state history, political alignment, and the multitude of interests in play within the state. In many ways, Alabama is very much unlike our other cases, yet in other respects the contextual elements in Alabama are very similar to our other cases. Alabama's decisions regarding the ACA are a result of the ways in which these contextual elements interacted and unfolded.

The state's political history has rightfully been the subject of other research, but much of it written before 1990 (see, e.g., Key, 1949/1984; Martin, 1975). Of particular interest in a political sense is that Alabama has been a one-party state for much of the 20th and early 21st centuries. An important part of the story, however, is that the "one party" has shifted from the Democratic Party to the Republican Party. Throughout that shift, the one constant has been ideological conservatism. Coupled with strong preferences for states' rights, small national government, and a policy preference for social control (see Elazar, 1984), the unique history and culture in Alabama can be tied directly to the state's stance on the ACA. Alabama was among the first states to file suit to block implementation of the law. Even within this setting, however, the early period of the ACA and its implementation in Alabama was marked by some signals, particularly from the governor (a Republican), that *parts* of the ACA might be acceptable.

We begin this chapter with an overview of the state's history as a means to set the context for our analysis of state action within the framework of the ACA. We then discuss the current context of state government, health care in Alabama, and state politics. The remainder of the chapter focuses on the specific events that led to the choices made in Alabama relating to the ACA. We conclude the chapter with some thoughts and observations regarding the manner in which the debate about the ACA unfolded in Alabama.

Background

Alabama lies in the Deep South of the U.S. and is often referred to as the "Heart of Dixie." Its 52,419 square miles of territory is bordered by Georgia to the east, Mississippi to the west, Tennessee to the north, and Florida and the Gulf of Mexico to the south. The state is marked by more than 1,500 miles of navigable rivers (EDPA, 2017), which aided greatly in the development of Alabama's agricultural industry. The port of Mobile, one of the most accessible deep-water ports along the Gulf Coast, dates to early Spanish exploration and has continued to serve as an important transportation and commerce hub on the central Gulf Coast.

Alabama's population in 2016 was estimated at roughly 4.9 million, and roughly half of that population lives in the five largest metropolitan regions of the state. The city of Birmingham, located in the north-central region of the state, is the largest city in the state in terms of population and has long served as the industrial and economic center of the state. Birmingham was known for many years for its steel production. Alabama produces a wide variety of agricultural products, ranging from poultry and beef to cotton, grains, soybeans, and vegetables. Other manufacturing in Alabama includes automobiles, aircraft, and steel fabrication.

Alabama has also suffered through the years with a combination of high poverty and poor health outcomes. In 2017, roughly 19 percent of Alabamians fell below the federal poverty line (Vollers, 2017), with poverty rates especially high in the rural counties in the south-central section of the state. County poverty rates ranged from a low of 8.5 percent in Shelby County (suburban Birmingham) to 40 percent in Perry County in the state's "Black Belt." In terms of health outcomes, Alabama was ranked 48th out of 50 states in 2018 for health outcomes (United Health Foundation, 2019a). Alabama reported an uninsured rate of 16 percent in 2010 (Chollett, Barrett, & Bell, 2011); that number had decreased slightly to 10 percent in 2017 (Kaiser Family Foundation, 2019). In terms of overall health outcomes, Alabama ranked 47th out of 50 states in United Health Foundation's 2017 state rankings (United Health Foundation, 2019b).

History and Culture

Alabama was established as a territory in 1817 and achieved statehood in December 1819, just four days after its neighbor to the west, Mississippi, was admitted to the Union. Largely an agricultural state, Alabama's rich soil, natural waterways and ports, and willingness to join its other southern neighbors in the slave trade meant that Alabama's economy and population grew at a steady pace. Later, with the discovery of deposits of both coal and iron ore, Alabama became a center of heavy industry in the largely agricultural South through its iron and steel production in and around Birmingham (Flynt, 1989). This ultimately led to a struggle for political power not only between urban and rural residents but also between wealthy and poor citizens. With the demise of the steel industry in and around Birmingham in the late 1970s and early 1980s, Birmingham "reinvented" itself to become the center of banking, finance, and insurance in the state. While the source of wealth for the "Big Mules"[1] (Key, 1949/1984) changed, the role of "Big Mules" in state politics did not. These tensions would show themselves again in the debate over the implementation of the ACA in Alabama.

Alabama was an early participant in the secession of southern states that led to the Civil War, declaring its independence in early 1861. However, the vote to secede was not completely one-sided, as roughly 39 percent of voters (Kizer, n.d.) expressed a preference to remain in the Union. Following the defeat of the Confederacy in the war, Alabama followed a political pattern very similar to other Deep South states. Reforms imposed by the Republican-led national government, including extending voting and landowner rights to former slaves, led to political domination by the Republican Party in Alabama, which, in turn, polarized most white citizens in the state. Following the end of Reconstruction, and in response to the perceived excesses of Republican efforts to enfranchise blacks, the Democratic Party became the stronghold of white Alabama citizens, and state government worked to enshrine segregation in law. Underlying this party and racial split was a struggle for political control of the state between populists and what V. O. Key (1949/1984) termed the "Big Farmers" and "Big Mules" (the "Big Mules" were the industrialists in the northern part of the state). While the Democratic Party in Alabama reigned supreme during this period, the various lines of cleavage throughout society led to intense intraparty political conflict in the state. Overlaid across this setting was a series of three state constitutional conventions (of the six so far in the state's history) that further sought to strengthen disenfranchisement of African Americans and assure continued political and social control by white citizens in Alabama (Martin, 1975). Moreover, these constitutions, particularly the constitutions of 1865, 1868, and 1875, all sought to create large numbers of constitutional state offices;[2] many of these offices continue to exist with separate constituencies as they have for many decades. The existence of multiple elected state offices not only allows for the formation of separate bases of political power but also provides a series of elected "stepping-stones" to progressively higher levels of elected office.

The importance of this history is the tension created by the existence of these separate, and largely independent, political positions. While Alabama is often (wrongly) thought to be monolithic politically (Daniel Elazar, 1984), for example, described Alabama as a strongly traditionalistic state), a closer examination reveals important vectors of internal disagreement that persist to the present. Indeed, the level of conflict in Alabama politics across party factions, regional sectionalism, and personality (Martin, 1975) virtually guarantees that disagreement will be not only strong but also plentiful. Knowledge of this history helps us explain the series of events that led to Alabama's opposition to the ACA in the 21st century.

As V.O. Key (1949/1984, p. 41) pointed out, "[i]t is not a long step from localism to a sectionalism based on a genuine diversity of interests." Alabama politics has always been characterized by localism, and winning support in one's home county is critical to any election process in the state (Martin, 1975). As Key (1949/1984, Chapter 3) noted 70 years ago, the sectionalism that develops from this localism tends to pit rural against urban, black against white, small landholdings against large landholdings, and conservatism against agrarian radicalism—a sectionalism that persists to the present time.[3] Whites in the largely slave-holding western part of the state required cooperation from white farmers in the northern part of the state to overcome the effects of Reconstruction and to emplace de jure segregation. While these cleavages are often most visible in party politics, they lead to very real differences in policy choices as well. Even in a one-party state, politics are not nearly as monolithic as they might appear.

Another interesting facet of Alabama politics is the reliance on "larger-than-life" political figures. In a culture that largely rewards a certain genteel approach to social life, Alabama has had its share of flamboyant political characters. "Big Jim" Folsom won the gubernatorial election in 1946 and again in 1954, not only in part because he was able to build a coalition across existing political and social divisions (Key, 1949/1984) but also in part because of his style: At 6 feet 8 inches tall, he towered over almost everyone. He campaigned with a wooden bucket (into which people placed money) with a promise he would clean out the state capitol. A hillbilly bluegrass band accompanied him to his campaign events (Martin, 1975). For many, Folsom was an unforgettable character and indicative of the conduct of state elections.[4]

The state of Alabama has a conservative heritage that dates back decades. The largely rural tradition coupled with the institution of slavery, participation of the state in the Confederacy, and years of post-Civil War disenfranchisement and de jure segregation have given Alabama a richly deserved reputation in this regard. This inherent conservatism has made Alabama (and much of the rest of the South) something of a bastion of Republican control since the mid-1990s. Between the onset of Reconstruction and the 1994 midterm elections, Alabama was a staunchly Democratic state, albeit an exceptionally conservative one. Alabama vehemently opposed school desegregation in the early 1960s, leading to then-governor George Wallace's famous stand in the "schoolhouse door" at the University of Alabama, refusing to allow black students to enroll. Wallace would later parlay this notoriety into a serious independent run for the presidency in the 1968 election, in which his stand on states' rights proved particularly enticing to many, especially in the South. Since politics in the South was still heavily Democratic, this split of the Democratic vote contributed to the defeat of Hubert Humphrey and victory for Republican Richard Nixon.

The South, in general, and Alabama, in particular, continued to be a bastion of Democratic support, albeit very much a conservative voice in Democratic politics. When the Republican Party gained control of the U.S. House of Representatives in 1994 for the first time since the 1950s, many elected Democratic members of Congress from the South switched party allegiance and became Republicans—a pattern that held in Alabama as well. The growing conservatism of the Republican Party appealed to many southern conservative Democrats, and voters were generally supportive of these party defections.[5] Alabama elected its first Republican governor since Reconstruction in 1986, and with two exceptions (Jim Folsom, Jr., in 1992 and Don Siegelman in 1998), all Alabama governors since then have been Republicans.[6]

In sum, Alabama has a rich history of strong party politics, overlaid with factionalism, regionalism, and conflict. When coupled to a constitutional setting that provides for a large number of statewide elected offices, and a flair for flamboyant personalities, we may conclude that Alabama's political and cultural setting is anything but simple and monolithic. These same forces come into play in the early 21st century when the state is faced with policy choices regarding the ACA: While the state eventually adopts a strong position of rejection of the ACA, the process of getting to "no" is a convoluted tale of a clash of party politics, regionalism, racism, and factionalism.

The Political Landscape

Alabama is a state currently dominated by conservative Republicans, a situation that was solidified in 2010 when the Republicans gained control of both houses of the state legislature for the first time since Reconstruction. Republican presidential candidates have carried the state, with two exceptions, in every election since 1960; since 2004 the Republican candidate has garnered at least 60 percent of the vote in Alabama. By every measure, Alabama is a solid "red" state. Six of the seven congressional representatives from Alabama are Republican; the lone exception represents the largely black 7th Congressional District in West Alabama and metro Birmingham (Orndorff, 2011, p. 8A).[7] This solid party control allowed state policymakers to oppose ACA implementation in the strongest manner possible and largely without effective opposition.

Alabama also has a high rate of uninsured citizens; about 16 percent of citizens have no health insurance (including Medicaid and Medicare). About 20 percent of citizens are enrolled in Medicaid (Orndorff, 2012a, p. 1A). There are more whites than blacks who do not have medical insurance, although a disproportionate percentage of minorities are uninsured (Chollet et al., 2011). These percentages follow, in the abstract, a similar pattern in most southern states. Set against a background of historical racism, the debate in Alabama ultimately pits urban versus rural representation; large, moneyed urban interests against rural populists; and Republicans against Democrats. While the rhetoric available in the public record is not explicitly bigoted or racist, the patterns of interests follow traditional cleavages in Alabama society.

Blue Cross/Blue Shield of Alabama (BCBSAL) is the leading provider in the Alabama insurance market (Tu, Carrier, Lechner, & Draper, 2013), controlling 92 percent of individual enrollees in the state.[8] The remaining 10 percent of the market share is split among other competitors, with the second- and third-largest providers together enrolling roughly 6 percent of individuals in the state (Chollett, Stewart, & Witmer, 2011, pp. 2–3). Moreover, BCBSAL is one of the largest businesses in the state, with revenues in 2013 of more than $4 billion (Walsh, 2013). This situation leads to a largely noncompetitive health insurance market. In 2013 a federal lawsuit was filed in Birmingham seeking an antitrust verdict against BCBSAL, in an effort to make the private health insurance market in the state more competitive.

Starting at "Maybe": The Early Debate in Alabama

Republican control of six of Alabama's seven congressional seats and two Senate seats virtually guaranteed strong opposition to the ACA in Congress. Indeed, the various congressional votes on the ACA reflect this control, with the representative from the 7th District (representing an urban area in and adjacent to Birmingham and extending into heavily black western Alabama) the only member of Alabama's congressional delegation to vote in favor of the legislation at some point in the process. In the final House vote on the ACA, however, all seven members of Congress from Alabama voted against the legislation. Alabama's two senators, Richard Shelby and Jeff Sessions, were particularly outspoken against the ACA, and both voted against the ACA. Shelby was elected to the Senate in 1986 as a Democrat, was reelected in 1992 as a Democrat, and then changed parties in 1994. He has been reelected since as a Republican and has been a staunch supporter of Republican policy positions. Sessions was first elected in 1996 as a Republican and reelected three times as a Republican. He resigned in 2017 to assume the role of the U.S. Attorney General in the Trump administration.

At the state level, the governor's mansion was in the hands of Bob Riley, elected in 2002 in a close race. Riley had first sought (and won) office in 1996, when he was elected to the House of Representatives from the 3rd Congressional District in eastern Alabama as a Republican. He was reelected as governor in 2006 by a comfortable margin. Although Riley had opposed the election of Obama in 2008, he made little effort to take a public stance on the proposal for the ACA. The law was not passed until Riley's last year in office. Riley was succeeded in office by another Republican, Robert Bentley.

Prior to the 2010 election cycle, Democrats held a slim majority in both houses of the state legislature. The Democratic majority had been steadily shrinking, and the 2010 election brought Republican control to both chambers for the first time since Reconstruction. As of this writing, Republicans hold 27 of 35 seats in the Senate and 77 of 105 seats in the House (BallotPedia.org, 2018). Most of the Democrats left in both the Senate and the House at this point were from largely black districts, and most of these were found in more rural parts of the state (the exceptions were heavily populated districts in Birmingham, Huntsville, Mobile, and Montgomery). Already a conservative body, Republican control of both houses of the legislature virtually ensured a firm shift to the ideological right.

The other important constitutional office in the state is the attorney general. As is the case in many southern states, the attorney general in Alabama is elected through a popular vote. As is also true for many states, the office of attorney general is often a stepping-stone for those seeking higher political office. The Republican Party had controlled the attorney general's office since the 1994 election, and the two attorneys general who served during the period of this study were thus both Republicans: Troy King served from 2004 until 2011 and was succeeded by Luther Strange, who served until 2017. It is also noteworthy that Jeff Sessions, who would later be elected to the Senate and become an outspoken critic of the ACA, served as attorney general in Alabama from 1995 to 1997, before stepping down to run for the Senate seat vacated by the retiring Howell Heflin (D- AL).

In sum, at the point the ACA was approved by Congress and signed into law by President Obama, the reins of government in Alabama were firmly in Republican hands. Given the conservatism inherent in Alabama politics, this virtually guaranteed a strong state response against the ACA—a reaction that did not disappoint. The phased implementation in the ACA served, perhaps, to mute a certain amount of outspoken criticism, but many politicians in Alabama still wasted little time in organizing their opposition. Among the first to take direct action against the ACA was the attorney general, Troy King. King's office began work to file a lawsuit in federal court to block implementation of the ACA; ultimately Alabama would join 12 other states in a joint lawsuit filed in U.S. District Court in Pensacola, Florida, to block implementation (Word, 2010). Although the attorney general of Florida, Bill McCollum, touted the lawsuit as a bipartisan effort, 11 of the 12 plaintiffs were Republican. The lone Democrat was James Caldwell of Louisiana.[9] The lawsuit challenged the constitutionality of the individual mandate and asserted that the ACA threatened state sovereignty. The district court judge ruled in favor of the states, as did the 11th Circuit Court of Appeals. The Obama administration appealed to the U.S. Supreme Court, which consolidated three cases into a single case challenging the individual mandate and Medicaid expansion. In a surprise ruling, Chief Justice John Roberts sided with the more liberal wing of SCOTUS, which upheld the constitutionality of the ACA.

King's tenure as attorney general had not been without conflict and controversy. In 2009, King and then-governor Riley were on opposite sides of an issue regarding forms of electronic gambling (Perrin, 2009), an issue ultimately settled by the Alabama Supreme Court in favor of the governor (Chandler, 2009).

In a separate incident, King was accused of improperly receiving and reporting gifts from Alabama Power Company (Sims, 2009). King ultimately reimbursed a portion of the disputed gift. King ran for a second term as attorney general in the 2010 election but was defeated by challenger Luther Strange in the Republican primary; Strange went on to win the general election in November 2010.

Meanwhile, outgoing governor Riley was unwilling to take a public stance on the ACA. Alabama's constitution limits sitting governors to two consecutive terms, and Riley maintained a generally low profile during the election. The Republican primary was something of a surprise, with a little-known state representative, Robert Bentley, winning a contentious primary over two better-known challengers. Bentley finished second (of three) in the first primary, where he beat Tim James, son of former governor Fob James.[10] Bentley faced Bradley Byrne in the runoff, in which Bentley defeated the favorite Byrne by 12 percentage points (Talbot, 2010). Bentley then defeated the Democratic nominee by a comfortable 15 percentage points and was sworn in as governor in early 2011.

Bentley had attended medical school at the University of Alabama–Birmingham, graduating in 1968. He served for a time in the U.S. Air Force as a general physician before returning to Alabama for a three-year residency at the University of Alabama. He then opened a dermatology practice in Tuscaloosa, which grew into one of the largest dermatology practices in the Southeast (Business Council of Alabama, 2012). Bentley first entered politics as a member of the state House, where he became known as an active advocate for a variety of medical issues and was largely responsible to a series of changes in Alabama's organ donor rules (Business Council of Alabama, 2012). With this background, many observers expected Bentley to take a stand on the newly passed ACA.

In many ways, Bentley did not disappoint, although his early actions were marked by a degree of indecision. The early period of Bentley's first term was marked by cautious support of parts of the ACA. Claiming expertise based on his career as a dermatologist, Bentley initially agreed that health care was too expensive and that cost control was important. He also created several special commissions to collect information and make recommendations regarding issues such as Medicaid expansion, the viability of a state exchange, and other issues. However, as his term wore on, Bentley took issue with the findings of many of these commission reports and ultimately became more strident in his opposition to the ACA.

The use of special commissions represents an interesting tactic on the part of Governor Bentley. On one hand, the governor could point to the commissions as evidence of careful consideration and adherence to a fact-based decision process. On the other hand, the use of commissions may also be seen as a delaying tactic to "buy time" while other efforts at the national level to block the ACA were made. Of note is the fact that while Governor Bentley generally praised the work of his commissions, he would later take issue with many of the findings and generally ignored the recommendations they presented. The specifics of these commission reports are discussed later in this chapter.

The composition of the commissions is also noteworthy. Although the commissions generally represented a cross section of interests within the state, the two commissions differed significantly in terms of the number of direct gubernatorial appointments. For the commission charged with making recommendations for a state insurance exchange, the governor retained authority directly to appoint only 3 of the 15 members. The Alabama Medicaid Advisory Commission, on the other hand, consisted of 33 members; 11 were appointed directly by Governor Bentley (Williamson, 2013). The composition of both commissions also reflects, in part, the divisions in Alabama society noted by Key (1949/1984), with both rural and urban interests on the committee.

From "Maybe" to "No": State Choices in Alabama

As detailed elsewhere in this volume, each state could take (or fail to take) several actions; taken together, these choices indicate the level of a state's support or opposition of the ACA. Although Alabama ultimately took strong action to oppose the ACA, the path to resistance was not as straightforward as one might otherwise think. Alabama's politics and prevailing political ideology certainly favored efforts to block the ACA, yet within the state there was both debate and dissent regarding the ACA.

Creation of a State Exchange

One of the early choices discussed in Alabama was whether to create a state insurance exchange or to default to the federal exchange. Early signals by Governor Bentley suggested Alabama might seek its own exchange. Indeed, the fact that Bentley offered public support for a state exchange seems to suggest at least a tacit acceptance of the ACA, which gave states a specific choice. The state Department of Insurance (ADOI) applied for two federal grants worth about $9.6 million to assist with planning for a state exchange (Rockefeller Institute, 2014). A portion of these funds was used to support the work of a commission created by Governor Bentley to make recommendations regarding the composition and operation of a state exchange. When announcing the creation of this commission, Bentley publicly expressed hope that Alabama would be able to meet the deadline of 2014 for the creation of the exchange. In his public remarks, Bentley said,

> What we're trying to do here is set up an Alabama health insurance exchange so people in the state, regardless of where you are in life—whether you are a young mother or whether you are a college student or whether you are an elderly person with a preexisting disease—you will be able to purchase insurance.
>
> (Chandler, 2011, p. 1D)

Moreover, Bentley went on to say that "even if the [ACA] had never been passed that this was something that we needed to look at" (Chandler, 2011,

p. 1D). He also expressed an opinion that adding insurance providers in the state would strengthen market competition.

Alabama Health Insurance Exchange Study Commission (2011)

In June 2011, Governor Bentley empaneled the Alabama Health Insurance Exchange Study Commission through the vehicle of Executive Order 17. The commission was charged with making recommendations on several related issues: whether the exchange should be housed within an existing state agency, a new agency, or a nonprofit entity; who should serve on the governing board for the exchange; an analysis of the resources needed for the Exchange; an analysis of the effects of interactions between the exchange and existing insurance markets; and the specific functions of the exchange (ADOI, 2011). What is noteworthy about this list is that the commission was not charged with recommending whether the state should create a state exchange or default to the federal exchange; the initial position was that Alabama would create its own exchange, and the purpose of the commission was to recommend ways to accomplish this. However, the commission ultimately included a recommendation in its final report.

The executive order created a 15-person commission. The governor chose the interests represented on the commission, although many of the participants were appointed directly by those interests. The governor did retain direct appointment authority for three positions. The interests included representatives from several facets of the Alabama health community, including representatives from the nonprofit, for-profit, and independent insurance markets (ADOI, 2011, p. 2). In his instruction to the commission, Bentley said, in part,

> Every Alabamian deserves access to affordable health insurance. My vision for the Alabama Exchange is to improve the health of our citizens by providing them with a gateway to purchase health insurance that best fits their needs while also promoting competition among health insurers.
> (ADOI, 2011, p. 1)

The language in this statement echoes an underlying theme of the commission, a theme that would also play an important role in the later commission on Medicaid expansion. Specifically, the focus of the commission was squarely on costs and affordability, particularly with regard to state budgets. Taken at face value, one might reasonably conclude that the governor was expressing at least tacit support for the ACA. Indeed, the co-chair of the commission (and chair of the Senate Health Committee), Greg Reed (R-Jasper), told *The Birmingham News* that the ACA requires an insurance exchange, and if the state failed to create an exchange, the federal government would create one. He continued on to say he would "rather see Alabama in control" of the process (Spencer, 2011, p. 1C).

The commission's report, issued under the auspices of the ADOI, was released in November 2011. Over the course of five meetings, the commission gathered information on the current state of Alabama's health insurance market, sources of health insurance coverage, stakeholder views on a state exchange, and possible functions for a state exchange. Based on the information collected and discussed, the commission included several recommendations in its final report. The first of these was not part of their initial charge: The commission's report recommended, by unanimous vote, the creation of a state exchange (ADOI, 2011). This finding is important for two reasons. First, the commission went beyond the issues covered in their initial charge. However, it is also reasonable to conclude that the recommendations made elsewhere in the report only make sense in the context of agreement about a state exchange. Second, the interests represented on this commission include representatives of all the major stakeholders in the health insurance market in Alabama. The representation also included stakeholders appointed to the commission by all the major political figures in state government, including the governor, the Speaker of the House, and the President Pro Tempore of the state senate.[11] One might reasonably conclude that the appointing authorities were unlikely to nominate commission members who might be indifferent or hostile to the interests of the appointing authority.

The second finding recommended that the state exchange employ a "free-market facilitator" model, in which any qualified provider could offer plans. The exchange would thus serve as a source of unbiased information for consumers to consult when making plan choices. Along with this, the commission recommended that the state create a single administrative entity to facilitate and oversee the state exchange. As a means to ensure that the exchange remains politically neutral, the commission recommended the formation of a quasi-public authority to implement and operate the exchange. In addition, the report noted that to place the exchange under the auspices of the ADOI would create a potential conflict of interest because ADOI is also charged with the regulation of the insurance market. The commission recommended against placing the exchange under the Alabama Medicaid Agency for fear that the state exchange would be seen by some as another welfare program (ADOI, 2011). The commission also recommended the formation of a governing board that would be relatively small so as to facilitate both deliberation and decision-making, but large enough to include representatives from the different health insurance interests in the state. To no great surprise, the list of recommended interests was very similar to the list of interests represented on the commission (ADOI, 2011, pp. 5–6).

The commission also considered the structure and operation of the exchange. The report recommended that the exchange develop separate risk pools for the small-group and individual market segments, as was the case in other states in the process of developing state exchanges. In a similar vein, the commission examined the interplay between a state exchange and existing public insurance programs such as Medicaid and ALL Kids.[12] The report concluded that the effect on these other programs would be minimal, although the ALL Kids program would lose enrollees as children in that program became eligible for

Medicaid. In a surprising move, the commission's report advocated (at least tacitly) for Medicaid expansion in Alabama, noting that

> [e]xtending Medicaid to additional low-income Alabamians will address the longstanding problem of workers who are either not offered employer coverage or who are likely to lose employer coverage when they change or lose their jobs. It could also address the problem of underinsurance among low-wage workers, even when insured.
>
> (ADOI, 2011, p. 7)

The commission also suggested that a function of the exchange could be to aid in the identification of citizens eligible for Medicaid. In a very real sense, the commission was recommending that the state expand the Medicaid program as available under the ACA and to use the exchange as a means to bring eligible citizens into the Medicaid program.

The final recommendation made by the commission addressed the costs of a state exchange and how those costs should be covered. The commission considered a total of five funding models, including support from the state's general fund, an assessment on hospitals and other health care providers, a fee added to all insurance policies sold in the state (including those sold outside the exchange), an assessment on companies selling health insurance in the state, and an assessment on small-group and individual plans sold through the exchange. The cost estimates for the exchange ranged from $34 million to $49.6 million in 2015, the first year of proposed operation. By a vote of 9–6 the commission recommended that the exchange be funded through an assessment on all small-group and individual plans; all six votes against unanimously preferred the option to assess only those plans sold through the exchange (ADOI, 2011, p. 11). In either case, the costs for operating the exchange would be recouped through the imposition of what amounts to a small user fee attached to sales of health policies. This recommendation meant that the commission was explicitly not recommending the expenditure of state funds to operate the exchange.

In sum, the governor's commission took a very positive stance regarding the creation of a state health insurance exchange. Moreover, with two exceptions, all the commission's recommendations enjoyed unanimous support of the commission's members.[13] The high degree of consensus among the major stakeholders in the state, coupled with the nature of the recommendations, suggests that the health insurance sector in the state fully expected the ACA to withstand the legal challenges. It also suggests a relatively high degree of support for both the individual mandate and for Medicaid expansion. The latter is particularly important inasmuch as the governor's charge to the commission did not include the question of Medicaid expansion. While no formal recommendation about Medicaid is included, the language in the report makes this position clear.

Early reaction was supportive of both the process and the recommendations. Yet behind the scenes, a debate was underway in the state as to whether the state's insurance market would be capable of supporting a viable state exchange. A report commissioned by the ADOI in 2011 reported that 59 percent of adults in Alabama received health insurance through their workplace. Moreover, about 19 percent of residents under age 65 received some sort of public coverage. Even so, about 16 percent of Alabama's non-elderly population was uninsured, and roughly 7 percent of residents were underinsured (Chollet et al., 2011). The report suggested that the ACA exchange would enroll nearly double the number of citizens in the individual insurance market. Roughly 671,000 non-elderly Alabamians were uninsured; the majority of the uninsured were white adults between 19 and 30 years of age, and roughly 80 percent lived within metropolitan statistical areas within the state (Chollet et al., 2011, pp. 2–5).

The major health insurance actor in the state, BCBSAL, dominated the market, with an 86 percent overall share of the health insurance market and a 95 percent market share in the small-group market (Chollet et al., 2011) in 2010. Although several other carriers offered plans in Alabama, only three (Golden Rule, 4 percent; United Healthcare, about 3 percent; and Humana, 2 percent) had a noticeable share of the market (Chollet et al., 2011, p. iii). Moreover, BCBSAL was the focus of a national antitrust lawsuit brought against all Blue Cross/Blue Shield plans nationwide and filed in federal district court in Birmingham (Rockefeller Institute, 2014). Chollet et al. (2011) concluded that there was little market pressure for insurers in Alabama to offer ACA-compliant plans, and most companies declined to grandfather existing policyholders to the extent allowed under the ACA. In a nutshell, the health insurance market in Alabama was not competitive, and it was unclear whether a state insurance exchange would be any more competitive. In fact, the issue of competitiveness was raised during state senate debate on a bill to create a state exchange, when Senator Dick Brewbaker (R-Montgomery) asked, "How many insurance carriers actually do business in all 67 counties? I only know of one" (quoted in Chandler, 2012a, May 9, p. 6B). Interestingly, the issue of market competitiveness was noticeably absent from the governor's Exchange Study Commission's report, and we could find no public statements by the governor pointing to a lack of competitiveness as a reason to default to the federal exchange.

When the state legislature convened for its 2012 session,[14] the Republican-controlled House passed a bill that would allow for the creation of a state exchange. However, Governor Bentley issued a threat to veto the bill (WSFA-TV, 2012) should the state senate pass the bill prior to the resolution of the pending case before SCOTUS challenging the constitutionality of the ACA. Alabama was a party to that litigation and was one of the early participants in the lawsuit. The bill was killed in committee in the Senate and was never brought up for a floor vote. A similar bill failed to pass in the following year's session. Yet the issue of a state exchange was clearly still on the minds of both the state legislature and the governor; Bentley signed a bill in May 2012 that prohibited the sale of health plans on a state exchange that offered coverage for abortion services except in certain cases (Rockefeller, 2014). These mixed messages on the future of a state exchange seemed to indicate a certain amount of indecision on the part of state policymakers.

Governor Bentley's public statements regarding the state exchange tended to waver from mild support to clear rejection. In an interview in February 2012, Bentley said he was "not very enthusiastic" (Orndorff, 2012b, p. 1C) about the plan reflected in the commission's report. He again cited the cost ($50 million, the high estimate made by the commission) and suggested that he may seek a revised or rewritten plan. In this case, the governor's objection seemed to be with the specifics of the plan offered rather than an objection to the idea of a state exchange. By mid-2012, Governor Bentley continued to express support for a state insurance exchange, but he also cautioned that Alabama would delay as long as possible before making its insurance exchange active (Chandler, 2012b, p. 2B). Part of this delay was due to the still-pending case of *NFIB v. Sebelius*, 567 U.S., 132 S. Ct. 2566, before SCOTUS challenging the constitutionality of the ACA. His plan was to bring the state exchange to fruition by executive order, given that the legislature was out of session until February 2013, and the federal deadline for the creation of the state exchange was late 2012. By mid-2012 Bentley became more strident in his hostility toward the idea of a state exchange, noting that the state could not meet the mandated deadline to create its exchange. He further suggested that Alabama should wait until after the presidential election in 2012, relying on the prospect that a Republican president and a Republican-controlled Congress would choose to repeal the ACA (Chandler, 2012c, p. 1C). As Governor Bentley's public opposition to the ACA grew stronger, he claimed he was relying on his experience as a physician to bolster his credibility for this position. He also cited his ideological position as an important factor but simultaneously claimed that his opposition was driven by factors other than politics (Chandler, 2012d, p. 10A). In the same statement in early October, Bentley said for the first time he would not comply with the federal deadline and would default to the federal exchange (Chandler, 2012d, p. 10A), a position he reiterated shortly after the 2012 presidential election and just days before the federal deadline to create a state exchange (Chandler, 2012e, p. 7A). When the deadline arrived for the exchanges to go active, Alabamians' options were those in the federal exchange.

It thus appears that Governor Bentley experienced a significant change in position regarding the viability and desirability of a state exchange. On one hand, having a state exchange could be considered a victory for states' rights advocates in that the state retains control over the content and operation of the exchange. The report from the governor's commission can be reasonably interpreted as a strong case for a state exchange (the vote of the commission was unanimous in favor), and the governor's early public remarks support this. Yet, in spite of the early position in favor and no real publicly available remarks to the contrary, Bentley shifted his position and took actions that effectively halted action in the state legislature to pass legislation to allow the creation of a state exchange. As the deadline for a state exchange grew nearer, comments by the governor grew more firm. In those remarks before the Birmingham Business Alliance, Bentley expressed solidarity with other Republican governors, including the governors of Texas, Florida, and Louisiana, saying, "If we stand together, I do believe Congress is going to have to look at this again . . . that will send a clear signal to all of our elected leaders in Washington that the health care bill should be changed" (Chandler, 2012e, p. 7A). The deadline passed without further action to create a state exchange, and Alabama thus defaulted to the federal exchange.

The process of getting from "maybe" to "no" illustrates the interplay of interests in the state. On one hand, the health community—hospitals, insurance companies, and doctors, among others—seemed to support the idea of the state exchange. From the standpoint of the direct providers, bringing thousands of new "customers" into the market for health-related services could not help but be an attractive prospect. The strong support for a state exchange among the members representing these interests is indicative of this support. In fact, even representatives of the legislature—a very conservative group—also supported many of the commission's recommendations. That the House passed a bill to create a state exchange and that a very similar bill was in process in the Senate further underline this support. However, when overlaid with a more populist, antigovernment view, it appears that the forces for states' rights ultimately were defeated by the populists. Rather than allow Alabama to control its own destiny with a state exchange, the antigovernment faction was willing to sacrifice that control for the hope that the ACA would eventually be overturned through the courts or through legislative action. Even after the 2012 election, this strategy seemed to dominate the public discussion.

Also noticeably absent from most of the public debate is any discussion of the benefits of the ACA to the citizens of Alabama. Although the commission's report detailed the likely benefit of a state exchange, the public debate remained focused on issues of constitutionality, the viability of the law, and the cost of the state exchange. Also notable is the central role played by Governor Bentley in the process. Alabama is generally considered to be a "weak governor" state[15] (Gray, Hanson, & Kousser, 2007), and the fact that the governor drove the public debate (and the outcome) is noteworthy. Bentley's status as "physician-governor" may have played a role, but his ultimate rejection of the consensus of the broader medical community in the state makes his actions all the more puzzling.

Medicaid Expansion

The issue of Medicaid expansion was somewhat less variable than the issue of a state exchange. Alabama has implemented a Medicaid program that barely meets federal requirements and is one of the most restrictive in the nation (Williamson, 2013), although nearly 20 percent of the state's residents receive Medicaid benefits (Chollet et al., 2011, p. iii; Orndorff, 2012a, p. 1A). In 2011, Medicaid covered more than half of all births in the state, as well as half of all children in the state (Williamson, 2013). Given the relatively large proportion of uninsured in Alabama, an expansion of Medicaid to cover more citizens would do much to expand health insurance coverage in the state.

A report written by health economists Becker and Morrisey (2012, p. 1) from the University of Alabama–Birmingham calculates a net state tax revenue increase of about $935 million if Medicaid were to be expanded. The report examines three different scenarios depending on the estimates of new enrollees in the Alabama Medicaid program between 2014 and 2020. Using the middle scenario, the report estimates an additional $11.7 billion in Medicaid program costs paid by the federal government, with an additional $771 million to be incurred by the state. The report notes that the actual state cost is likely to be somewhat lower, due to lower costs for uncompensated care, as well as mental health and other services otherwise provided by the state to the expansion population (those who would be newly covered under Medicaid expansion) under current policy (Becker & Morrisey, 2012, pp. 3–4). With a net influx of nearly $20 billion in new economic activity in the state, Becker and Morrisey predict an increase of about $935 million in new revenue to the state (using the middle scenario; the low and high estimates are $749 million and $1.58 billion, respectively). In short, the study predicts a net gain in state revenue of about $160 million, after paying the state portion of the new Medicaid bill.

Elsewhere, a separate study commissioned by the Alabama Hospital Association estimated the total economic impact of Medicaid expansion in the state. As was the case with the report offered by Becker and Morrisey, the estimates produced by Addy and Ijaz (2013) included three different estimates depending on the number of new enrollees in the expanded Medicaid program. Using the middle scenario, Addy and Ijaz (2013, p. ii) predicted increased business activity of about $28 billion; a doubling of state GDP; and 30,700 new jobs created across multiple sectors of the state's economy. The study was publicly questioned by Governor Bentley, who dismissed the findings as doubtful (Ranaivo, 2013) and "bogus" (Stein, 2013, p. 11A). He went on to say,

> The jobs are already there. You're not creating jobs. You're not creating new people by bringing all this money in. You have the doctors already there. The nurses are already there. You don't produce a new doctor in a year. I went to school 24 [*sic*] years to become a doctor. You don't produce these type people immediately.
>
> (Cason, 2013, p. 10A)

At the same time, the Alabama Hospital Association used the report's findings to announce a coalition to advocate for Medicaid expansion, thus pitting at least parts of the state's health and medical community against the physician-governor's position on the issue. Bentley's opposition to Medicaid expansion had been fairly constant; in 2012 he vowed to oppose Medicaid expansion because of the tax burden, saying that the ACA "is the single worst piece of legislation to be passed" in his lifetime (quoted in Beyerle, 2012). Although the governor's Medicaid commission had yet to issue its report, it seems clear that, at least in his public stance, Governor Bentley had rejected both a state exchange and Medicaid.

Other voices in the state spoke in favor of Medicaid expansion. David Bronner, the chief executive officer of the politically influential Retirement Systems of Alabama, stated it was irresponsible for the state not to accept the federal money (Rawls, 2013a). The disagreement led to charges that the governor sought revenge by instituting new controls over the investment authority held by Bronner (Rawls, 2013b), a charge the governor denied. Bronner had been at odds with the governor and claimed that the dispute was also the result of Bronner's refusal to hire a member of Bentley's staff. Bronner had referred to governors who refuse federal money as "idiots" (Rawls, 2013b), thus linking the two issues. The state's chief medical officer and chair of the Alabama Medicaid Advisory Commission, Dr. Don Williamson, was another voice in favor of Medicaid expansion (Maetz, 2013). In the political realm, the Birmingham Metro Chapter of the NAACP, the Greater Birmingham Ministries, and Progressive Democrats of America planned and conducted marches in October and December 2013 to protest the governor's refusal to accept an expanded Medicaid program in Alabama (Stein, 2013, p. 11A). In spite of the opposition to his position, Governor Bentley continued to defend his opposition to Medicaid expansion. In November 2012, he announced that the state would not participate in Medicaid expansion. "I will not expand Medicaid as it exists under the current structure because it is broken . . .," said Bentley (Chandler, 2012e, p. 7A). He continued to maintain that his obstruction to the ACA was a matter of political philosophy, rather than political expediency. Moreover, even after the presidential election in November 2012 and the defeat of Republican candidate Mitt Romney, Governor Bentley continued to believe that the ACA would be overturned by Congress, regardless of conventional wisdom—"they're wrong," claimed Bentley (Chandler, 2012e, p. 7A).

On October 25, 2012, Governor Bentley formally established the Alabama Medicaid Advisory Commission, chaired by Dr. Don Williamson, the state health officer. Created by Executive Order 35, the commission was charged with developing options to reform the Medicaid program in Alabama. There were four specific areas that the commission was to address: an analysis of the financial needs of the program, the creation of a sustainable model of finance for the program, new or innovative models of care and service delivery, and methods to increase transparency and fairness in the program. It is noteworthy that the charge to the commission did not include the specific question of Medicaid expansion. There were 33 members representing 15 separate interests, along with representatives from the state legislature (both House and Senate), as well as several executive branch state agencies. Of the 33 members, 17 were appointed directly by the governor. The committee met seven times and issued its report in January 2013.

The commission made a total of eleven recommendations. None of the recommendations directly addressed the issue of Medicaid expansion but focused instead on more technical aspects of the current state Medicaid program, as per the governor's charge to the commission. The recommendations included items such as the establishment of regional patient care networks in the state, the ability for regional care networks to contract with private managed-care providers, legislation to create a cap on state Medicaid spending, actions to crack down on fraud and abuse in the Medicaid program, and measures to increase transparency in the program. A closer look at the report, however, provides a compelling case for Medicaid expansion in Alabama. The report cited a growing demand for Medicaid services, the comparatively low level of services currently provided, and general inflation in the health care sector (Williamson, 2013). Still, the report stopped short of any recommendation regarding Medicaid expansion under the ACA (indeed, the ACA is never explicitly mentioned in the report). However, the commission's chairperson, Dr. Don Williamson, remained an advocate for Medicaid expansion (Maetz, 2013, p. 2F).

Meanwhile, Attorney General Luther Strange continued his legal efforts challenging the constitutionality of the ACA. Along with other Republican attorneys general, Strange signaled Alabama's opposition to the individual mandate and Medicaid expansion, cases that ultimately failed. Still, Strange's office continued to resist the ACA, a position that Strange converted successfully into a temporary appointment to fill Jeff Sessions's U.S. Senate seat when Sessions accepted President-Elect Trump's invitation to serve as attorney general of the U.S. However, in the Republican primary to fill the seat, Strange was defeated by Roy S. Moore, the controversial former two-time chief justice of the Alabama Supreme Court, unabashed Trump supporter, and general political firebrand.[16]

In the end, Governor Bentley continued to state publicly that Alabama would not expand Medicaid under the ACA, and indeed, Alabama has held that stance up to this point. In his final year in office Bentley was the subject of rumors and investigations, which included charges of an extramarital affair and misuse of campaign funds. Bentley resigned under threat of impeachment in April 2017 and was replaced as governor by Lieutenant Governor Kay Ivey, who was sworn into office the same day Bentley resigned. Bentley also pleaded guilty to two misdemeanor charges centered around the misuse of campaign funds. Faced with an ongoing scandal, the issue of Medicaid expansion effectively fell off the policy agenda.

As is the case with a state exchange, the outcome of the debate over Medicaid expansion can be explained through the interplay of interests, and populists versus the "Big Mules." The need in Alabama for an expanded Medicaid program is, to many observers, self-evident, but the debate was focused firmly on issues of cost. On one hand, advocates for expansion argued that the benefits of expansion greatly outweighed the additional state costs. These arguments were rejected out of hand by the populists, who saw Medicaid expansion as the uncontrolled growth of another "Big Government" program that Alabama could ill afford. The dismissal by the populists of the studies that suggested the net benefits of expansion outweighed the costs, without contrary evidence, illustrates this point. There were no studies or estimates that were offered to counter the available data; rather, the available data were simply dismissed as "bogus."

State Legislation

Since 2010, the state legislature has been controlled by the Republican Party. One of the earliest statements of opposition to the ACA from the legislature was the passage of a bill in June 2011 to put before state voters a constitutional amendment to allow employers, health care providers, and individuals to opt out of any health care system. A direct challenge to the ACA, the amendment would effectively bypass the governor from the decision process if approved by voters (White, 2011, p. 10A). The amendment would "prohibit any person, employer, or health care provider from being compelled to participate in any health care system" (ballotpedia.org, 2018). The amendment appeared on the November 6, 2012, ballot[17] and passed by a comfortable 59 to 41 percent margin (ballotpedia.org, 2018). While many observers saw the initiative as largely symbolic, it was a clear statement of opposition to the ACA. As one state senator stated, "[t]he people of Alabama don't want any part of Obama's national legislation" (White, 2011, p. 10A).

Although not itself a direct rejection of the ACA by the state legislature, the intent of the legislation to place the issue on the ballot was a calculated political move with little downside. If the amendment passed, the legislators could claim they did not block the ACA; the people of Alabama did so. The governor could also claim that his actions in opposition were simply an expression of the will of the people, although we could find no public statements to this effect. If the amendment failed, the legislature could still vote to block implementation, even if the governor did not block implementation through executive action. One could reasonably conclude that the governor's actions regarding the ACA, especially after the 2012 election, were likely driven by a populist response to the amendment as a rejection of the ACA by the citizens of Alabama. While it is difficult to show a causal link, Governor Bentley's position on the ACA seems to have become firmer and more strident following the 2012 election results.

The state legislature was also charged with developing legislation to enable the creation of a state insurance exchange and to pass needed insurance market reforms. Governor Bentley initially signaled support of a state exchange (Chandler, 2011, p. 1D), and the House began work on a bill to create a state exchange during the 2011 legislative session. That bill passed the House but later died in committee in the Senate. There were two factors that led to the effective withdrawal of the bill from consideration. First, Governor Bentley threatened to veto any bill that created a state exchange before SCOTUS ruled on the constitutionality of the ACA, a threat that the Senate appeared to take seriously. Second, the bill came under fire after some in the Senate questioned whether the legislation would create a virtual monopoly for BCBSAL. Several lawmakers noted that BCBSAL was the only company in Alabama that would qualify to join the exchange and that the result would not be an open marketplace (Chandler, 2012a, p. 6B). Said State Representative Greg Wren (R-Montgomery), "We absolutely want an open marketplace. If only one company could qualify, that's not an open marketplace" (Chandler, 2012a, p. 6B). A similar bill was introduced in the state legislature in the 2012 session, but that bill also died in committee. As the deadline for the creation of a state exchange neared, Governor Bentley signaled a willingness to create a state exchange by executive order, an action that was largely unchallenged in the legislature. The state legislature showed no interest in creating market reforms to encourage a more robust insurance market in the state. In spite of the dominance of Blue Cross/Blue Shield, and the fact that at least one other insurer declined to enter the small-group market, the legislature refused to consider legislation to entice additional actors into the health insurance marketplace. In many ways, Alabama's position on the ACA was thus left to the governor, with minimal action, input, or guidance from the state legislature.

It is also interesting to note that, unlike other states, Alabama's legislature did not enact any legislation in direct opposition to the ACA. While the bill placing the issue in the hands of Alabama voters and the bill banning the sale of health insurance policies that included abortion coverage can reasonably be construed as "not ACA-friendly," the legislature did not pass legislation banning a state exchange or refusing to expand Medicaid. Rather, the legislature generally sidestepped direct legislative confrontation. As the Rockefeller Institute (2014, p. 7) field team suggest, it is possible that the attitude of the legislature was "one of 'we're just not going to bother with this.'"

Conclusion

In sum, Alabama represents a state at the extreme end of the scale of opposition to the ACA. In spite of evidence that the ACA would be beneficial to citizens, the state's economy, and state revenue, strong partisan opposition ensured that the ACA would be resisted by every means possible. The lack of a robust competitive private insurance market in the state complicated the process, but intentional delays and active partisan opposition mean that Alabama stands as the exemplar case for a state in opposition to the ACA. Still, it is also clear that Alabama's path to "no" was anything but straight and uncomplicated. Instead, the process by which policymakers in Alabama considered the ACA and its requirements was very much dictated by a combination of interests, politics, culture, and traditional social and political cleavages in the state.

It is particularly notable that the interests in the battle over the ACA mirrored the interests described by V.O. Key (1949/1984) 60 years earlier. The "Big Mules" in the relatively wealthy areas of the state (led by Birmingham and the surrounding counties) were more or less in direct opposition to the rural, populist, antigovernment interests in other parts of the state. Indeed, the populist rejection of studies showing net gains for Alabama through the ACA, and the conflicts over costs, are indicative of this cleavage. Governor Bentley, himself a titular member of the "Big Mules" camp by virtue of his profession, was nonetheless swept into office by a strong populist voting bloc. It is likely that the governor's early indecision about the ACA was due, at least in part, to a tension between his professional life and his political life. As the owner of a large medical practice in the state, one may conclude that Bentley would himself been the recipient of increased business revenue as thousands of new consumers suddenly entered the health care market. Yet, at the end of the process, the governor became one of the more outspoken opponents of the ACA in Alabama—he essentially became the "face" of opposition.

The division of political power across a number of elected positions in the state also may have contributed to the choices made by the state. Alabama was an early party to the lawsuit challenging the constitutionality of the ACA; it appears that the decision to become involved in the suit was made by the attorney general. Even after Troy King was replaced by Luther Strange, Alabama's stance on (and participation in) the lawsuit remained constant. Both King and Strange were elected on the strength of the rural, populist vote, and both likely saw the ACA as a clear overreach of the federal government's power. The legislature's actions are somewhat less clear in that the legislature seemed generally content to stay in the background and allow the governor and the attorney general to fight the public battles. This is likely due to the fact that Alabama's legislature is a part-time body and is only in session a few weeks each year. Events in the battle over the ACA were happening quickly, the legislature was out of session for most of the period, and the governor did not see fit to call for a special session to address health care reform.

Finally, the Alabama case illustrates the complexity of state policy action and the multitude of actors and interests who ultimately shape policy outcomes in ways dictated by long-standing patterns. These patterns are the result of the unique circumstances in the state's history and in the particular ways political interests developed within the state. Those patterns have remained remarkably consistent over time, and largely resilient to change. The net result is a series of patterns and actions that led from "maybe" to "no" on the question of the ACA.

Notes

1. The term *Big Mules* is the name given to the industrialists in and around Birmingham (Key, 1949/1984). With a different source of wealth and a different lifestyle, the "Big Mules" emerged as a separate political force in Alabama politics, a societal cleavage that persists into the 21st century.
2. There are currently 18 separate state offices elected in statewide elections in Alabama. In addition, Alabamians elect two national senators through statewide votes.
3. It is important to note that Key makes the point that the conservative agrarian stronghold is in the Black Belt (western Alabama). Although named for the character of the soil in the region, it is also home to a large African American population. Because of a historical reliance on Jim Crow laws and political disenfranchisement,

politics in this region have focused on maintenance of social and political control, leaving agrarian interests in the rest of the state to take a more radical agrarian approach to politics. See Key (1949/1984, Chapter 3).

4. It is noteworthy that "Big Jim" Folsom's son, Jim Folsom, Jr., was elected governor in 1992, largely by invoking the name of his famous father.
5. Woodward (2013) suggests that the "southern strategy" pursued by Republicans in the 1980s was crucial to this shift. Many southern white conservatives were threatened by the emergence (and activism) of black voters, which helped split support for the Democratic Party. Party identity became almost an issue of race as more whites abandoned the Democratic Party in favor of the Republicans. The Republican platform offered a more conservative alternative; thus, the intersection of ideology and race reinforced the shift.
6. Fob James had first been elected governor as a Democrat in 1978 but changed his party allegiance and ran successfully as a Republican candidate for governor in 1994.
7. The 7th Congressional District also includes much of the city of Birmingham, which is also predominately Black.
8. The next nearest state in terms of market share control is Michigan, in which Blue Cross/Blue Shield controlled about 67 percent of the market. Only four other states have a single company that controls more than 60 percent of the market (Walsh, 2013).
9. It is worth noting that James Caldwell was first elected as a Democrat but later changed his party affiliation to Republican during Bobby Jindal's term as governor. Caldwell thus became the first Republican to hold office as attorney general in Louisiana since Reconstruction.
10. Also in the primary was Roy Moore, another example of larger-than-life characters in Alabama politics. The former chief justice of the Alabama Supreme Court, Moore was removed from office for violating a federal court order to remove a statue depicting the Ten Commandments from the rotunda of the Alabama Judicial Building. Moore ran for governor in 2006 and 2010, losing in the primaries on both occasions. He was elected again to the Alabama Supreme Court in 2013, before being suspended in 2016 for his refusal to uphold a SCOTUS ruling on same-sex marriage. Moore ultimately resigned from his seat on the Alabama Supreme Court in 2017 and ran for the U.S. Senate seat vacated by Jeff Sessions, narrowly losing to Democrat Doug Jones after charges of sexual misconduct with underage females against Moore emerged shortly before the election.
11. However, we should also note that the governor in Alabama is also chief legislator; in addition to other constitutional powers, the governor chooses both the Speaker of the House and the President Pro Tempore of the Senate (Martin, 1975). In this case, the governor's appointees are given appointment power for the commission members.
12. ALL Kids is the name given to the Alabama program created under the CHIP. ALL Kids provides coverage administered by BCBSAL to qualified children younger than 19.
13. In addition to the aforementioned question of who should pay for the exchange, the commission split 10–2 on a relatively minor issue of whether to recommend that Alabama change its definition of "small employer" at the outset or wait until 2016 to make the change at the time required by the ACA. The 10 votes were in favor or retaining Alabama's then-current language, which defined a small employer as a business employing between 2 and 50 people. The ACA definition would have expanded the definition to include businesses employing up to 100 people.
14. The Alabama legislature is in session a total of 30 "legislative days" over a 105-day period, beginning in February in the year following an election and in March

in other years. All members of the House and Senate stand for election at the same time, and serve four-year terms. The governor has the authority to call the legislature back into session for up to 12 additional "legislative days" days to address legislative issues specified by the governor (BallotPedia.org, 2018).

15. A weak governor state is a state in which gubernatorial power is constitutionally limited beyond that found in other states. Power given to governors in other states is typically given to the state legislature instead. See Schlesinger (1965).
16. As noted earlier in Note 10, Roy Moore's political career has been checkered and full of controversy. His image fits well with the Alabama tradition of larger-than-life, memorable political figures, and his career has been filled with actions to support a strong conservative agenda. In addition to the events mentioned previously in this chapter, Moore garnered national attention during his Senate campaign by openly wearing a pistol to campaign rallies.
17. This amendment was one of eleven amendments on the ballot for the November election. The current state constitution has been in place since 1901 and has the distinction of being the longest, and most amended, of all state constitutions (Martin, 1975).

6 Dueling Sentiments

Michigan and the ACA

The story of Michigan is not unlike many of its neighboring midwestern states, areas rich with natural resources that developed into industrial manufacturing hubs to capitalize and, in many cases, exploit these resources. Throughout its development, Michigan has seen its fair share of ups and downs. In many ways, the battle over health care in the state has mirrored this trend of conflict and opportunity. The health care debate in Michigan has been influenced by this shared history by the challenges wrought on a region when the jobs dry up, by the corresponding increase in poverty, and by the outsized influence of third-party actors, predominantly unions, in state affairs. All these issues together make the study of Michigan's response to the ACA fascinating, because unlike in many other states, the health care debate in Michigan has rarely followed party lines.

Background

Michigan is the 10th-most populous state in the country and has the largest land mass east of the Mississippi River. With the sheer size of the region comes an abundance of natural resources and economic diversification. Michigan borders four Great Lakes (Superior, Michigan, Huron, and Erie) and features nearly 65,000 inland lakes and ponds, which means that a person in Michigan is never more than 6 miles from a freshwater source and within 85 miles of a Great Lake. The northern part of the state, including the Upper Peninsula, relies heavily on tourism and a service-driven economy, boasting more than 3,200 miles of freshwater coastline, greater than 100 recreational bike trails, and more lighthouses than any other state in the country (Michigan Tourism, 2017). The southern half of the state is known for industry and manufacturing and is home to the "Big Three" American automobile manufacturers (General Motors, Ford Motor Company, and Fiat Chrysler), which for a time, were the largest three automobile manufacturers in the world (Vlasic, 2011), and all headquartered within the Detroit city limits.

Michigan boasts seven cities with populations of greater than 100,000 residents with the city of Detroit, in Wayne County, pacing the state at more than 700,000 residents (U.S. Census Bureau, 2010). This number nearly matches the combined total population of the next six largest cities throughout the state. The headquarters of the state's manufacturing base and the encompassing Wayne County, Detroit accounts for nearly 20 percent of Michigan's total population. Like many of its midwestern neighbors, Michigan, especially Detroit, was built on blue-collar, manufacturing jobs. For a time, Detroit was one of the most populous and prosperous cities in the world, but like many of its fellow industrial-based midwestern brethren has faced several challenges over the past 50 years.

History and Culture

Beginning roughly in 1903 with the opening of Ford Motor Company, industrial growth within the city and state was rapid. By 1920, Detroit had become the fourth-largest city in the country but with all the expansion came increasing tensions along racial and jurisdictional lines. The Great Migration, a period during the 20th century in which more than 6 million African Americans moved from the rural South to the more industrialized Northern cities in search of opportunity, served to increase growing racial tensions in the region. This migration also coincided with the growth of unions and labor representation. The Great Depression slowed growth, but this proved to be temporary as the war effort once again ramped up the need for manufacturing. Eventually, the rapid growth, continuing migration, and exceedingly poor working conditions came to a head in several bloody protests and race riots (Baulch & Zacharias, 1999).

With the war finally over, the growth of labor unions began to increase steadily as the battle for increased profit sharing and safer working conditions took center stage. Soon after, the rapid growth resumed; this time fueled by the Federal Aid Highway Act of 1956 and the resulting construction of the Interstate Highway System. The creation of the highway system proved to be a major boon for Detroit because it provided substantial manufacturing demands, as well as greatly increased recreational and vehicular travel options. Ultimately this proved to be the high point for Detroit and the surrounding region; simmering racial tension, union conflict, globalization, and increased competition all conspired negatively to impact the automobile and manufacturing industry across the city and state after this high point.

Like many of its midwestern industrial peers, Detroit (and, in turn, much of Michigan) experienced substantial challenges adapting to the deindustrialization of the country, and increased foreign competition in the latter half of the 20th century. Over the last 40 years, Detroit has lost more than half of its population and for the first time in nearly 170 years fell outside of the 20 most populous cities in the country (MacDonald, 2016). The precipitous population decline was tied directly to the loss of hundreds of thousands of manufacturing jobs over the past few decades (Stock, Udow-Phillips, Ogundimu, & Ehrlich, 2010). Many of these jobs were union positions and included collectively bargained health care coverage options. When the factories closed, the jobs left, and the unions folded. Roughly 40 percent of the citizenry left behind (nearly 4 million citizens) were uninsured or receiving some form of public subsidy (Stock et al., 2010). As catastrophic as this was, the carnage was compounded by generations of public corruption (Baldas, 2013).

While Detroit receives much of the credit and blame for the fortunes of the state of Michigan, the state capital, where much of the governing policy is crafted, sits 90 miles west in Lansing, located almost directly in between Lake Michigan to the west and Lake Huron to the east. Lansing was not always the capital; it actually succeeded Detroit in that honor in the middle of the 19th century. After Detroit was surrendered during the War of 1812, state lawmakers decided it prudent to move the capital inland in order to increase the distance from the Canadian border and to spur development in the state's interior (Michigan State Senate, 2018). While the move was initially contentious, land was cheap, and Lansing eventually grew to be the fifth-largest city in the state.

To a lesser degree, Lansing experienced a similar history to Detroit in that the city became an industrial powerhouse in the early 20th century with the founding of the Olds Motor Vehicle Company, better known as Oldsmobile, in 1897. Oldsmobile continued for more than 100 years in Lansing, tracing the peaks and valleys, much like its larger counterparts to the east before ultimately being shuttered by General Motors in 2004. In addition to being the state capital, Lansing has one other factor working in its favor that Detroit did not. Lansing is home to a major public research institution in Michigan State University. One of the country's original land-grant universities, Michigan State offered diversification, funding, and research that were mostly absent in Detroit and other areas as manufacturing disappeared (Sallee, Rosaen, & Anderson, 2007).

The Political Landscape

The Role and Impact of Unions

Over the past century in Michigan, unions have held a prominent and influential role in state government and politics. The birthplace of the American automobile and long the epicenter of American manufacturing, Michigan has enjoyed a long and hard-fought history of collective bargaining, until recently. There has been a sustained effort over the past several decades to dismantle union effectiveness at the federal level. The legal ramifications of these actions coupled with a massive downturn in the state economy tied directly to the erosion of American manufacturing and the closing of several large automakers in the state have made union influence a shell of what it once was.

Nowhere is this more evident than in looking at the United Automobile Workers (UAW). Long one of the most influential and powerful organizations in not just the state but the country, the UAW has seen membership decline from roughly 1.5 million in the mid-1970s to 400,000 in present day. The decline in influence and representation is not unique to the UAW; total union membership within the state is at historic lows with fewer than 700,000 registered union members in Michigan. This issue was further exacerbated in 2013 when, to the shock of many, Michigan became a "right-to-work" state, further dissipating what little remaining political clout unions had maintained. Historically, union membership was strongly correlated with higher wages and benefits; unions held substantial political capital to influence decision-making and shape policy throughout much of the 20th century. By the time health care reform was again gaining traction on the national stage, in early 2007, union influence was on the verge of irrelevance.

The ACA

The ACA has proved to be one of the most contentious policy issues in recent memory. The divisions, at least initially, were mostly by party line; which is surprising since the general framework of the law was based on Republican proposals and allowed for substantial state discretion is the implementation period. There proved to be several challenges of the legal, partisan, and political variety that sparked heated and long-lasting debate across the country and within the state of Michigan over whether to support the legislation and, if so, how to best implement the provisions.

Studying the response and implementation in Michigan provides perhaps one of the most interesting and illuminating perspectives on the decisions states had to make and, more important, the factors that ultimately influenced that process. Michigan is a state where there was a great need for health care with, as previously mentioned, more than 40 percent of the state population uninsured or receiving a subsidy. It would seem that the Medicaid expansion proposal was tailor-made for a state like Michigan, yet soon after the ACA was signed into law, Republican attorney general Mike Cox joined 13 other states in a lawsuit challenging the law's constitutionality. Attorney General Cox made this decision on his own, in opposition to other state party leaders. Interestingly, fellow Republican governor Rick Snyder, in defiance of Cox's decision, opted provisionally to expand Medicaid using a Section 1115A waiver. This waiver allowed Michigan to implement state-mandated modifications to the federal legislation and create a state–federal partnership to administer Michigan's new health insurance exchange. Michigan became just one of five Republican-controlled states to expand Medicaid at the time and was one of four states to use the Section 1115A waiver to modify federal regulations.

Michigan provides for an interesting case study due to the historical and contextual factors previously outlined but also, and perhaps more important for this discussion, due to the alternative stances taken within the state in response to the ACA. Based on prior research, one would expect Michigan to have opposed initial implementation of the ACA along party lines (Travis et al.,

2016), yet the opposite happened. Partisanship played a pivotal role in ACA-related decision-making in Michigan, but unlike in several other states, it does not appear to have been the primary factor. State Republican leadership was split on the issue, which was rather unique given what was transpiring across the country. Legislators fought bitterly for one side or the other, often buoyed by several special interest groups or local organizations.

One of the most influential special interest groups, and one that is at least somewhat unique to Michigan, is the UAW. The UAW not only collectively fought and bargained for highly competitive salaries and benefits that were among the best in the country but also changed the culture in Michigan. Michigan became a unionized state, a state where workers' rights played a critical role in decision-making. Over time, however, jobs began to be outsourced and factories closed. By the mid-1970s it had become clear that Michigan, like the rest of the country, was entering a period of postindustrialization (Bell, 1976). By the late 1990s, private-sector unionization had shrunk to levels equal to the early 1930s and the Great Depression (Moody, 1997). The decline in unionization was a direct result of the shrinking labor market and disappearing workforce (Moody, 1997). Despite the decline in representation and influence, the union foothold and culture were still very much present in the ACA discussions. Much of this played out in a way that did not necessarily value one organization over another but gave a voice to several influential outside organizations during the contentious decision-making period.

Like many states in the same situation, Michigan's response to the ACA was greatly influenced by partisanship and third-party actors. However, the narrative diverged in Michigan, unlike other states, because there was substantial disagreement within each party on what actions to take and how to do it. There is little denying the need for health care in Michigan, due to large subsidy rates, high unemployment, and low income yet where many other states actively opposed expansion, Michigan was effectively split on the matter. While the divide influenced and slowed action, it also led to a drawn-out and nuanced response to the legislation.

State leadership took several conflicting, supportive, and oppositional measures when it came to joining lawsuits, expanding Medicaid, and administering a state exchange. The most visible divide was between the Republican attorney general and the Republican governor, each of whom took vastly different positions on the ACA. Their divergence resulted in conflict and opportunity and provided a forum in which allegiances varied and decisions played out in real time in the public arena. The political environment became polarized to a degree that had not been seen at the local level in decades; congressmen and their families received death threats in response to their favor of the legislation, and vandals destroyed property throughout the state (Spangler, 2010). Within the legal arena, Michigan became party to several lawsuits while at the same time attempting to expand Medicaid and create a state-run exchange; this was all done with a unified executive and legislature.

Putting a Price on Citizenship: Early Opposition to the ACA in Michigan

After little more than a year of hearings, forums, and arguments, the ACA was signed into law on March 23, 2010. Much like it had been at the federal level, the discussion at the state level in Michigan was contentious. Proponents of the legislation cited several disturbing trends plaguing the American medical system, in particular, the exceedingly high cost of care, that, at best, contributes to ineffective, redundant, or inappropriate care and, at worst, to the more than 80,000 deaths a year caused by medical mistakes (Dolsen, 2009). Those opposed to the legislation were generally fiscal conservatives who argued against the increased financial commitments and uncertainty of where the money would come from. "Some opponents said the new law amounts to a 'government takeover' of health care. Some said it violates the Constitution. Others said it will cut the benefits on which Medicare recipients depend, or will explode the deficit" (Levin, 2011). The truth was and has been obscured, and in many cases, politics trumped need (Mayer et al., 2015). The foundational cleavages were further deepened by the substantial uncertainty that surrounded the law. The delayed rollout and substantial discretion that was afforded to the states in support and opposition further fueled skepticism and uncertainty about how to proceed at all levels of government.

This climate of uncertainty led many, including high-ranking officials in Michigan, to oppose the ACA. What makes Michigan so interesting is that it was not unified opposition among party lines like many other states. Michigan employs a republican form of government with three separate but equal branches: the executive, judicial, and legislative. In most state matters, the final decision-making power resides with the governor. The governor is elected on the same ticket with the lieutenant governor, who is considered the first-in-line executive should something befall the governor. The second and third in succession line, the secretary of state and attorney general positions, are also elected concurrently with the governor and lieutenant governor.

When President Obama signed the ACA into law in March 2010, Michigan was led by Democratic governor Jennifer Granholm. Granholm took office in 2003 and was nearing the end of her two-term limit, which ran through 2010. Governor Granholm was in support of the ACA and began proceedings to formally and legally expand health care in Michigan. However, with less than a year left in office, Governor Granholm was limited in her political capital with regard to what she was able to accomplish. The biggest challenge to the Granholm administration, and one of the more interesting ACA-related conflicts after passage, came from Michigan attorney general Mike Cox. Unlike Governor Granholm, who was nearing the end of her political career, Attorney General Cox was a Republican with future political ambitions.

Cox and Granholm had clashed previously in their near decade together in Michigan state leadership. In the early 2000s, Governor Granholm supported the University of Michigan's use of racial preferences in its admissions policy, essentially allowing the University of Michigan to legally discriminate in terms of student admittance; Attorney General Cox openly opposed. When the Michigan Civil Rights Initiative went to a vote in 2006, it was passed overwhelmingly, resulting in a ban of the use of racial and gender preferences at state institutions. Interestingly this was decided at the ballot on November 7, 2006, the same day that Governor Granholm won reelection. This was a win for the attorney general, and a very public and humiliating loss for the governor, who had yet even to begin her second term.

Almost immediately following President Obama signing the law into passage, several lawsuits were filed challenging its constitutionality. One of the most serious threats to the law was what came to be known as the *NFIB v. Sebelius* suit, which primarily challenged the constitutionality of the individual mandate and whether the federal government could legally require citizens to purchase health insurance under the commerce clause. Despite vocal and legal support of the ACA from Governor Granholm, Attorney General Cox, who just two months later would announce his candidacy for governor, entered Michigan into the NFIB lawsuit, Cox stated that it was in an effort "to stop President Obama and Congress from forcing Americans to buy a product as the price of citizenship" (Sellek & Yearout, 2010). Governor Granholm, along with Governors Gregoire (D-WA), Ritter Jr. (D-CO), and Rendell (D-PA), responded in support of Attorney General Holder and upholding the health care legislation, stating that the legislation was "the single most important reform of our health care system in decades" (Bell, 2010).

The timing of Cox's decision and his candidacy announcement suggest that it may have been more of a political strategy, geared to capitalize on growing disdain for the Obama administration and to galvanize the support of the fledgling Tea Party movement for his upcoming gubernatorial bid (Cox, McMillin Woo Reform, 2010).

In addition to the debate that raged between Governor Granholm and Attorney General Cox, in Michigan, there were several third-party actors that played substantial roles in the ACA decision-making process leading up to the implementation. The Thomas More Law Center, a conservative, Christian, public interest law firm headquartered in Ann Arbor, also played a major role in state opposition to the ACA.

Founded in 1999 by Domino's pizza magnate Tom Monaghan, the center is named for English philosopher and statesman Thomas More, who is perhaps most famous for his opposition to the Protestant Reformation and his resistance to the monarchy's split from the Catholic Church, a stance that ultimately cost him his life. In more recent history, the Thomas More Law Center has taken up a number of high-profile conservative causes across the country and has litigated several controversial cases in the past two decades. Charged with preserving "America's Judeo-Christian heritage, defending the religious freedom of Christians, and restoring time-honored moral and family values" (Thomas More Law Center, 2018), the More Law Center was quick to come out against the ACA, filing suit on October 7, 2010.

The Thomas More Law Center suit was filed on behalf of Michigan residents in an effort to challenge the mandate and enforcement requiring individuals to purchase health care or be subject to fiscal penalty. The suit named four defendants by name, Barack Obama, Kathleen Sebelius, Eric Holder Jr., and Timothy Geithner (the president of the U.S., secretary of the HHS, U.S. Attorney General, and secretary of the Treasury, respectively). Speaking on behalf of the More Law Center, Counselor Robert Muise buoyed Michigan attorney general Cox's actions, stating,

> Congress has authority to do any number of things to improve health care. But the Constitution limits Congress to what it can impose on individuals. We are here because the Congress violated the U.S. Constitution by forcing individuals to engage in a commercial activity.
>
> (Guthrie, 2010)

The two lawsuits set the stage for the divide that would characterize the implementation of the ACA in the state of Michigan. Attorney General Cox's decision to join the NFIB lawsuit further solidified the battle lines between those in support and those in opposition of the health care reform; interestingly this action, along with many of the other most divisive, took place after the legislation had already become law. These debates would play out in courthouses, town halls, and other public spaces, in Lansing and throughout the state over the coming months.

Beyond the theatrics, rhetoric, and specter of political ambition that contributed to Attorney General Cox's decision to sign on to the NFIB lawsuit was the legal question of whether the attorney general had standing without the support of the governor to engage in such an action. With the lines drawn, a power struggle ensued between Attorney General Cox, a Republican, and Governor Granholm, a Democrat, both of whom were trying to promote their agenda before being term-limited out of office in 2011. While acknowledging there was little she could do about Cox's participation in the NFIB suit, Governor Granholm publicly disputed Cox's authority and "his assertion that he was acting on behalf of the people of Michigan" (Bell, 2010). A representative for Cox maintained that the attorney general was acting within his constitutional authority in joining the lawsuit.

Support and opposition mostly fell along party lines, but some of the more biting criticism of Cox's action came from Robert Sedler, a professor of constitutional history at the Wayne State University Law School. Sedler argued that Cox's specious claim that Congress exceeded their regulatory authority was little more than an attempt to pander to the growing Tea Party contingent in advance of his run at the governorship (Cox, McMillin Woo Reform, 2010). Citing decades of well-established case law, Sedler noted that "the Supreme Court has repeatedly since 1923 rejected challenges to the federal government's regulatory authority" (Cox, McMillin Woo Reform, 2010). Despite the growing sense and accusations that Cox's actions were little more than a strategic maneuver to further his political ambitions, Governor Granholm acknowledged there was little she could do about Michigan's participation in the suit; however, she did push back by authorizing through executive order the creation of the Health Insurance Reform Coordinating Council (Jones, 2014). The Health Insurance Reform Coordinating Council was set up to oversee the implementation of the health care law in Michigan. Led by Community Health Director Janet Olszewski and consisting of seven additional members from varying state agencies, the council assisted in the ongoing implementation through 2014 (Barks-Hoffman, 2010). Governor Granholm's executive order also created the Office of Health Insurance Consumer Assistance within the state agency that oversees insurance companies and state banks. With these actions, Governor Granholm made it clear that despite Attorney General Cox's actions, Michigan was moving forward with the law.

Both Cox and Granholm left office in early 2011. Cox was replaced by fellow Republican Bill Schuette, and Granholm (a Democrat) was succeeded by Republican businessman Rick Snyder. At least on the surface, this appeared to be a victory for the conservative contingent opposing the health care legislation. Surprisingly, however, little changed; Attorney General Schuette maintained support for the NFIB lawsuit that was slowly working its way through the courts, and Governor Snyder, breaking from his party, continued Granholm's support of health care reform.

The suit brought by the Thomas More Law Center was the first to be resolved and the first court decision on the constitutionality of the law across the country. In the ruling, U.S. District Judge George Steeh "refused a request for an injunction to put a stop to preparations for implementing the Affordable Care Act" (UPI, 2010). At issue was whether the federal government, and specifically Congress, could mandate citizens obtain health coverage and penalize those who failed to do so. After deliberation, U.S. District Court Judge George Steeh held that the individual mandate was permissible under the Commerce Clause of the U.S. Constitution, refusing the requested injunction and dismissing two of the six claims brought forth. In support of the decision, Steeh stated that "the minimum coverage provision, which addresses economic decisions regarding health care services that everyone eventually, and inevitably, will need, is a reasonable means of effectuating Congress's goal [to address growing costs and increase coverage]" (Pelofsky, 2010). Counsel Robert Muise expressed confidence that the case would continue on to SCOTUS, stating, "I think it's important that this decision be reversed to prevent Congress from overreaching the way it did in passing the original mandate" (UPI, 2010). Muise and the Thomas More Law Center appealed to the 6th Circuit Court of Appeals who ultimately denied the review, effectively putting an end to the challenge in July 2012.

Just prior to the dismissal of the More Law Center suit, the U.S. Supreme Court heard and ruled on the NFIB lawsuit. By early 2012, Michigan, like several other states that chose to support or oppose the lawsuit, was under new leadership. Republican attorney general Bill Schuette maintained much of the stance and views of his predecessor, Mike Cox, in support of the lawsuit. Cox, attempting to parlay his opposition into additional publicity and support, failed to make it out of the Republican primary for governor, finishing a distant third. Running on a bipartisan platform, businessman Rick Snyder won the Republican nomination and ultimately the governorship over the outspoken Democratic mayor of Lansing, Virg Berneo. Much to the chagrin of Cox and Schuette supporters, Governor Snyder moved to sustain his Democratic predecessor's efforts to expand health care throughout Michigan.

While the politics of the administration changed, the debate remained very much the same, at least until SCOTUS's ruling. On June 28, 2012, in a 5–4 decision, the court upheld the law by recognizing the individual mandate as a valid extension of Congress's taxing power. The court did hold that it is unconstitutional to tie state funding to Medicaid expansion, in effect coercing state compliance. This ruling effectively ended the initial major challenge to the legitimacy and constitutionality of the law, overnight rendering the efforts of several opponents in Michigan and throughout the country moot. SCOTUS's decision to strike down the provision tying funding to Medicaid expansion, and making expansion a state issue, ultimately ensured that the next battle over health care would be one fought over whether to accept or decline Medicaid expansion funds.

The Role of Leadership in State Government and an Unpopular Expansion

With significant disagreement in the upper reaches of government and several legal battles playing out over the future of the ACA, Michigan took a "wait-and-see" approach to the issue of Medicaid expansion. Those in favor of health care reform and Medicaid expansion were generally Democrats and several influential professional health care organizations. Those opposed to Medicaid expansion not only were generally Republicans but also included several powerful labor and religious organizations, as well as a handful of outspoken Tea Party representatives.

Again, the decision over Medicaid expansion came down to leadership. Republicans held the majority in the Michigan legislature; however, Republican governor-elect Rick Snyder, an influential businessman, broke party ranks and offered his support of the legislation. Governor Snyder's stance effectively stymied the efforts of political opponents to derail the legislation in the state and led to a holding pattern that would not be resolved until the resolution of the NFIB lawsuit and the reelection of President Obama.

When SCOTUS ruled to uphold the ACA in June of 2012 it was seen as an affirmation of the legislation, and the main challenge was over. Local health officials championed the verdict while cautioning that the sheer complexity of the legislation and the required undertaking would not necessarily be a smooth process (Swidwa & Matuszak, 2012). Mariane Udow-Phillips with the Center for Healthcare Research and Transformation (CHRT) characterized the legislation as a critical step in the right direction, stating that "[i]t's not a perfect law, but it's a foundation that we can build from and that's really important" (Sekaran, 2012).

The last hope for opponents to the ACA was a change in leadership during the 2012 election season. Naturally, the largest issue was what would happen with the new health care legislation; a vote for Democrats meant preserving and expanding on what was already done, whereas a vote for Republicans meant dismantling and replacing key provisions of the legislation. Again the debate was heated at all levels of government with several third-party actors trying to sway on-the-fence voters. With less than a month before the election, the CHRT, along with two University of Michigan economists, released a highly influential report on the benefits of health care reform to the State of Michigan. The report concluded that by proceeding with the established implementation of the ACA and by further expanding Medicaid, the State of Michigan could save nearly $1 billion in the first decade of the law's implementation (Guenther, 2012). The report found that through a combination of federal funds and reductions in uncompensated care, the legislation would curb escalating health care costs and result in 10-year savings to the state between $840 million and $1.4 billion, depending on the number of enrollees (Guenther, 2012). Furthermore, by expanding Medicaid, CHRT concluded that the legislation would also extend coverage to more than 600,000 Michiganders, many of whom lacked health care, relied on emergency rooms and contributed to the skyrocketing insurance costs due to the lack of any preventative measures (Guenther, 2012).

While the CHRT findings were startling, the impact on the election was harder to discern. Within the state, President Obama and incumbent Democratic senator Debbie Stabenow were reelected. In the House, Democrats lost one seat, while at the local level, Democrats picked up four seats in the state legislature with Republicans maintaining a slim majority.[1]

After the NFIB ruling reaffirmed the constitutionality of the ACA, President Obama won reelection, and Michigan maintained a Republican majority, the debate began to turn to the issue of what to do about Medicaid expansion within the state. The question of whether to expand generally followed party lines and, based on which, one would have expected Michigan to further oppose the ACA by rejecting Medicaid expansion. After the court's ruling in the NFIB case, Republican governor Rick Snyder released a statement criticizing the ACA, stating that "the health care law fails to make important reforms needed in our health care system, has been a serious detriment to our economic recovery, and imposes significant new taxes on businesses and the American people" (Snyder, 2012). Despite his qualms, Governor Snyder was one of the first Republican governors nationwide to express public support of the ACA and Medicaid expansion, stating that it was his responsibility to move forward with expansion as soon as possible to ensure Michigan would be best able to take advantage of expiring federal funds and retain as much creative institutional control as possible. Snyder continued, stating,

> This makes sense for the physical and fiscal health of Michigan. Expansion will create more access to primary care providers, reduce the burden on hospitals and small businesses, and save precious tax dollars. It also puts Michigan rather than Washington in the driver's seat in terms of implementation, which allows us to better address Michigan's specific needs.
>
> (Young, 2013)

While Snyder went against his party and their wishes, there were several others in support of his actions, and these organizations included: AARP Michigan, Michigan Association of Community Mental Health Boards, Michigan Association of Health Plans, Michigan Health and Hospital Association, Michigan Osteopathic Association, Michigan Primary Care Association, Michigan State Medical Society, and the Small Business Association of Michigan.

One of the more prevalent arguments from ACA opponents has been the declining federal subsidy and how states would deal with the shortfall. The ACA guaranteed the federal government would cover 100 percent of newly enrolled Medicaid recipients (in states choosing to expand) through the year 2016. Beginning in 2017, the funding rate would drop to 95 percent of the total cost with subsequent yearly decreases until 2020 when the federally funded amount would reach 90 percent and remain there in perpetuity. Opponents took issue with where the money would come from when the federal subsidies declined, and whether the federal government would even follow through with all the pledged funds. When the issue was raised in the Republican-controlled state legislature, Governor Snyder responded by highlighting the projected savings that Medicaid expansion would bring the state; with the surplus, Snyder vowed "to earmark half those savings into a fund until 2020 that would be tapped when the federal government's share of the financing gets smaller in future years under Obamacare" (Young, 2013).

Despite Governor Snyder's efforts, there remained substantial discussion and uncertainty over whether Michigan would actually expand Medicaid. The issue created strange bedfellows, aligning Republican governor Snyder with Democratic leadership and several state health care and progressive policy organizations. On the other side, Republican attorney general Schuette, picking up where his predecessor, Mike Cox, left off, along with Republican state leadership, made the case to reject Medicaid expansion in the name of fiscal conservatism.

Several legislative sessions and town hall meetings were held, during which third-party groups clashed over the best way to move Michigan forward. A number of prominent health care professionals, organized as Michigan

Physicians United, came out in support of reform with some reservations. Saginaw neurosurgeon Gerald Schell stated,

> Physicians practice medicine with the burden of excessive medical malpractice insurance and the constant fear of trial lawyers seeking unbelievable and unwarranted cash awards, of which a large percentage goes to the attorney that sued. Physicians often feel pressure to order excessive testing merely to cover their bases and help guard against malpractice claims. This leads to reductions in quality, a less efficient system, and unnecessary and unsustainable financial burdens to society.
>
> (Engel, 2009)

The lack of tort reform remained a cause for concern for Michigan Physicians United and an issue that was cited as unresolved due to little more than politics. In addition to physicians groups, several business advocates, including the Michigan Chamber of Commerce and the Small Business Association of Michigan, came out in favor of expanding Medicaid as a measure to control the state's response to the legislation (Eggert, 2012a). By expanding Medicaid and including several contingency clauses that would allow the state to later reconsider its decision should the need arise; proponents argued it was a no-lose situation (Eggert, 2012a).

Despite the support from the business community, universities, health care organizations, and Governor Snyder, there was still a vocal and influential contingent opposing Medicaid expansion. Dating to the 2010 election, Republicans have enjoyed a majority in both chambers of the state legislature. Around this time the Tea Party came to prominence within the state and ardently opposed health care reform and Medicaid expansion. Local Tea Party member Isabelle Rockford argued that the law "is hugely expensive and puts the country on a horrifying path to financial ruin" (Eggert, 2012a). The Mackinac Center for Public Policy (MCPP) was also leading the charge against Medicaid expansion. Citing the familiar refrain of uncertainty regarding federal and state obligations, as well as how many people would actually be covered, the MCPP instead advised for a wait-and-see approach to expanding Medicaid (McHugh, 2013). The MCPP further cautioned that state politicians and the public should be wary of much of the information in support of reform, stating that it comes from one of two sources:

> [t]he first are . . . bureaucrats, who look favorably upon a massive expansion of the program they run. The other are hospitals and their lobbyists, who covet the increase in taxpayer dollars heading their way if the states choose the expansion.
>
> (McHugh, 2013, p. 4A)

When it was finally time to vote on whether to expand Medicaid, it was immediately apparent just how divided the different factions were. The MCPP raised the point that "Obamacare" and Medicaid expansion were often discussed synonymously, but in reality the questions around each were quite different, a distinction that the Snyder administration attempted to stress in order to distance itself from the unpopularity of "Obamacare" (Gilbert, 2013).

The Snyder administration's Medicaid expansion proposal was pitched as a customized plan for the residents of Michigan. In an effort to reframe the issue as one of state reform, not federal expansion, Snyder spokesperson Sara Wurfel elaborated that the Healthy Michigan plan deviated from the federal option to the extent it required separate federal approval. It became an issue of state responsibility achieved through the federal framework; Wurfel went on to state that the customized approach to expansion allowed Michigan to "control costs by focusing on personal responsibility and wellness, reducing the burden of uncompensated care that shifts costs onto businesses and taxpayers, and helping our citizens access affordable care" (Gilbert, 2013).

When Snyder's Healthy Michigan proposal finally made it to the House floor, officially House Bill 4714, it was passed without much opposition despite the consternation of many in the Republican-controlled chamber. Republican Representative Joe Haveman of Holland, Michigan called it the "toughest vote" of his career, if for little more reason than the perception that he supports Obamacare (Haveman, 2013). Representative Haveman continued that he "believes the Affordable Care Act makes our state's health care worse and increases costs on all of us, the Michigan Medicaid Reform plan improves care and lowers costs" (Haveman, 2013).

Representative Haveman's views and disdain for reform were echoed by many of his colleagues in the House, but ultimately the fear of missing out on financial incentives and the ongoing effort that distinguished Medicaid from the polarizing discussion of Obamacare were enough to support expansion.

Upon moving to the Senate, the debate was more protracted. During the initial committee meetings, Governor Snyder's "Healthy Michigan" plan failed to make it out of session. It was only after the initial "no" vote that sessions were added, and legislative leaders were able to reach a compromise. While it was a clear best-case-scenario win for Democrats, Governor Snyder again tried to distinguish between the ACA and the Medicaid expansion component by asking "that all Michiganders step back and look to say this isn't about the Affordable Care Act. This is about one element that we control here in Michigan that we can make a difference in here in people's lives" (Davey, 2013, p. A14). By framing the issue as one of reform and choice and attempting to distance themselves from the unpopularity of the federal reforms, legislative leaders were able to accumulate the necessary votes to pass in both the state house and senate (Fangmeier, Jones, & Udow-Phillips, 2014).

Despite many Republican lawmakers voting in favor of expansion, the animosity of being stuck between a rock and a hard place was palpable. Soon after voting in favor of Medicaid expansion, Republican senator Mike Kowall of White Lake criticized the ACA as taking away individuals rights and decisions, creating more "red tape" for small-business owners, and penalizing those who choose not to purchase coverage. Senator Kowall likened the decision to choosing the best of two evils, stating that "[i]f Michigan did not form its own plan, the Affordable Care Act would harm our taxpayers and would result in employers leaving the state" (Oosting, 2013).

Fellow Republican Senator Howard Walker from Traverse City delivered the following statement before voting in favor of expansion:

> The Affordable Care Act, also known as Obamacare, is one of the worst pieces of legislation passed by our United States Congress in many years. It takes health care decisions away from our people; it penalizes those who choose not to purchase health care coverage; it places new mandates on small business owners; and it cuts funding to our local hospitals and health care providers, among other negative aspects.
>
> (Oosting, 2013)

Senator Kowall and Walker's opinions were far from unique within their party. Several others were worried that their actions would be construed as a tacit endorsement of Obamacare and that runaway costs would ultimately prove its undoing (Davey, 2013).

Despite the many concerns, the financial implications were simply too great to be ignored and on April 1, 2014, Michigan became the 24th state to expand Medicaid under the ACA, offering coverage to more than 440,000 previously uninsured Michiganders (Families USA, 2016). Despite the vote of support, the process was contentious, not just across parties but within; as Jonathan Oosting (2013) highlights, Republicans "aren't fighting over support for Obamacare—publicly, at least, they're fighting over who hates it most."

In keeping with the narrative that there was a line distinguishing Medicaid expansion from Obamacare and that a vote for one was not an endorsement of the other, Governor Snyder pushed for additional creative control over the state Medicaid expansion. In many ways, this was viewed as a compromise between the Republican governor Rick Snyder (in favor of expansion) and Republican legislators (split with a strong Tea Party opposition). By expanding Medicaid through a Section 1115 demonstration waiver on April 1, 2014, the state retained greater autonomy in designing the implementation of the expansion, as well as offering a break from the federal legislation and polarization of "Obamacare." A Section 1115 demonstration waiver gives states added flexibility and design responsibility for how they implement and administer service to Medicaid populations. The waiver effectively gives states latitude to operate outside of the bounds of federal law, assuming they can demonstrate the need of such programs and justify how they would serve the population to the extent that they gain federal approval. Both Republicans and Democrats had some familiarity with the waiver as prior leadership had utilized a similar process to expand coverage to needy adults (Musumeci, Rudowitz, Ubri, & Hinton, 2017).

Michigan's demonstration waiver was the first of a two-part waiver process that provisionally expanded Medicaid within the state while providing a termination clause requiring the program to be self-sustaining. Through 2016, the federal government funded 100 percent of state Medicaid expansion costs. Beginning in 2017, however, the funded amount progressively decreases to 90 percent of associated costs in 2020. The Michigan waiver calls for the capital saved by the federal funding to be set aside in order to cover the state's increased funding obligations beginning in 2017. Early analysis projects state savings to continue through 2020 when Michigan will be responsible for 10 percent of total expansion costs (Snyder, 2013); however, not everyone agrees on these projections and whether the federal funding will continue unabated (McHugh, 2013).

Michigan's use of the Section 1115 demonstration waiver effectively allows the state to take further control and responsibility of the Medicaid expansion process. The waiver was used as both a carrot and a stick, of sorts—designed to appease those with fiscal concerns over expansion, as well as those worried about reelection. The waiver provided a way to further customize the implementation of the law and Medicaid expansion in a manner in which the state was able to retain authority while also providing termination options, should it come to it.

"Tie-Barred": Opposing a State Exchange

The ACA provided the option for states to create their own state insurance exchange or simply default to the federal system. The insurance exchange would be designed to be the "one-stop shop" for the delivery of the new legislation. The federal government not only created a baseline exchange but also offered states the opportunity to create and customize their own exchange to the needs and circumstances within the state. For the most part, the states were highly supportive of the state exchange option, viewing it as a way to maintain autonomy and regulatory authority within their jurisdiction (Dinan, 2011). However, in some cases such as that of Michigan, the decision on whether to create a state insurance exchange was highly politicized.

As polarizing as the discussion over the ACA was in Michigan, it was of little surprise that the conversation over creating an insurance exchange was as difficult as it proved to be. Governor Snyder, along with proponents of the state-run option advocated for the process as a way to retain autonomy and as much creative control as possible. Much like in the prior debates over the lawsuits and the Medicaid expansion decision, the process was heated and highly partisan. Again, Attorney General Schuette led the primary opposition to the state exchange option, urging state lawmakers to proceed carefully and not rush into creating an exchange. As momentum for a state exchange grew, Attorney General Schuette continued to urge patience, pivoting from outright rejection to a delayed-action approach, while waiting to see if the law would eventually collapse. This was similar to the tactic advocated by the MCPP during the Medicaid expansion debate (McHugh, 2013). In defending his calls for delayed action, Attorney General Schuette took to disparaging federal deadlines and the frequency with which they are often extended, at one point likening the deadlines to a three-dollar bill, both of which are phony (Eggert, 2012b).

The state exchange issue originally came up in the fall of 2011 when the state senate voted in favor of creating a state-run exchange. Half of the Republican senators voted in favor of the state exchange. From this point moving forward, Attorney General Schuette was successful in controlling the agenda, at least with regard to the insurance exchange aspect of the law within the state. At his urging, lawmakers in the House (Republican majority) failed to take up action on the issue until after the NFIB SCOTUS ruling and President Obama's reelection that fall.

From a deadline perspective, Attorney General Schuette's campaign was especially problematic. November 15, 2012, was the established deadline to qualify for federal funding in assistance with creating a state exchange. By urging members of the House to delay action until after the presidential election on November 6, it left little more than a week for the bill to pass the House in order to secure federal funding. At this point there was vocal support, and it seemed like a foregone conclusion that the Republican-led House would vote for the state exchange, if for no other reason than to limit federal involvement.

When the bill was introduced to the House, it was "tie-barred" to another controversial bill banning abortion coverage. The process of tie-barring, as defined by the Michigan State Legislature (2018), is "[a] device to condition the effectiveness of legislation on the enactment or passage of other specified legislation." This was a tactical maneuver by hold-out Republicans that effectively bound the issue of a state-run insurance exchange with a total ban of abortion coverage under the new law. A vote for a state exchange was now essentially a vote in favor of banning abortion in the state. With little more than a week to address the bill, this action effectively doomed the state-run insurance exchange proposal from the start.

These actions brought outrage from across the state, in particular, from the Planned Parenthood Advocates of Michigan, and the bill ultimately failed to make it out of the Health Policy Committee (Fangmeier et al., 2014). Republican House Speaker, Jase Bolger stated that there were simply "too many unanswered questions for the committee to feel comfortable with a state-run exchange" (Bouffard, 2012).

Expressing disappointment, Governor Snyder quickly moved to file paperwork creating a state-partnership marketplace in order to comply with federal funding deadlines. The state-partnership exchange is one of four options permitted under the ACA. Viewing the four options as a scale, the extreme left mark would be the state-based marketplace. This is where the state has complete autonomy in the design, maintenance, and operation of the exchange; this is what proponents in Michigan were pushing for. Moving to the right on the scale is the state-based marketplace federal platform (SBM-FP). The SBM-FP is for all intents and purposes a state-run exchange; however, it still runs on the federally facilitated marketplace IT platform. Next is the state-partnership marketplace (SPM); this is what Governor Snyder defaulted to after it became clear that the push for the state-based exchange was in vain. The SPM allows states to conduct some plan management and offer minimal consumer assistance at the state level, while all other exchange functions and enrollment are handled at the federal level. The final marketplace option, on the far right of the scale, is the federally facilitated marketplace. This is the most generic, a one-size-fits-all approach within which the federal government takes over all enrollment responsibilities from the state.

In an attempt to maintain some modicum of control when the state-run marketplace was no longer an option, Governor Snyder wrote HHS Secretary Kathleen Sebelius outlining his plan for the state–federal partner exchange. Snyder stated that Michigan would "perform the plan management function of a partnership exchange, as well as the consumer assistance function," with additional responsibilities to be determined at a later date (Snyder, 2013). This letter effectively brought to a close the incredibly condensed and chaotic battle over the creation of a state-based marketplace in Michigan.

Conclusion

Health care reform in Michigan, much like across the country was fraught with challenges. The issue impassioned citizens and inflamed lawmakers on each side of the aisle, and while partisanship was the primary dividing line, in Michigan it was not a firm one. The case of Michigan is unique and informative because it highlights the sheer complexity of federal policy implementation. It highlights the partisan divisiveness that has become increasingly common in our society, and it highlights the interplay between citizens, third-party actors, and local and state government officials.

Michigan is a prime target example of the population the ACA was designed to reach. An area where much of the wealth has moved from urban cores to neighboring suburbs and even out of state, where jobs have dried up and the population has aged. With all these factors, the number of uninsured and underinsured has skyrocketed, fueling a substantial drain on service quality and capacity. Prior to the passage of the ACA, Michigan had nearly 40 percent of its population either uninsured or receiving some level of subsidy. By almost all accounts the existing system was failing in Michigan, insurance costs were rising faster than inflation, and much of the population was becoming even more at risk.

The ACA was designed to address these issues by offering health insurance to all qualifying individuals. The inclusion of a mandate would serve the purpose of balancing the risk pools and ensuring there were enough young healthy individuals to balance out the older sicker pool. The problems, however, began to surface almost immediately. Much like at the federal level, in Michigan, combatants were generally aligned by which side of the aisle they sat on. From the very beginning it was a partisan issue, with Republicans and Democrats both arguing for fiscal responsibility, but having vastly different definitions and paths toward achieving that goal.

When the ACA was signed into law, Michigan had a Democratic governor, Jennifer Granholm. Citing popular reports that the ACA could save the state roughly $1 billion over a decade and help insure more than 600,000 Michiganders (Guenther, 2012), Governor Granholm quickly offered support. What makes Michigan so fascinating though is what happened next. The Republican attorney general Mike Cox challenged Governor Granholm's authority by making Michigan party to several lawsuits challenging the constitutionality of the ACA. This was an unprecedented action and set the stage for a fierce battle between Republicans and Democrats moving forward in the state.

As steep as the partisan divide on the issue had become, what happened next was perhaps even more surprising. Governor Granholm was succeeded by Republican businessman Rick Snyder, giving Republicans control of the state legislature, the attorney general's office, and the governor's mansion, yet Governor Snyder chose to break party ranks and support the ACA. This set the stage for a long drawn out back-and-forth battle.

Republicans framed the debate as one of fiscal responsibility, for not wanting to be on the hook for future cost increases should the system prove unsustainable. The Democrats attempted to compromise by selling the idea of being able to craft the implementation of the law in a way to minimize state risk and maximize coverage. Ultimately, the Democrats and Governor Snyder prevailed but not before a long and protracted argument between the two parties and several influential third-party actors, including Tea Party representatives, the local business community, and Planned Parenthood.

The decision-making within the legislative body proved to be interesting as it varied between support and opposition measures with respect to each component of the ACA, despite a substantial Republican majority within each chamber. In the debate over Medicaid expansion, it was the House that took the support initiative with the Senate holding out; during the discussion over the state exchange, the Senate quickly supported the notion while the House was exceedingly slow to move on the issue. The actions of members within each chamber on the two different issues provide a remarkable contrast. Republicans in both legislative bodies were loath to support the legislation for fear of what being associated with Obamacare would do to their conservative credentials and primarily how it would impact their chances at reelection. What transpired at the urging of attorneys general Mike Cox and Bill Schuette was a sense of plausible deniability, where conservatives in each chamber were able to both speak out and vote against the different implementation aspects of the law before ultimately passing it with minor changes to protect themselves against future blowback.

Few states were as divided as Michigan over the ACA. What seemed like a simple math problem, tallying Republicans and Democrats became so much more than that. The sheer complexity of the policy process was on full display at each level of state and local government. The chaotic nature with which the state was split on support of the ACA, both joining lawsuits and attempting to push forward the law; the slow struggle toward Medicaid expansion that resulted in many conservatives voting to expand Medicaid, all the while condemning Obamacare; and the perfectly timed obstructionist effort to disrupt the state exchange that resulted in Michigan missing out on both jobs and funding. The case of Michigan illustrates the complexity, partisanship, and bitterness that go into policymaking and implementation. In Michigan, like so many other places, the issues were about more than state need and the overall health of the citizens; it came down to a fight over ideology and resources, much like it always has.

Note

1. Michigan elects state senators every four years. There was no Senate election in 2012.

7 Live Free or Die

New Hampshire and the ACA

New Hampshire represents a shifting view of the ACA. During the initial implementation, New Hampshire was in absolute unwavering opposition to the legislation. This was not totally unexpected, as New Hampshire holds a long-held tradition of limited government that led to the initial knee-jerk reaction of opposing all aspects of the ACA. However, shortly after the initial implementation, control of the legislature swung to the left after large gains in the House. This allowed the Democratic governor, Maggie Hassan, to expand Medicaid through a waiver allowing for private distribution of Medicaid services. Medicaid expansion, one of the foundational dimensions of the ACA, has been one of the main foci in New Hampshire and has been the source of a great deal of discourse.

Similar to the other three states in this book, the story of New Hampshire is best viewed by taking a deeper look at the decisions made in reference to the law. Support or opposition for any legislation can be quantified by a simple yes or no, while quantitative methods have a great deal of utility; often there are underlying stories that tell a richer story. In the case of New Hampshire, it is the long-held, unique political traditions and culture that have influenced decision-makers most often. New Hampshire is the oldest state in this book and accordingly has some of the most embedded political traditions.

The chapter begins with an overview of the history, political traditions and unique government structure of New Hampshire that are at the core of most of the decisions made in reference to the ACA. The chapter then examines the decisions and processes specific to the ACA in the context of the political arena of New Hampshire. The chapter ends with some concluding remarks about the unique atmosphere of the ACA implementation in New Hampshire.

Background

Modern-day New Hampshire is bordered by Quebec, Canada, to the north, in the east by Maine and the Atlantic Ocean, Massachusetts to the south, and Vermont to the west. New Hampshire is commonly known as the Granite State due to the extensive granite formations in the White Mountain region that offer year-round recreation activities for locals and visitors alike. The ski season in

New Hampshire regularly extends into late spring. Perhaps the most famous portion of the White Mountains, Mount Washington, is the tallest peak east of the Rockies. The Mount Washington Observatory was created as a nonprofit research facility in 1932. Mount Washington is the home of some of the most extreme weather on record. This observatory is designed to provide a facility to better understand weather and climate variations. The Mount Washington Observatory provides a steady stream of academic researchers to this area year-round that supplement the traditional visitors pursuing outside activities (Mount Washington Observatory, 2018).

According to the U.S. Census Bureau (2018), New Hampshire currently has a population of approximately 1.3 million people and enjoys the highest median income in the country at $76,620. The population is overwhelmingly homogenous, with the American Community Survey (2017) estimating the population at 94 percent white. Along with a high median income, New Hampshirites enjoy an extremely high level of health. The United Health Foundation (2019a) ranks New Hampshire as the eighth-most healthy state in the nation.

New Hampshire, the northernmost of the original colonies, traces its history back to a 1623 English land grant. Captain John Mason, along with several other Englishmen and Scots, were granted this land with the intent to set up a fishing colony alongside the Piscatuaqua River. Under the direction of the English government, a series of towns were developed in an effort to mimic the stereotypical English community found in the homeland. In those early days, New Hampshire came under the rule of several governors. Benning Wentworth was perhaps the most influential, serving from 1741 to 1766. Wentworth was responsible for developing more than 100 communities. These towns contained plots for more than 30,000 families, allowing for the population to almost triple. Succeeded by his nephew, Sir John Wentworth, the tradition of developing what is now known as New Hampshire continued. Sir John Wentworth went on to develop roads, charted an accurate map of the colony, created the state militia, and assisted in the founding of Dartmouth College. Loyal to the Crown, he fled to Nova Scotia when the first shots of the Revolution were fired and remained active in Nova Scotia politics until his death (New Hampshire Department of State, 1977).

New Hampshire citizens take great pride in the historical contributions of their state and those who have called New Hampshire home. New Hampshire became the first of the 13 colonies to declare its independence and develop its own state constitution. It was New Hampshire's ninth and deciding vote that ratified the U.S. Constitution. New Hampshire citizens have made significant contributions to the foundation of the country. New Hampshire provided the first vice president, John Langdon, who later became president of the Senate. The Battle of Bunker Hill, the first great battle of the Revolutionary War, was fought primarily by New Hampshire troops. Three original signers of the Declaration of Independence were from New Hampshire and the father of the U.S. Navy, Revolutionary War Naval Commander John Paul Jones, was also a New Hampshire resident (New Hampshire Department of State, 1977; Daniell, 1981).

In an effort to create a safer environment early New Hampshire settlers quickly sought to create towns as an extension of their plantations. It was believed by coming together into tight-knit towns "their goals of effective governance, economic prosperity, and stable social and religious institutions" (Daniell, 1981, p. 39) would be easier to achieve. While there were early setbacks, that desire to build strong communities first sought in the formative years laid the groundwork for the political traditions found in contemporary New Hampshire. Organized local governments were centered around the concept of the town, with the townspeople responsible for most community affairs. This rejection of the gentry class and the formation of self-governing towns in which each citizen had a say in local affairs worked well for these settlers. There was a division of labor with committees to handle day-to-day affairs. The town also allowed for an organized response to public safety, disease, or natural disasters.

By 1680 the population of New Hampshire grew to just over 2,000, and most residents were involved in the very prosperous agriculture trade. Town leaders declared open land close to town as community property, planting, caring for, and harvesting crops were a community affair. The townspeople divided the labor among themselves with all doing their fair share and sharing in the profits. Agricultural goods were sold to other communities within New Hampshire and eventually exported back to the Old World. The abundant timber and access to the coast also spurred the growth of another lucrative business in New Hampshire, shipbuilding (Daniell, 1981). Many of these industries still remain in a New Hampshire that remains very prosperous; in 2017 the U.S. Census Bureau (American Community Survey, 2017) reports New Hampshire to have the highest per capita income of all the states.

New Hampshire has a long-standing political tradition that supports limited government and is extremely cautious of involving government at any level in policy choices. The political view of New Hampshire citizens can be characterized by the idea government should be minimally involved in day-to-day activity, and any policy interventions should be a local action rather than a state or federal initiative. It is in this sense that New Hampshire responded to the ACA. While Republicans in New Hampshire were wholeheartedly in opposition to the act in any form, Democrats supported finding a route to implement health care reform in a way that met New Hampshire's long-standing tradition of fiscally conservative limited government (Rockefeller Institute, 2015).

History and Culture

New Hampshire may have the most politically active citizens in the nation. The lower chamber of the House has 400 representatives, in a state with just over 1.3 million citizens. This makes the New Hampshire state legislature the third-largest legislative body in the world, behind the U.S. House of Representatives and the British Parliament. This exemplifies the state's intense interest in the process of governing; one out of every 3,300 New Hampshire citizens is a state representative. To put the size of the New Hampshire House in perspective, California has 80 members of the House, one for approximately every 485,000 citizens. However, the New Hampshire Senate has only 24 members, the fourth smallest in the nation. A 24-member Senate equates to just 13 "no" votes necessary to stop a bill (Jacobson, 2013; New Hampshire Executive Council, 2018).

The governor in the Granite State is elected every two years, one of just two states to have a two-year cycle (neighboring Vermont is the other). There is another unique aspect to New Hampshire state politics, the Executive Council. A throwback to colonial days, the Executive Council was crafted by King Charles II to gather feedback and report back on the actions of John Cutt, the first appointed royal governor of the territory. In January 1776, New Hampshire's state constitution was signed; it called for the abolishment of the governor's office, replacing it instead with the five-member Executive Council. This Executive Council was elected by the citizens and acted as the upper branch of the legislature. The office of governor was put back in place in 1784 and renamed the president; the Executive Council was moved from the legislature to the executive branch to act as oversight of the president (governor). This time, the Executive Council was tasked with reporting back to the people on the actions of the executive rather than to King Charles II. Today the Executive Council remains and acts as a fourth branch of government as provided by the New Hampshire Constitution. This is a unique check on the state's top executive and certainly influences the decision-making process of the governor. The Executive Council is a living symbol reminding the world of New Hampshire's lack of trust in government (New Hampshire Executive Council, 2018).

The Executive Council has five members who are elected independently of each other and of the governor on the same two-year cycle as the governor. Under the state constitution, the governor and the council are granted veto authority over each other. No state business becomes effective until approved by the governor and a majority of the council. Although the Executive Council cannot act independently, it has the authority to veto any actions or nominations of the governor (New Hampshire Executive Council, 2018). The two-year election cycle, coupled with the power of the Executive Council, may have created one of the least powerful governors in the nation (Pew Charitable Trust, 2007).

These characteristics make New Hampshire state government so unique. Jacobson (2013) describes New Hampshire's state government as "transparent, and obscure, rigid, and unruly, with an unusual degree of checks and balances" (p. 1). Tom Rath, a former New Hampshire attorney general, describes New Hampshire politics as being void of major scandals, with little or no corruption, and fairly transparent (Jacobson, 2013). The New Hampshire system is a good fit for the people of New Hampshire. Not only is the New Hampshire State House large; but it is also unusual in that members are paid only $200 a year. The benefit of such low pay is the diversity of citizens it attracts, career politicians are replaced by retirees, college students, and citizens with flexible job schedules, such as attorneys or real estate agents. Members elected to both the House and Senate are elected biennially. (Jacobson, 2013).

Another proud political tradition in New Hampshire is the hosting of the nation's first presidential primary election every four years. New Hampshire has only one metropolitan area, Manchester, with most of the population concentrated on the southern border closest to Massachusetts. Having citizens dispersed throughout the state has created a unique atmosphere of "retail politics" (Vavreck, Spiliotes, & Fowler, 2002). Retail politics is best described as reaching citizens through town meetings, and religious or economic organizational meetings. Rather than touching large amounts of potential voters through large media outlets as is the norm in most states, politicians campaigning in New Hampshire need to get out and shake hands and make direct personal connections in order to be successful. Having New Hampshire state citizens so involved in politics at the state level has changed campaigning strategy in New Hampshire. New Hampshire's retail politics "requires campaigns to accommodate deeply ingrained local traditions regarding the accessibility of candidates" (p. 596). In the 2000 presidential primary, John McCain visited New Hampshire early and often, attending 114 town-hall meetings. Vavreck et al. (2002) argue this made the difference in McCain's victory in New Hampshire over Bush in the Republican primary. Although New Hampshire voters do not have the final say in picking the nominees from each party, they take great pride in revealing the candidates' platforms and setting the tone for the primaries to come (Steger, Dowdle, & Adkins, 2004; Kaufman & Kaliner, 2011).

Unlike other states, most candidates for the House spend less than $5,000 during the election process; some candidates have won campaigns with no money spent at all. This low economic barrier to entry and the large size of the chamber, combined with the extraordinary level of checks and balances that come along with the Executive Council, have created the unique character of New Hampshire politics (Jacobson, 2013).

The ACA

President Obama signed the ACA into law in early 2010. The objective of the law was to provide health care to all Americans as well as address certain parts of health care responsible for escalating health care–related costs. As could be expected there was a great deal of discourse centered around this new groundbreaking law. The majority of the discourse was fueled by a bitter partisan divide. The structure of the funding of Medicaid expansion and the mandate that required individuals to purchase and maintain coverage or face tax penalties became the two portions of the act that became the center of this discourse and resulted in several federal lawsuits. SCOTUS ruled the tax penalty a lawful congressional action; SCOTUS also ruled that each state could choose whether to expand Medicaid. These court decisions devolved several decisions from the federal government to each state. In addition to giving states the option to expand Medicaid, states were given the option to develop their own health care exchange or default to the federal exchange. Several states crafted legislation in symbolic support or opposition to several other portions of the act, creating an atmosphere of either contempt for or encouragement for the future of health care (Mayer, Kenter, Lucero, & Morris, 2018).

At the time immediately prior to the ACA becoming law approximately 158,000 people (10 percent of the population) in the state were uninsured, one of the lowest in the country. Between Medicaid expansion and coverage through the marketplace, the ACA would provide financial assistance to insure 7 out of 10 (69 percent) uninsured non-elderly residents of New Hampshire, leaving 3 out of 10 (31 percent) of the uninsured ineligible for direct assistance. These residents have an income above the limit for tax subsidies or are eligible for employer-based plans but opt out. However, initial estimates suggest insurance available in the marketplace without a subsidy will be less expensive than policies available currently (Kaiser Family Foundation, 2014).

In 2012, after the lawsuits were settled the ACA was initially implemented. Democrats were achieving a great deal of success at the polls. New Hampshire has traditionally been a staunch Republican stronghold. After almost two decades of losses, Democrats picked up a substantial number of the 400 House seats to gain a majority. Democrats also began chipping away at the long-held Republican control of the state senate as well. Although the Republican Party maintained a slim majority in the Senate, New Hampshire had developed into a true bipartisan legislature. Despite the gains by the Democratic Party, the initial response to the ACA was overwhelmingly negative. New Hampshire failed to develop a state health care exchange, instead choosing a federal–state partnership exchange. They chose to not expand Medicaid, and they passed several laws intended to impede the implementation and administration of the ACA.

With the election in 2013 of Governor Maggie Hassan, a Democrat, New Hampshire saw two Democratic governors elected back to back for the first time in more than 150 years (Rockefeller, 2015). A Republican majority returned to both the House and Senate in 2014, demonstrating just how volatile the political landscape in New Hampshire was at the time the ACA was rolled out. Regardless of which party is in control of New Hampshire politics, one thing remains static: New Hampshire has always had a strong preference for local control of policy decisions and a long-held practice of limiting government involvement in the daily life of its citizens.

Early in the implementation process it became clear that, if the ACA was going to gain any traction in New Hampshire, it would have to be framed as a private option every step of the way. This private option was successfully implemented by Pennsylvania and Arkansas when they accepted federal funds to expand Medicaid under a Section 1115 waiver, and New Hampshire's ACA supporters were watching those states closely. To further emphasize how much of a "third rail" accepting federal funds for health care in New Hampshire is, State Senator John Reagan, a Republican, refused to even acknowledge the term *Medicaid expansion*, opting to frame the issue as a premium payment plan for people who had been priced out of the health care market.

After watching the success (and lack of political fallout) from Pennsylvania's and Arkansas' private option plan, New Hampshire politicians began to soften their once unwavering opposition to the ACA.

State Legislation

The ACA has become President Barack Obama's signature contribution to the historical policy issue of health care reform. Obama ran his campaign on this issue and eventually signed it into law on March 23, 2010. The bill passed by seven votes, with all 178 Republican members of the House voting against the bill (Travis et al., 2016). It was expected that New Hampshire's Republican-led legislature would follow in their federal colleagues' footsteps and oppose the ACA at every opportunity.

The Granite State has a long-standing political tradition that supports the notion of limiting the involvement of government in the everyday business of her citizens. Historically New Hampshire lawmakers have gone to great lengths to avoid big government in policy choices. Citizens of New Hampshire have long shared the belief that the free market, rather than government actors, should drive policy decisions. The reaction to the ACA was no different in that the citizens of New Hampshire were extremely cautious of the federal government's involvement in health care at the local level. Republican state legislators were overwhelmingly opposed to the ACA in any fashion, while Democrats supported a compromise that supported the implementation of some of the prescribed federal reforms as long as they were in terms that were seen as agreeable to New Hampshire's political tradition of fiscally conservative limited government (Rockefeller Institute, 2015).

The Republican majority in the legislature was able to pass several statutes intended to impede the implementation and administration of the core components of the ACA. Governor Lynch quickly realized he had little support from the legislature, so he added $1 million to the legislative agenda to fund the implementation of a state-run health care exchange. Republican legislators quickly asserted their unanimous opposition by passing HB 601, which countered the governor's legislation by limiting the amount of ACA associated funding they could accept from the federal government. HB 601 cut the funding by 66 percent ($666,000), enough that creating a state exchange became impossible. By limiting the funding in this manner, the bill effectively vetoed creating a state exchange without having to vote on it. House Speaker William O'Brien, a Republican, went as far as to suggest New Hampshire return the grant to Washington to help reduce the federal debt (Langley, 2011).

Additionally, HB 601 created the Joint Health Care Reform Oversight Committee to oversee all aspects of the ACA. HB 601 also made the insurance commissioner a direct report to the five-member all-Republican Executive Council. This portion of the new law put the Executive Council in position to approve or deny any decision in reference to the ACA (New Hampshire Legislature, 2011).

The legislature also passed HB 1297, outlawing the creation of a state exchange and greatly limiting state involvement in any exchange created in the state. HB 1297 did allow for state agencies to deliver very limited functions of a federal exchange. Governor John Lynch's successor, Governor Maggie Hassan, a Democrat, would later exploit that small portion of the law and create a state–federal partnership exchange, which allowed the state to maintain some control over the management of plans and consumer support. HB 1297 also authorized a 12-member Health Exchange Advisory Board. The governor, insurance commissioner, health and human services commissioner each nominated four individuals to this board, all of whom had to be confirmed by the Executive Committee. The responsibility of the Advisory board was to represent the interests of individual citizens and businesses utilizing the health care exchange (New Hampshire Legislature, 2012).

In addition to substantive policy, legislators passed SB 148, a symbolic law intended to relay legislators' opposition to and undermine the success of the ACA. This second bill prohibited the individual mandate and its related penalties and fines from affecting New Hampshire citizens. (Rockefeller Institute, 2015). SB148 was signed into law in the summer of 2011 without the governor's signature. Governor Lynch understood this law was a strictly symbolic attempt to further oppose the ACA. The penalties and fines for not complying with the individual mandate are administered by the Internal Revenue Service, and New Hampshire legislators have no control over who receives penalties assessed by the Internal Revenue Service (Fahey, 2011). William O'Brien, Speaker of the House, added to the rhetoric by stating that

> the vast majority of New Hampshire residents have rejected ObamaCare and they want this outrageous federal takeover of our health care system to end immediately. These new state laws protect New Hampshire citizens from a blatant intrusion into their freedom by forcing them to buy health insurance or potentially go to jail.
>
> (p. 1)

O'Brien was well aware of the symbolic nature of SB148 but continued to play to the established tradition of limited government while fanning the flames of the anti-Obama right. The Republican majority spun Governor Lynch's refusal to sign SB148 as supporting the Democratic strategy of taking over a large portion of the economy by supporting the ACA. O'Brien argued that Governor Lynch was assaulting the liberty of all New Hampshire citizens by supporting the ACA (Fahey, 2011; Rockefeller, 2015).

New Hampshire lawmakers passed several laws that were in direct opposition the ACA. These laws took several well planned avenues to impede the federal law whether it was through limiting the funding the state could accept to advertise the pending exchange (HB 601), outlawing a state-run exchange (HB 1297), or the symbolic act of insulating New Hampshire citizens from any federal penalty associated with the individual mandate. New Hampshire lawmakers made it clear they were opposed to federal government's involvement in the day-to-day activity of her citizens.

Medicaid Expansion

During the implementation phase of the ACA, New Hampshire was among the states that chose not to expand Medicaid. This was an expected decision given New Hampshire's tendency to avoid policy choice that would increase the federal government's involvement in the day-to-day activity of New Hampshire. In 2014, two years after initial implementation, Governor Hassan, a Democrat, was able to draft a bipartisan expansion plan that she hoped would please legislators on both sides of the aisle. Hassan's plan proposed to use federal dollars to buy private health insurance for those uninsured citizens; the plan would allow Medicaid expansion while giving the appearance of little government involvement (Mayer et al., 2018). However, this plan would need to be approved by the Centers for Medicare and Medicaid Services (CMS) as a Section 1115 Demonstration Waiver.

Medicaid is a partnership between the federal government and states. The federal government provides matching funds to the state's expenditures while the state is responsible for administering the daily operations of the program. States must meet certain core requirements of the program in order to continue to receive the federal funding. With this partnership in mind, Section 1115 waivers are traditionally agreed on through extended negotiations between the secretary of HHS, the CMS, and the state and require reapproval every five years. Although not specifically codified in the law, it has been an informal policy of the HHS and the CMS that the waiver be revenue neutral, that is, adding no additional costs to the federal government. The budget neutrality of the waiver is usually implemented by establishing a per capita limit on funds over the five-year life of the waiver. This shifts the risk of extending past the federal guidelines to the state.

The Centene Corporation, an existing New Hampshire health care insurance provider, created Ambetter Health to be the sole provider of the private option to service the needs of those who entered the market through the proposed Medicaid expansion (Sanders, 2017). Crafting a plan in this matter allowed the legislators to provide a much-needed benefit to New Hampshire's underserved population, while maintaining the image of keeping the federal government, and, more specifically, President Obama, out of New Hampshire's day-to-day affairs.

Governor Hassan's proposed private option would allow New Hampshire citizens to accept expanded Medicaid funds to be used to purchase private health insurance. At the time this plan was proposed the Executive Council was composed of three Republicans and two Democrats. The first hurdle for Governor Hassan was to convince the Executive Council to approve the plan before it moved to the legislature. Because of the private option, the plan received overwhelming bipartisan support at all levels of government and was quickly approved. This agreement allowed New Hampshire lawmakers to give the much-needed appearance of limited government while allowing close to 150,000 uninsured New Hampshire citizens access to much-needed health care. Presenting the private option expansion in such a manner allowed New Hampshire to provide insurance for its deserving citizens and still have the sense they have not "caved in" to Obamacare. The expansion plan also included a sunset clause that mandates the program end if federal funding dips below 100 percent, the sunset clause and the private option would be the two largest issues needing approval from the CMS (Mayer et al., 2018; Kaiser Family Foundation, 2015a; Rockefeller Institute, 2015).

Governor Maggie Hassan's Medicaid expansion Section 1115 waiver was approved by the CMS, and on August 15, 2014, New Hampshire officially offered health care through existing Medicaid managed-care plans. These plans used federal dollars to pay the premium directly to existing state plans. In the first three months, approximately 18,000 citizens enrolled in the expanded Medicaid health plans. However to comply with the authorizing New Hampshire state law an 1115 waiver was needed to be applied for and approved so that participants could be enrolled in Marketplace Qualified Health Plans (QHPs) in order to be a true private option (Kaiser Family Foundation, 2015a).

In 2016, the now-Republican-controlled legislature applied under the Obama administration for another Section 1115 Medicaid waiver. This second waiver sought to add several addendums to the existing expansion program. The first was a work requirement that would require able-bodied participants to be employed a minimum of 30 hours a week. Those who were not employed would be required to be seeking employment or be enrolled in an authorized job training program. The waiver further sought permission to add a copayment to Medicaid recipients who used an emergency department of a hospital for nonemergency care. And last, the waiver application included a requirement that recipients of expansion benefits submit a state-issued driver's license or identification card to prove their New Hampshire residence and, separately, to submit two forms of identification to verify their U.S. citizenship (American Health Line, 2016). This 2016 Section 1115 waiver met none of these requirements as interpreted by the Obama administration and was denied. As part of the denial of the waiver, the CMS cited the proposed changes "could undermine access, efficiency, and quality of care provided to beneficiaries and do not support the objectives of the Medicaid program" (American Health Line, 2016, p. 1). Despite the denial of changes, the existing expansion was allowed to continue as is.

In 2017, with the Trump administration firmly in place, the new governor, Chris Sununu, a Republican, requested another amendment to the original Section 1115 waiver. This amendment sought permission to require recipients of New Hampshire's Medicaid expansion that are between 19 and 64 years of age take part in at least 100 hours a month of "community engagement activities." These activities include community service, job training, or actual employment (Solomon, 2018; DeWitt, 2018). This waiver application was less restrictive than the previously denied waiver application. Sununu's waiver had a lower work requirement, removed the copayment for nonemergency visits to the emergency department, and removed the identification requirement. However, this Section 1115 waiver application included an ultimatum stating that if it was not approved by May 30, 2018, the Medicaid expansion program would be closed entirely. On May 7, 2018, the secretary of HHS, CMS, and New Hampshire's governor, Chris Sununu, announced the Section 1115 waiver was successfully negotiated and granted to New Hampshire. Governor Chris Sununu praised the waiver, stating that "today's announcement by CMS authorizing New Hampshire's Medicaid work requirements is a transformative step towards a more thriving workforce" (DeWitt, 2018, p. 1). Governor Sununu went on to state that with the CMS's help, New Hampshire now has "the most robust work requirement in the nation" (DeWitt, 2018, p. 1). Governor Sununu went on to argue that "work requirements help lift able-bodied individuals out of poverty by empowering them with the dignity of work and self-reliability while allowing states to control the costs of Medicaid programs" (Solomon, 2018, p. 1). Sununu stated that work requirements "help people gain the skills necessary for long-term independence and success. We are committed to helping more people get into the workforce, as it is critical not only for individuals but also for our economy as a whole" (p. 1).

Seema Verma, the CMS administrator, also issued a statement supporting the waiver and mirrored Governor Sununu's sentiment: the key to ending poverty and increasing access to health care revolved around people returning to the workforce. Verma suggested the work requirement supports the core "objectives of the Medicaid program" (Solomon, 2018, p. 1). Verma congratulated Governor Sununu's "commitment to join me in improving the lives of Medicaid beneficiaries by creating a crucial link to work and community engagement" (DeWitt, 2018, p. 1). Verma went on, supporting the Trump administration's rhetoric by stating that President Trump has helped create "one of the strongest job markets in our nation's history and we want to make sure able bodied, working-age adults receive the necessary skills to join our growing workforce" (p. 1). The approved waiver included exemptions for participants who are parents or caretakers of a dependent child of any age who is disabled. The waiver also included an exemption for participants with chronic or acute health diagnoses that would make them unable to meet the work or community engagement requirement. The CMS administrator argued that by including these individuals in the waiver, it would have a "detrimental impact on Medicaid beneficiaries' access to coverage and care" (Verma, 2018, p. 5).

New Hampshire was the fourth work requirement waiver approved by the Trump administration to date; Arkansas, Indiana, and Kentucky are the other three. This is in sharp contrast to the Obama administration, which consistently denied any work requirement waivers. Jake Leon, the public information spokesman for the New Hampshire Department of Health and Human Services, states that of the approximately 50,000 New Hampshire residents eligible for Medicaid, 45 percent are currently working part-time or full-time jobs, leaving approximately 27,000 recipients affected by the 1115 waiver.

Previous research by Mayer and Kenter (2014) and Barrilleaux and Rainey (2014), suggest party control of the governor's office is significant when examining Medicaid expansion. The research argues that Republican governors are drivers of opposition to the act. In New Hampshire, Governor Hassan, a Democrat, was a proponent of Medicaid expansion in her time as governor. Upon taking over control of the executive mansion, Governor Chris Sununu, a Republican, began an attempt to dismantle the ACA in New Hampshire. Sununu's administration quickly directed their efforts at dismantling the Medicaid expansion plan that Hassan developed across party lines. Sununu reapplied for a more restrictive Section 1115 waiver that included a work requirement under the belief there is a positive relationship between working and increased health. The research on health and work suggest it is the quality and stability of the particular job that influences the work–health relationship. The Kaiser Family Foundation (2018b) suggests that low-paying, unstable employment may have a negative impact on individual health.

It was the policy of the Obama administration to deny work waivers. That administration believed the objective of Medicaid was to promote health, not just provide health care coverage. Conversely, the Trump administration immediately granted work requirement waivers to Kentucky, Indiana, Arkansas, and New Hampshire. The Trump administration believes that forcing people to work to be eligible despite the quality or stability of the job will increase their level of health. With that work requirement comes the symbolic gesture of removing "free riders" from the system, making government benefits available only to those who make a contribution to the economy (Kaiser Family Foundation, 2018b). The debate about the relationship between working and health, along with the question of whether Medicaid's objective is to promote health or to provide health coverage, will be the basis for future legal and ideological debates to come.

State Exchange

The health care exchange is one of the cornerstones of the ACA. The act encouraged states to develop a state-administered exchange that would be tailored to the distinct needs of that state's citizens and small businesses (Travis et al., 2016). Creating a state exchange was the source of a great deal of partisan discourse in New Hampshire, and was yet another intersection where the structure of the ACA clashed with the political culture and traditions in the state. Although the basic premise of the state exchange was to allow for local control of exchanges, it was the federal mandate to develop the exchange that raised the ire of New Hampshire politicians who fought bitterly to impede the creation of an exchange in any fashion (Rockefeller, 2015).

In 2011 Governor John Lynch proposed accepting an initial $1 million grant from the federal government to begin the process of creating a state-run health care exchange. Governor Lynch argued that in keeping with New Hampshire's political tradition the only option was to develop a New Hampshire state-run exchange that would allow New Hampshire to regulate the insurance business within its borders with the least amount of outside influence (Lynch, 2012). Lynch's time in the Executive Mansion was overshadowed by an Executive Council that was unanimously Republican (5–0), which limited his decision-making. The Republican-led legislature responded with HB 1297 that explicitly prohibited the state from running the health exchange; however, the language in the law allowed certain functions associated with the federal exchange to be performed. New Hampshire remained steadfast against creating a state-run exchange and chose to allow the federal–state partnership exchange to become the marketplace for New Hampshirites looking to fulfill the individual mandate. The partnership style of exchange was a compromise of sorts, it allowed the symbolic opposition to the ACA by refusing to comply with the preferred state-run exchange, while still allowing some local control of the health care reform efforts.

The New Hampshire Insurance Department (NHID) was tasked with providing the bare necessities necessary to allow for the implementation of the exchange. The NHID, established in 1851, was the first insurance regulatory agency established in the country. The NHID is responsible for regulating all aspects of the insurance industry statewide. The commissioner is appointed by the governor and approved by the Executive Council and serves a five-year term (NHID, 2018). Even with the minimal assistance in implementation provided by the state, the exchange was still classified as a federal–state partnership with the state administering the federal exchange. Although technically this is a federal–state exchange, state involvement in implementation was kept as a secondary (and sometimes tertiary) duty of the NHID staff, with the intent of impeding the implementation and the success of the act as much as possible (Rockefeller, 2015). The NHID outsourced the minimum amount of work necessary to remain in compliance with the federal regulations. In an effort to further exert its opposition of federal interference with local affairs, the NHID turned down several million dollars offered by the federal government intended to advertise the exchange. However, the NHID director did transfer a small amount of available federal funds earmarked for outreach and education to the New Hampshire Health Plan (NHHP) to fund the implementation of the exchange. The NHHP is a quasi-governmental organization designed to administer the state's high-risk insurance pool. The director of NHID felt the NHHP was uniquely suited for the task of implementing the exchange since it has experience with high-risk populations such as those on Medicaid. This transfer of responsibilities resulted in a request for proposals to find a company to assist in the public outreach portion of implementing the exchange to be released less than one month prior to the launch date (Rockefeller, 2015). The public outreach efforts were limited in comparison to other New England states and were limited to a website that provided several success stories and links to three social media sites (Covering New Hampshire, 2018).

These lackluster efforts were met disapprovingly by some New Hampshire lawmakers, who accused the NHID and the NHHP of trying to circumvent their efforts to provide health care through the ACA. This hybrid management arrangement allowed state-level influence on what was intended to be a federal process, in this case, state-level interference with the process (Rockefeller Institute, 2015; Mayer et al., 2018). New Hampshire was steadfast in maintaining as much control as possible over the health care insurance marketplace in order to impede progress every step of the way.

The NHID's influence did not stop at the development stage of the exchange. It continued to impede the rollout of the ACA at every opportunity it had. During the required pre-rollout education phase intended to provide New Hampshire citizens information on the affordability and accessibility of the plans offered on the exchange, NHID continued to work at a snail's pace in an effort to impede the progression of the ACA. NHID contracted with Louis Karno and Company, one of the fastest-growing companies in the state, with a reputation for innovative advertising campaigns. However, the advertising campaign for the New Hampshire exchange, "Covering New Hampshire" (coveringnewhampshire.org), had limited impact (Rockefeller, 2015). The medium chosen to reach citizens was a web-based media campaign centered on a YouTube channel containing seven videos that received 3,044 total views. There was no traditional television or radio advertising as in other states. This high-powered advertising firm produced an uncharacteristically low-key advertising campaign (Rockefeller, 2015).

At the time of implementation of the exchange, Anthem Blue Cross and Blue Shield was the only health care provider in the state. Anthem initially offered 11 different plans: 5 bronze-level, 3 silver-level, and 2 gold-level plans and a catastrophic direct access plan (New Hampshire Insurance Department, 2014a). Out-of-pocket deductibles and premiums for these plans were among the highest in the country (Ramer, 2013; Rockefeller, 2015). NHID officials argued these were expected premiums due to the low population of the state coupled with Anthem already providing 90 percent of the plans in the state (Rockefeller, 2015).

Further complicating the rollout, in an effort to maximize profits, Anthem's plans had a very narrow network of providers. The plans offered on the exchange only covered 16 of the 26 hospitals in the state. This narrow network was the cause of substantial disagreement among hospital administrators, the NHID, and Anthem. The excluded hospitals geographically covered the most economically disadvantaged citizens in the state. Hospital administrators also criticized the NHID for allowing the process to go on with little or no transparency as compared to other New England states (Rockefeller, 2015).

The Anthem coverage offered on the exchange was challenged administratively by a patient who argued that Anthem's coverage did not meet the state's minimum standards. The plaintiff's petition argued that by purchasing Anthem's insurance, she would then be required to change health care providers as well as travel a considerable distance to an in-plan hospital. NHID ruled against the petitioner and in favor of Anthem. The state ruled that the coverage provided by Anthem on the exchange met the minimum standards set forth in the state laws (New Hampshire Insurance Department, 2014b). Although New Hampshire complied with the federal minimum standards, the lack of competition is the main cause of the high premiums. Since the unsuccessful legal challenge, two other providers, Harvard Pilgrim, and Minuteman have since begun offering coverage through the exchange in New Hampshire (Sanders, 2017). The additional providers afford New Hampshire citizens with an expanded network of health care providers.

Conclusions

It quickly became clear to Governor Lynch that the federal involvement as mandated by the ACA was contradictory to New Hampshire political traditions and any political move made in support of the ACA was going to be met with resistance. Lynch continued to argue that by turning their backs on the ACA, the lawmakers were doing a disservice to their constituents. By creating a vibrant, well-designed health care exchange run by New Hampshirites for New Hampshirites, they would better service the needs of the state. The governor faced unwavering opposition to the ACA, and it soon became clear that New Hampshire lawmakers were more inclined to support symbolic opposition to the ACA than to create an exchange that took into consideration the specific needs of the citizens they were elected to serve (Rockefeller Institute, 2015). It would take the work of a talented diplomat to allow New Hampshire to keep her political traditions and provide health care for those in need. The future of the ACA looked bleak in New Hampshire (Mayer et al., 2018).

From the very beginning, the citizens of New Hampshire have been highly suspicious of the ACA. The state lawmakers not only chose not to create a state exchange; they also took it one step further and passed a law banning a state-based exchange forcing the development of a state–federal partnership exchange. They showed their continued opposition to the ACA by refusing to expand Medicaid, as well as passing laws opposing the individual mandate and related tax penalties. The initial actions were overwhelmingly in opposition to the ACA. However, in 2014 a bipartisan effort was successful in crafting a Medicaid expansion plan under a private option that the federal government approved under a Section 1115 waiver. Public perception of support and opposition to the ACA in New Hampshire has remained relatively stable since inception with very little variance. Republicans continue to chip away at dismantling the act while Democrats continue to look for diplomatic solutions to health care reform that will adhere to the free-market traditions of the state. Governor Hassan was able to break the legislative stalemate with her private option of Medicaid expansion. This solution allowed for the perception of offering a "private, free market solutions to policy problems, offering legislators who opposed the ACA an opportunity to harvest federal dollars while standing in opposition to Obamacare" (Rockefeller Institute, 2015, p. 26). This bipartisan decision to expand Medicaid shifted New Hampshire from opposition to the ACA to being slightly supportive as measured by previous research

(Mayer et al., 2015; Travis et al., 2016; Mayer et al., 2018). The 2018 amendment of the Section 1115 waiver allows the current conservative state legislators to play to their base by continuing to show symbolic opposition to "free-loading" Medicaid recipients while parroting the Trump administration's talking points of creating the most vibrant economy in recent history.

Currently, Republicans have control of the senate, house and governor's mansion in New Hampshire (National Conference of State Legislatures, 2018). It is expected the ACA will continually be dismantled at every opportunity. New Hampshirites can expect continued limited information about the enrollment process and other inaccurate claims about "Obamacare." A 2014 survey by Myers and Strategic Services reports 47 percent of the remaining uninsured are not registered to vote and self-report as politically disengaged (Rockefeller, 2015). It will take significant victories by Democrats in the next election cycle to move the needle towards New Hampshire providing well-thought-out health care through the ACA.

8 Taking the Lead

California's Endeavor for Universal Health Care

California, like many states in the country, had a strong need for health care reform to help cover millions of state residents without insurance placing a financial strain on state resources. Unlike other states, however, partisan debates over the ACA were limited, and a majority of state citizens supported the legislation. The combination of bipartisan and citizen support allowed California state legislators to approach health care reform aggressively and with enthusiasm, acting as a model for all other states attempting to create state exchanges and expand Medicaid. Overall, the story of ACA implementation in California is one of bipartisan cooperation and innovation.

This chapter begins with an overview of California, emphasizing its diversity, need for expanding health insurance coverage, and its political environment, optimal for health care reform. The remainder of this chapter focuses on California's role in the *NFIB v. Sebelius* federal lawsuit, as well as the choices surrounding the implementation of its state market exchange and Medicaid expansion within the state. The chapter ends with a summary of the events that led to the existing health care structure in California.

Background

Home to 39 million people, California is the most populous state in the nation and the third-largest geographically, spanning 156,000 square miles (State of California, 2018; Kaiser Family Foundation, 2015b). Despite the state's large size, one third of California consists of forests, and as a result, 95 percent of the population resides in urban areas, with half of Californians located in 5 of the 58 counties in the state (Kaiser Family Foundation, 2015b). California has many areas of industry that are spread throughout the state, such as education, finance, government, health care, manufacturing, technology, transportation, utilities, tourism, and agriculture. The diverse industries thrive in different parts of the state depending on their needs geographically. For example, the agriculture region of California exists in the Central Valley, which is located in the middle of the state and is where many crops and farm-related goods like asparagus, grapes, lettuce, oranges, rice, shelled almonds, tomatoes, milk, and cream are produced (Litwin, 2017).

California also has many unique attractions that draw tourists to the state every year. The number of tourists visiting the state grew every year between 2009 and 2016, with travel spending equaling $126.3 billion in 2016, generating $10.3 billion in travel-related state and local tax revenues in the same year (Easter, 2017). Tourists flooding into the state often visit Hollywood, Beverly Hills, Disneyland, Pebble Beach, Venice Beach, and Laguna Beach in the southern part of the state and Napa Valley, Lake Tahoe, San Francisco, and Yosemite in the northern part of the state (Litwin, 2017). The education system in California also draws people to the state with many high-caliber universities, including public school University of California, Los Angeles; private schools like Stanford and the University of Southern California; and 112 community colleges (Litwin, 2017). Technology is also a big attraction for individuals interested in tech jobs and innovation, and people in this field typically flock to an area known as Silicon Valley. Silicon Valley is located outside of the San Francisco Bay Area, and many major technology companies, including Apple, Google, HP, and Intel, are located there, which has brought a great deal of wealth and job growth to the area. Between 2010 and 2019 jobs in Silicon Valley increased by 29 percent (Silicon Valley, 2011; Avalos, 2018).

History and Culture

California's population boomed with the discovery of gold in 1848. Known as the gold rush, the hope of fortune led to an influx of young men relocating to the state and the spread of people and industry throughout California (Clay & Jones, 2008). The pursuit of wealth in the 1800s represents the beginning of fluctuating wealth within the state highlighted by moments of economic crisis followed by times of economic prosperity. In the 1990s, the dot-com bubble led to a similar flood of people into the state following wealth, increasing the state's population by more than 4 million people (Quay, 2014). There have also been periods of economic downturns, as was the case when the dot-com bubble burst, but the state has been resilient and proved itself to be an economic powerhouse. Not only has California become the largest economy in the U.S., but it has demonstrated economic dominance on a global scale, producing $2.44 trillion of economic output in 2015, which rivaled the economic output of France in the same year. If included in the 2015 world GDP rankings, California would have ranked sixth, ahead of France, India, Italy, and Brazil (Gray, 2012).

The rush of individuals to California for the gold rush not only helped the state financially but also intensified immigration to the state, a trend that has become a strong part of California's current narrative. Since 1920, immigration rates have averaged 1,000 people a day in California, with an average of 300,000 immigrants moving to the state since 1980 (Quay, 2014). In the present day, much of the California population is grouped together in the same areas geographically, but the population of California is highly diverse and includes the largest populations of the four major ethnic groups: whites, Latinos,

Asians, and American Indians. California has the second-highest population of minorities behind Hawaii, with 61.5 percent of the state classified as non-white. Latinos are the most predominant ethnic group in the state with a population of 15 million, which is slightly more than single-race whites, who have a population of 14.9 million (Walters, 2015). Furthermore, more than 10 million immigrants, a quarter of the U.S. immigrant population, call California home. Moreover, 27 percent of Californians are foreign-born, which is twice the national average. Of the foreign-born residents, almost half are naturalized American citizens, and an additional 26 percent have legal status through green cards or visas; however, the remaining 25 percent are undocumented (Hayes, 2017).

Although many of the immigrants living in California are from Latin American countries, 53 percent of the immigrants moving to the U.S. between 2011 and 2015 were from Asian countries and only 22 percent were from Latin American countries. The foreign-born population has contributed to the California economy, however, and makes up a majority of the California workforce with 64 percent of the labor force born outside the U.S. compared to 63 percent of laborers born in the U.S. Despite their activity in the labor force, immigrants made 14.8 percent less on average than their U.S.-born counterparts (Hayes, 2017). Although California has more diversity than most other states, the poverty rates by race and ethnicity are consistent with the national average. The cost of living ranks within the top four in the U.S., which may make it difficult for low-income individuals to live comfortably in the state (Kaiser Family Foundation, 2015b). Since 2015, poverty rates in the state have decreased, but 4 in 10 residents are living in or near poverty (Bohn & Danielson, 2017). Income disparity is evident, and blacks and Hispanics are more likely to live below the poverty line than are whites and Asians (Kaiser Family Foundation, 2015b).

The Political Landscape

The political landscape in California is much less diverse than its culture. The state is politically left-leaning with consistent Democratic control of the state legislature. The governorship of the state has been held by Republicans, but the policies passed during Republican state executive power indicated a much more moderate stance than Republican governors in conservative states (National Conference of State Legislatures, 2017). In California there is an east/west divide with many conservatives residing in the eastern, more rural areas of the state and with most of the very liberal individuals residing in the San Francisco area. The location of conservatives in rural areas is the norm in most states in the nation, but many of the conservatives in rural California identify as moderate conservatives. California also has many people that identify as independents, but the left receives the benefit of this distinction as independents are most likely to support Democrats in elections (McGhee & Krimm, 2012).

The State of Health Care in California

The political nature of the state does not absolve California from disparities in health access and health outcomes. White individuals in California are more likely to smoke but less likely to report experiencing fair or poor health, poor mental health, diabetes, or living as overweight or obese compared to blacks and Hispanics. Access to care is also more readily available to the white population, and they are more likely to have regular access to medical care than are Hispanics or Asians. Access to care extends beyond racial lines, and income disparity is evident between those who live in rural areas compared to those who live in urban areas of the state. Individuals living in poorer, more rural counties, especially those in the north and central valley, have a lower life expectancy, worse health behaviors, limited access to clinical care, and unhealthier environmental factors (Kaiser Family Foundation, 2015b). California has proved to navigate the challenges associated with diversity adequately, however, and ranks above the national average for population health at 17th. The state also ranks in the bottom five for their rates of smoking, obesity, and physical inactivity and has experienced a 54 percent decrease in violent crime since 1990. California faces many environmental health challenges, however, that are unique to the state, like high levels of air pollution and severe droughts that have lasted for unprecedented periods (Kaiser Family Foundation, 2015b).

California, the ACA, and Health Care

Despite the above average health of California residents, state legislators had significant incentive to move forward with the ACA when President Barack Obama signed it into law on March 23, 2010. In addition to the state's unique lack of conservative diversity, leading to few political objections, California had the most uninsured individuals of any state in the country prior to the implementation of the ACA, which facilitated support for the health reform policy. Non-elderly individuals in California accounted for 14 percent of all non-elderly uninsured people nationwide (Kaiser Family Foundation, 2015b). Half of individuals with insurance were covered by employer plans, while one fourth were covered by Medi-Cal or an alternative public plan. Only a specific group of low-income adults were eligible for Medi-Cal, and there were few alternative affordable insurance options (Kaiser Family Foundation, 2015b). The diverse composition of the state also highlighted problems with disparity and health insurance. Non-Hispanic whites were two times as likely to have health insurance compared to non-Hispanic blacks, and Hispanics are three times less likely to have insurance compared to the white population. One reason for this is that since the 1970s, Hispanics and blacks have experienced a decline in insurer-sponsored health coverage and instead are more likely to rely on publicly funded insurance programs (Kirby & Kaneda, 2010).

Under the ACA, many of the populations that struggled to enroll in affordable health care programs and receive regular access to health care would have been eligible for ACA-funded insurance, alleviating pressure from the state and its citizens. Prior to the ACA, 85 percent of health care bills that were not paid for by the patient were covered by public funds, ultimately making California communities responsible for gaps in health insurance coverage (Kirby & Kaneda, 2010). Employers would also benefit from the new legislation and experience a 6 percent decrease in the amount they spend on employee health care by 2016 (Long & Gruber, 2011).

Overall, the ACA would provide coverage to most individuals in need. It was projected that the uninsured population by 2016 would consist of 11 percent of people that had coverage but lost it; 13 percent would represent documented residents that did not need to adhere to the individual mandate; 36 percent of individuals that chose to take the tax penalty and not enroll in health insurance; and 40 percent would be undocumented workers that were not able to receive ACA benefits (Long & Gruber, 2011). Although undocumented immigrants were ineligible for coverage under the ACA, they would still benefit from the program. Many immigrants (especially the undocumented) receive medical care through Federally Qualified Health Care Centers, and the ACA allocated $11 billion to these health care providers. Moreover, $200 million was dedicated to outreach and navigation during phase one of implementation, which allowed for the expansion of clinics that served undocumented individuals (Lopez-Sanders, 2017).

In the end, the need and benefits that would result from the ACA, as well as the political makeup of California, helped the implementation of the ACA become a bipartisan issue instead of a political battle, which was not the case in many other states. Nonetheless, California faced many barriers such as the fight to support the constitutionality of the ACA, creating and implementing a state exchange, and expanding its Medicaid program while trying to provide Californians with affordable access to health insurance.

Perseverance, Uncertainty, and Innovation: California and the *NFIB v. Sebelius* Case

In 2009 the cost of uncompensated medical care was roughly $62.1 billion nationally. Despite the concern over unpaid medical services, many states were vehemently against the ACA and felt Congress overstepped its constitutional authority by enacting the minimum coverage and Medicaid expansion requirements (Bazar, 2012). Having the highest rate of uninsured individuals in the country, California depended on the legislation, and the funding it provided, to implement health care reform in the state. With the lawsuit ongoing, it was unknown if the law would be upheld, completely rejected, or if only pieces of the original bill would survive. The ruling was critical to the success of health care reform in California, and if the SCOTUS upheld the ruling of the 11th Circuit, then the health care plan in California would need to be completely revisited. Despite existing in a "cloud of uncertainty" as State Senator Ed Hernandez referred to the situation, California continued to implement parts of the

ACA and make substantial changes to their existing health care system (Bazar, 2012).

While new changes in the health care system were being designed and tested, California took steps to ensure that its opinion on the ACA would be heard during the SCOTUS case, the *NFIB v. Sebelius* (secretary of HHS). On behalf of the state of California, the California Endowment took on the legal fight to argue for the constitutionality of the ACA. The California Endowment is a private organization that operates statewide in California with the purpose of increasing access to affordable care for all Californians, especially underserved populations. The California Endowment also researches heavily in the areas of social science and public policy to produce work that stresses the benefits increasing access to care will have on individuals and communities (Reilly, 2011; California Endowment, 2012). To argue their case in court, the California Endowment hired lawyer Kathleen Sullivan, one of the country's top appellate advocates (Notable Representations, 2018).

Joining 12 other states and a number of health organizations, Sullivan petitioned SCOTUS to reevaluate the 11th Circuit's ruling on the individual mandate (Ross, 2012). On October 28, 2011, Sullivan filed an amicus brief supporting Congress's authority to regulate health care, arguing that Congress did not act beyond its authority or violate the enumerated powers. Moreover, according to precedents set previously by SCOTUS, the Necessary and Proper Clause allows Congress to enact laws that are not explicitly stated in the enumerated powers in situations of uncertainty. Additionally, Sullivan argued that for Congress to exercise its authority under the Commerce Clause, it simply needed to demonstrate that there was a rational basis for its conclusion that the collective actions of individuals had an impact on interstate commerce.

Sullivan further argued that, based on rights given by the Necessary and Proper Clause and the Commerce Clause to Congress, the 11th Circuit Court made two errors when ruling against the constitutionality of the individual mandate. The first mistake occurred when the court ruled that the minimum coverage requirement does not regulate behavior at the point of consumption (Health Happens Here, 2018). Sullivan argued that the legislation was associated with the consumption of economic resources because the ACA, when in effect, would change when uninsured and underinsured individuals accessed the health care market. People without adequate insurance may forgo treatment because the cost of care is much higher for individuals without insurance than it is for people with health insurance. Therefore, uninsured people often put off seeing a health care professional until they are very ill (Brief of the California Endowment, 2011; Ross, 2012). Uninsured patients are also more likely to seek care in emergency rooms despite the fact that this is the most expensive way to receive routine care for both the individual and the state (Health Happens Here, 2018; California Endowment, 2012; Higuera, 2018).

Sullivan contended that Congress could have rationally concluded that the decision of an individual not to acquire health insurance is an economic choice that affects interstate commerce, especially when the cost of treating the uninsured is much higher than treating those with insurance. Congress could have also concluded that because the activities of distributing, purchasing, and consuming health care accounts for 17.6 percent of the GDP, that it was within the rights given to the legislative branch to regulate health care. Sullivan further argued that the problem of uninsured patients is exacerbated in California due to a federal law that requires emergency rooms to accept all patients in need regardless of their ability to pay. Therefore, the high cost of uninsured patients paired with the requirement to treat patients creates a tangible link between regulating the choice of citizens refusing to buy health insurance and interstate commerce (Brief of the California Endowment, 2011).

According to Sullivan, the second error stated in the amicus brief was the 11th Circuit Appellate Court's statement that the individual mandate was not an essential component of the ACA but, instead, a provision that acted to counteract the possible consequences of the ACA once it was fully implemented (Brief of the California Endowment, 2011). In a follow-up amicus brief filed in January 2012, Sullivan provided empirical evidence that supported the California Endowment's argument that the individual mandate was critical for the success of the ACA. The brief also supported the argument that the individual mandate is Congress's attempt to regulate health insurance and that, without the requirement, expanding access to affordable care would be deterred because it would be more difficult to increase the number of people with health insurance and reduce health-related costs (Ross, 2012; California Endowment, 2012). If the individual mandate was not approved, then healthy people may not enroll in health insurance exchange programs, which would make the program more expensive for those that did enroll because the cost would be shared by a smaller number of people (Bazar, 2012). Additionally, Sullivan argued the act of taking away restrictions on individuals with preexisting conditions would increase costs for insurance companies, and the individual mandate would help incentivize insurance companies to join state exchange's and add competition (Bazar, 2012).

Patrick Johnston, CEO of the California Association of Health Plans, explained the ACA as a "three-legged stool" with three critical parts: the billions of dollars in federal funding that is necessary to expand coverage, the individual mandate that requires people to purchase health care, and guaranteed coverage that prevents health insurance companies from denying coverage to an individual for any reason. Johnston argued that if one of the legs were removed, California would have a difficult time recovering and could not move forward with its plan to reform health care as planned (Bazar, 2012). Additionally, with 1.4 million uninsured Californians in the state, Sullivan argued, the ACA would be 54 percent less effective in California if SCOTUS failed to uphold the minimum coverage requirement (California Endowment, 2012). In 2006, the state of California was responsible for $9.6 billion in unpaid health care because 37 percent of care provided to uninsured or underinsured individuals was not covered by a patient, a charity, or a government program. The onus was then placed on individuals with private insurance as health care providers and insurance companies try to make back some of their lost money. In 2009, this equated to an additional cost of $1,400 for families and $500 for individuals who were privately insured (Health Happens Here, 2018).

In the end, SCOTUS ruling in favor of the constitutionality of the individual mandate allowed California to continue reforming their health care system. With the decision finalized, California was able to take advantage of federal programs and extend access to care for individuals of low income who previously did not qualify for Medicaid. Combined with the state exchange that allowed people of middle to high income to receive affordable health care, California was set to create and implement a comprehensive health care system that would be available to all residents in the state.

Starting Strong: Covered California

In many ways the stakes for implementing the ACA were higher in California than any other state due to the high number of non-elderly, non-insured residents living in the state. California would be potentially providing insurance to 3.4 million additional Californians through the state exchange, more than any other state (Bindman & Schneider, 2011). California had the unique advantage of being progressive in their approach to implementing the ACA due to Democratic control of the state legislature and the presence of a moderate Republican governor who supported the legislation. Additionally, state citizens demonstrated support for the ACA, with 52 percent of Californians expressing support for the ACA when polled in 2010. This was more than 38 percent of residents who were against universal health care. Support of the ACA also grew as the implementation process moved along and the state exchange opened and began operating in 2014. In 2015, 62 percent of Californians favored the health care legislation and opposition decreased to 33 percent (Seipel & Calefati, 2015).

This support, along with the bipartisan support in the state legislature allowed California to be aggressive in their implementation of the law. Subsequently, September 30, 2010, yielded two significant firsts for California on the road to universal health care. California became the first state to create a state market exchange with the passage of Assembly Bill (AB) 1602 and Senate Bill (SB) 900, which launched the California Health Benefit Exchange, and Arnold Schwarzenegger became the first Republican governor to demonstrate support for the ACA (Benen, 2010). This is not surprising, however, as Schwarzenegger had tried and failed in 2007 and 2008 to create a universal health care system (Diamond, 2013).

After starting the ACA planning process, Schwarzenegger's second gubernatorial term ended in 2011, and his successor, Jerry Brown, a Democrat, continued the work of implementing the ACA. In 2012 Brown called a special legislative session to ensure that policies were in place to facilitate the execution of the ACA in California. In July of 2012, Brown informed the HHS that California would run a state-based health insurance exchange marketplace, and HHS gave California conditional approval on January 3, 2013 (Kaiser Family Foundation, 2013e). Two major steps were taken once California was given approval for their exchange. First, the California marketplace was established as an independent quasi-governmental organization that would exist without any formal association with state or federal agencies (Kaiser Family Foundation, 2013f). Second, it was determined that the market exchange would be overseen by a five-member California Health Benefit Exchange Board, which would be chaired by the secretary of California Health and Human Services (who would act as a voting, ex officio member). Additionally, the governor would select two members, and the Senate Committee on Rules and the Speaker of the Assembly would each pick one member. The law for selection criteria mandated that nominated members be an expert in an area relevant to the health insurance exchange, such as an expert in individual or small-employer health coverage, health benefit plan administration, or health finance. Additionally, board members would need to terminate all conflicts of interest such as relationships with insurance carriers, health care providers, health care facilities, or trade associations related to health exchange entities (Kaiser Family Foundation, 2013f).

The first five board members were Diana Dooley, Kimberly Belshe, Paul Fearer, Susan Kennedy, and Dr. Robert Ross (California Health Benefit Exchange, 2012). As the secretary of California Health and Human Services, Diana Cooley was the first chair of Covered California (Weinberg, Kallerman, & Carhart, 2014). Governor Schwarzenegger selected Kimberly Belshe, who was his secretary of the California Health and Human Services Agency from 2003 to 2011 and the deputy secretary of the Health and Welfare agency under Governor Pete Wilson. Schwarzenegger also selected Susan Kennedy, who was his chief of staff while he was governor (York, 2010). The Senate Committee on Rules, specifically President Pro Tempore Darrell Steinberg, selected Dr. Robert Ross, who was the president and chief executive officer of the California Endowment and who had previously acted as the director of Health and Human Services for San Diego County (Ross, 2018). Speaker of the Assembly, John A. Perez, chose Paul Fearer. Fearer was chair of the board of directors of the Pacific Business Group on Health (PBGH) from 1997 to 2012 and had served as chair and as a board member of PacAdvantage, a small business health benefit exchange that was a subsidiary of PBGH (California Health Benefit Exchange, 2012; California Health Benefit Exchange, n.d.).

The new health organization was very active in terms of searching for funds to propel the ACA implementation. The agency was awarded an Exchange Planning Grant, a Level 1 Exchange Establishment Grant, and a Level 2 Exchange Establishment Grant worth $674 million. Overall, by aggressively pursuing market exchange–related grants offered by the federal government California received roughly $910 million in contributions to its state exchange, which was more funding than any other state in the nation (Kaiser Family Foundation, 2013e). Having secured the money to build its state exchange, the board moved forward. The name "Covered California" was formally given to the market exchange in October 2012 (Kaiser Family Foundation, 2013f). From the very beginning, California was adamant that the state's health care exchange serve as a model for all other state exchanges. As a member of the board, Kim Belshe led and made decisions with the guiding principle, "2014 is tomorrow" (Diamond, 2013).

Keeping this standard in mind, California took steps to set a strong foundation for Covered California, including creating a system that would allow Covered California to negotiate for the lowest rates for small businesses and individuals. Covered California was set up as an "active purchaser," which meant establishing contracts with insurers, negotiating rates, and standardizing benefits could be done selectively, which worked to incentivize improvements to the health delivery system (Weinberg & Kallerman, 2017). Fewer than half of state exchange plans were active purchasers (Scheffler, Kessell, & Brandt, 2015). The ability of the exchange to be selective in its negotiating and contract tactics led to Covered California insurance premiums that were among the lowest in the country (Weinberg & Kallerman, 2017).

Unlike other states with only a few insurance plans to choose from, there was a great deal of competition in California, and 11 insurance companies agreed to participate in the marketplace. Anthem Blue Cross of California, Blue Shield of California, Health Net, and Kaiser Permanente, however, received 93 percent of the statewide market share in 2014 (Scheffler et al., 2015). California would only fund subsidies for insurance companies that participated in the state's market exchange, which incentivized providers to offer coverage in the exchange in order to attract more people to their companies (Weinberg & Kallerman, 2017). With such a high number of insurance companies participating, most Californians had access to three insurance choices, with some having up to seven options depending on the region in which they lived. Some areas in the state had a difficult time providing numerous insurance options, especially places where there were few hospitals or one dominant medical group. This often led to higher insurance prices because the state exchange was unable to negotiate. This was the case in Northern California, where rates were up to 30 percent higher than in Southern California where diverse hospital systems were more readily available (Weinberg & Kallerman, 2017).

Covered California and its active purchaser agreement also benefited California health insurance companies with the three largest health insurance companies in California accounting for half the profits reported under the ACA in 2014. Blue Shield of California reported $107 million in profits, Kaiser Permanente $66 million, and Anthem Blue Cross reported $9 million dollars. Not all states experienced California insurance companies' level of success, however. In 2014, insurance companies across the U.S. totaled a profit of just $362 million but reported $2.87 billion in losses, which highlighted the success of California's insurance companies (Terhune, 2015). The high profit margins in the state compared to the rest of the country led critics to question whether the governing board of Covered California could have negotiated better rates for those that had enrolled in the state exchange.

Consumers were given several health care plan choices at varying rates represented by the four metal tiers mentioned in Chapter 3 and were able to select a plan that best fit their lifestyle and gave them some control over the price of their health care. In California, individuals selecting the bronze option paid 40 percent, while the plan covered 60 percent. Silver covered 70 percent of the plan, gold covered 80 percent of the plan, and platinum plans covered 90 percent of the plan while the individual was only responsible for 10 percent (Health for California, 2018). In 2014, when the ACA was just beginning, 62 percent of Californians chose to enroll in silver plans, 26 percent enrolled in bronze plans, and only 12 percent of new consumers chose to enroll in either the gold or platinum plans (Scheffler et al., 2015). The metal tiers also helped avoid confusion as individuals enrolled in health care programs. Simplicity was emphasized by the members of Covered California to facilitate the application process. In October 2011, the state passed a law requiring the usage of one application that would be used throughout the state both electronically and on paper. The law also simplified the identification and citizenship verification requirements and increased cooperation with other government-offered programs (Kaiser Family Foundation, 2013f). These policies were implemented with the intention of making the marketplace easy to navigate by reducing barriers to health insurance for individuals interested in receiving government-provided health care insurance.

The decision of Covered California not to wait for the ruling of *NFIB v. Sebelius* to begin reforming California's health care system gave the state significant advantages once the individual mandate was upheld in SCOTUS. One significant benefit of the proactive action by Covered California was the opportunity to select the best personnel in health care to design, create, and support their market exchange. California was much further ahead in its implementation process, so there was little competition for the best talent. The director of Covered California, Peter Lee, said that "from top to bottom, Covered California has an all-star cast" (Diamond, 2013). Additionally, while other states were rushing to create insurance exchanges by 2014, California's early start allowed Covered California to be put together slowly with time to build and test the new policies that were being put in to place. Another major benefit was the ability to build a strong and efficient state exchange website and not default to contingency website plans like Oregon and Colorado were forced to do. Problems with the federal insurance exchange further highlighted the benefits of having the time to test systems, knowing that many people would be flooding the system as soon as they were able (Diamond, 2013).

Although much of the success of implementing the ACA in California was due to bipartisan cooperation, tensions built between the Democrats and Republicans in 2013 when President Obama gave states the choice to allow residents to keep their individual insurance plans for 2014. Had Covered California voted in favor of the extension, then people would have had the option to stay on their existing plans for an extra year instead of being forced to choose between the market exchange or a tax penalty. In order for states to let people keep their insurance for one extra year they had to meet three requirements: The state must approve the extension, insurance companies must approve the extension, and insurance companies must agree to provide health insurance for those choosing to enroll in the state exchange. The Covered California board voted unanimously against the extension that would benefit 900,000 individual insurance policyholders and instead moved forward with enrolling individuals into state-managed plans (Seipel & Calefati, 2013).

Not only did this decision lead to tension between Republicans and Democrats but also within the Democratic Party. Dave Jones, the state's insurance commissioner, was furious and called the decision "a disservice to California consumers" (Seipel & Calefati, 2013). The board members were accused of favoring insurance companies over California residents. There would have been steep repercussions for the insurance companies had the board approved the extension; however, the insurance providers would have lost millions of dollars by offering their plans for the same rates in 2013 and 2014 (Seipel & Calefati, 2013). Although the backlash was considerable, many policymakers defended denying the extension. President Pro Tempore of the State Senate Darell Steinberg felt that the success of the ACA implementation justified refusing the extension because the option of several competitive plans had led to the daily enrollment of at least 100,000 Californians, which was higher than any other state in the nation. Diana Dooley, secretary of the California Health and Human Services Agency and Covered California board chair, also defended the decision, stating, "If we ask the insurance plans to take everyone and insure everybody with no screens or preexisting conditions then we have to have everyone buying some level of health insurance to meet their responsibility to the system" (Seipel & Calefati, 2013).

Overall, the decision to refuse an extension by the Covered California governing board paid off, and during the first enrollment period, 1.395 million residents registered in the market exchange (Weinberg & Kallerman, 2017). Enrollment was also boosted and then stabilized due to financial grants that California was able to obtain, which helped 48 community organizations help citizens enroll in Covered California. Additionally, the negotiation of lower insurance rates for small businesses and individuals took stress off consumers and made insurance companies more willing to offer their services. By the end of the first enrollment period, California demonstrated that it had truly become the model for other states looking to implement a state exchange.

A Head Start: Medi-Cal

California founded its Medicaid program, Medi-Cal, in 1966, providing health care to low-income residents. Prior to the implementation of the ACA, eligibility for Medi-Cal was limited to families with children, seniors, and disabled individuals. Sixty-two percent of the Medi-Cal expenditures were used for children and adults with disabilities, while 38 percent went towards nondisabled children and adults. Adults who lived below the poverty line without children often did not qualify for Medi-Cal (Johnson & Metzker, 2017). Prior to the ACA, the Medi-Cal program had two delivery and payment structures with half of the beneficiaries covered by managed-care plans and the other half covered by fee-for-service agreements that paid health care providers for each service they provided (Lee & McConville, 2011). Managed-care programs involve a contract between Medicaid and managed-care organizations (MCOs) that allows MCOs to receive a predetermined per-member-per-month payment for the delivery of health care and additional services (Centers for Medicare & Medicaid Services, 2014). After the implementation of the ACA, more counties adopted managed-care programs, which allowed individuals with disabilities and seniors to move from fee for service arrangements to managed-care programs so their care would be better coordinated, would cost less, and would be more easily monitored (Lee & McConville, 2011).

Although the passage of the ACA was embraced by the state of California due to its ability to improve access to care, there were significant concerns that the state could not handle the flood of people into Medi-Cal as the state was already facing a budget crisis. Prior to the ACA and the expansion of Medicaid, Medi-Cal cost $45 billion dollars a year to operate, and it was anticipated that the new eligibility requirements would add an additional $3 to $4 billion to this cost by 2020 (Kieber-Emmons, 2011). The expansion of Medicaid extended coverage to non-elderly adults that were at or below 138 percent of the FPL, which qualified an additional 1.4 to 3.6 million adults for Medi-Cal, and it was expected that 750,000 to 910,000 additional people would enroll in Medi-Cal before 2019 (Wang & Trivedi, 2017; Lucia, Jacobs, Watson, Dietz, & Roby, 2013; Kieber-Emmons, 2011).

Additionally, Medicaid coverage has demonstrated that it increases the longevity of beneficiaries and increases health through preventative care so people live longer and therefore stay enrolled in Medicaid longer (Lucia et al., 2013). Despite the health benefits, the new financial commitments to Medi-Cal occurred at a time when California was already making cuts to their Medicaid program in order to save the state money. Moreover, in January 2011, Governor Brown proposed making $1.7 billion in cuts to Medi-Cal in an attempt to overcome a $22 billion deficit in the state budget. A similar cut to funds was attempted by Governor Arnold Schwarzenegger in 2008 but never came to fruition because it was held up in federal courts (Bindman & Schneider, 2011). Included in the proposed Medi-Cal cuts was an additional decrease of 10 percent in funds that would be given to physicians and clinics (Bindman & Schneider, 2011).

A 10 percent decrease in funding for clinics and physicians would exacerbate an already-significant problem for Medi-Cal patients. California was already struggling to attract enough doctors to provide efficient and adequate care. This problem existed in part because California ranked 47th in payments to Medicaid physicians, so many California doctors were reluctant to take on Medi-Cal patients, resulting in one Medi-Cal doctor for every 200 beneficiaries. State health care demands were expected to increase by 70 percent and to successfully manage this increase California would have to add 350 new physicians who would accept Medi-Cal patients (Bindman & Schneider, 2011). Although the state had concerns over affording the expansion of Medicaid and an increase in Medicaid physicians, the federal government had a plan that would alleviate financial stresses and pay 85 percent of Medi-Cal costs between 2014 and 2019. This amount included paying 100 percent of the health care spending costs for newly eligible beneficiaries, 50 percent of the costs for those that were eligible prior to the ACA but never enrolled, and 88 percent between 2015 and 2019 for children who are eligible for California's Children's Health Insurance Program, Healthy Families, but did not previously enroll, which would be an increase from 65 percent in 2014 (Lucia et al., 2013).

Despite the impending health policy changes in California, Governor Brown's primary concern was tackling the state's budget crisis. He began soon after he entered office, trying to overcome a decade of recurring budget deficits to create a surplus for the 2013–2014 fiscal year. Two main policy proposals helped the state save money. First, the governor introduced a plan in 2011 to shift authority from the state to local governments in several areas, including public safety, mental health, substance abuse treatment, and protective services. Second, despite promises to expand Medicaid in the state, Brown initiated the 10 percent provider rate cut to Medi-Cal after the 9th Circuit Court of Appeals upheld his proposal in May 2013 (Kaiser Family Foundation, 2013e). The savings from both changes combined reduced the state's general fund spending by $16 billion.

Although Brown had pushed for cuts to Medi-Cal, he decided to transition 875,000 children enrolled in Healthy Families to Medi-Cal beginning in January 2013, which also acted as a cost-saving measure. The transition took place in four phases over one year and had the goal of simplifying eligibility and coverage requirements, improving the coverage offered to children, and reducing or eliminating premiums for beneficiaries that had low income. It was projected that the state would save $58.4 million in the 2013–2014 budget year, and $72.9 million every year after (Kaiser Family Foundation, 2013e). The budget cuts led some to worry that California would not provide ample funds for ACA outreach and enrollment efforts. The California Endowment, the same organization that filed an amicus brief in support of the ACA, provided the state a $26.5 million grant to educate and inform people about their health insurance options. This grant provided the possibility for California to apply for federal funds that would match the amount, giving $53 million to the state to assist vulnerable populations with the Medi-Cal enrollment process (Kaiser Family Foundation, 2013e).

Despite the financial and personnel concerns, the California legislature formally voted to expand Medicaid in June 2013, which would allow individuals to enroll in Medi-Cal in 2014. Long before the vote, however, California had begun preparing for the influx of newly insured residents. California joined Connecticut, Minnesota, New Jersey, Washington, and the District of Columbia as the first states to enroll in the federally funded Medicaid Section 1115 waiver program (Kaiser Family Foundation, 2015b; California to Expand Medicaid, 2013; Goberstein, Gonzales, & Sommers, 2015). California's waiver was approved by the federal government in November 2010, several months after the ACA was passed, and was known as a "Bridge to Reform" program because it allowed approximately 500,000 low-income individuals to gain insurance coverage and access to health care (Lee & McConville, 2011). California would receive $10 billion over a five-year period to help prepare for Medicaid expansion in 2014. Due to the waiver, adults between the ages of 19 and 64 living at or below 138 percent of the FPL could begin receiving coverage prior to 2014. The intention of the waiver was to ease the rate of health care cost increases within the Medi-Cal program (California Bridge to Reform, 2010).

Shortly after California's acceptance into the program, State Senator Steinberg and Assemblymen Elaine Alquist and John Bill sponsored SB 208 and AB 342, which allowed California to begin implementing the 1115 waiver (California Bridge to Reform, 2010). One of the first steps taken was to distribute funds to the counties by creating low-income health plans (LIHPs). LIHP's provided California counties with two program options, Medicaid Coverage Expansion or the Health Care Coverage Initiative. Counties could also choose to implement both programs. The Medicaid Coverage Expansion program provided coverage to non-elderly and nonpregnant residents living at or below 133 percent of the FPL who were not previously eligible for Medicaid. The Health Care Coverage Initiative extended coverage to non-elderly and non-pregnant adults with family incomes ranging from 133 to 200 percent of the FPL. The federal government would match 50 percent of all funds available for Medicaid Coverage Expansion programs and 50 percent of Health Care Coverage Initiative programs up to $630 million (Kaiser Family Foundation, 2013e).

Under these programs, LIHPs would provide insurance to individuals until they could transfer to Covered California or Medi-Cal when the programs began in 2014 (California 1115 Waiver, 2011). Counties that wanted to start LIHPs had to meet a minimum requirement for health care and mental health services and improve the standards of their comprehensive indigent care programs due to new ACA guidelines (Lee & McConville, 2011). Additionally, AB 342 established guidelines that required LIHP enrollees to enroll in medical homes. Medical homes involve using a single health care provider that is tasked with coordinating the patients' care and tracking their medical records. Counties creating LIHP's also had to increase their geographical accessibility and increase cultural understanding that would help improve care for California's diverse population (Lee & McConville, 2011). The Bridge to Reform program once again highlighted physician availability problems because the new guidelines for Medi-Cal were strict and made it mandatory for patients seeking primary care to be given a new patient appointment within 20 days (Kieber-Emmons, 2011). In addition to creating LIHPs, the funds would be used to manage and facilitate the process of strengthening the infrastructure of public hospitals and making improvements that would allow more people to be served safely and efficiently. Specifically, $3.3 billion would be allocated to public hospital safety net programs, $2.9 billion to expand coverage to low-income individuals, and $3.9 billion to cover uncompensated health care costs (California Bridge to Reform, 2010).

The $3.3 billion was provided through a Delivery System Reform Incentive Pool, which prioritized four areas: infrastructure development, innovation and design, population-focused improvement, and urgent improvement in care. Infrastructure development focused on improvements in the area of technology, tools, and human resources. Innovation and redesign created and funded new and innovative care delivery models. Population-focused improvements prioritized 5 to 10 high-burden conditions affecting low-income patients and came up with new and efficient ways to treat these diseases. Last, the urgent improvements focused on the implementation of interventions and measurements that could be realistically executed to increase the standard of care for patients over a five-year period (Kaiser Family Foundation, 2013e). This process allowed health care providers to create new strategies and test them before the full implementation of the ACA would begin in 2014 (California Bridge to Reform, 2010). For example, 6 percent of all California acute hospitals treat roughly half of the state's uninsured population in need of hospitalization every year. These hospitals also rely on ambulatory services to provide primary and specialty care to uninsured individuals enrolled in Medi-Cal. The funds from the waiver were used to improve existing programs at these six hospitals so they would be prepared to treat the newly eligible health care applicants, in addition to the 3 million people that were expected to remain uninsured (Bindman & Schneider, 2011).

On January 1, 2014, Medi-Cal was officially expanded, and low-income adults, including those transferring from LIHPs, were now eligible to enroll in the program. The insurance benefits were similar to those offered by Covered California, including a comprehensive set of benefits referred to as essential health benefits, but were often provided at little to no cost to individuals and families (Kieber-Emmons, 2011). Under Medi-Cal, 21 plans were offered and varied by county, but many counties also offered commercial plans with insurance from companies like Anthem Blue Cross, Kaiser, Health Net, and Molina (California Bridge to Reform, 2010).

Medicaid expansion also addressed physician shortages. The new program provided a more stable funding stream, which in theory would be more attractive to medical personnel and result in an increase of physicians in low-income areas, helping to overcome Governor Brown's 10 percent provider rate cut (Lucia et al., 2013).

Guidelines outlined in the ACA made it mandatory to pay physicians Medicaid fees equal to Medicare rates for 146 primary care services in 2013 and 2014. Nationally, Medicaid physician fees for primary care would increase by an average of 73 percent, but because California's fees were so low, its Medi-Cal physician fees increased by 136 percent to be compliant with the pay guidelines set by the ACA (Kaiser Family Foundation, 2013e). Fees were not implemented with the start of the LIPH programs, however; California had until summer 2013 to begin increasing physician payments, six months after doctors expected to receive their pay increase. Although the increased payments would be paid back retroactively, the delay caused uncertainty among Medi-Cal doctors, and some health care professionals decided to steer clear of Medi-Cal, especially with the cuts to Medi-Cal by Governor Brown (Robeznieks, 2013).

Unlike many other states, the decision to expand Medicaid occurred with little partisan turmoil or debate. California Republicans did have concerns, however, over whether the state would be able to support the expansion of the Medicaid program in the long term. Federal support stemming from the ACA will start being reduced beginning in 2020, which will lead to a loss of $25 billion for Medi-Cal funding by 2027, $23 billion of which is directly tied to federal funding. The loss of funds is projected to add $10 billion to the General Fund by 2027 (Lucia, Jacobs, & Bindman, 2017). Cumulatively, the state's health care system will lose $130 billion in state and federal Medi-Cal funding between 2020 and 2027 if California is unable to find alternative sources of funding to make up for the federal contributions. In this case, the state may be forced to exercise the option to end open enrollment in 2019 and not allow new beneficiaries into the expanded Medi-Cal program. This would lead to a significant loss in coverage for Californians with 3.7 million fewer residents enrolled in Medi-Cal because beneficiaries would be unable to re-enroll in the program if they lost eligibility, even briefly (Lucia et al., 2017).

Despite the worst-case scenario presented by the Republicans, Democrats maintained that the taxpayers of the state would continue to take on the burden of the uninsured population if the Medicaid program was not expanded. This is significant due to the number of uninsured individuals in the state (California to Expand Medicaid, 2013). Additionally, the money contributed by the federal government for Medicaid would increase state tax revenues, which would help make up for some of the money being spent on Medi-Cal, potentially offsetting 42 percent of costs in 2014. New jobs created as a result of the ACA would also generate funds likely leading to an upturn in California's economy (Lucia et al., 2013). In the end, the Democrats and Republicans compromised and agreed that the state legislature could revisit their policy on Medicaid expansion if federal contributions dipped below 70 percent (California to Expand Medicaid, 2013).

Overall, the state of California was able to overcome budget and personnel problems to add additional low-income adults to Medi-Cal. Taking advantage of federal funds, California was able to expand access to care for many people previously ineligible for Medicaid through LIPHs prior to the 2014 open enrollment period and worked through budgetary problems to increase the number of people receiving care through Medi-Cal.

Conclusion

California represents a state fully in support of health care reform. Secretary Dooley's focus on making California the "lead car" nationally in the process of creating and rolling out the Covered California exchange is reflected in the enthusiasm in which state policymakers approached the ACA (Weinberg et al., 2014). Whereas many other states were taking steps to fight the legislation in court after the ACA was signed into law, California became one of 13 states to support the health care reform law by filing an amicus brief in favor of the individual mandate (Ross, 2012). Undeterred by the ongoing court battles, California wasted no time beginning its health care reform by expanding coverage to non-elderly and nonpregnant residents living at 133 percent of the FPL by taking advantage of a federal waiver that allowed low-income individuals to join county-based health care programs and become part of California's health care system sooner. This move provided access to care for uninsured and underinsured people in the state prior to 2014 and allowed the state to prepare and ease into the influx of new patients that would be entering the health care system once the ACA was fully implemented.

Despite the state's willingness to implement the ACA, there were several obstacles to overcome. Budget concerns are a prime example. Prior to the passage of the ACA, Governor Schwarzenegger had proposed cuts to Medicaid in an attempt to reduce the budget deficit. In 2011, Governor Brown made a similar proposal to cut $1.7 billion to their Medicaid program, Medi-Cal (Bindman & Schneider, 2011). Part of the proposed cuts included a 10 percent cut to physicians and clinics, which gave physicians little incentive to serve low-income residents in California creating a physician shortage for Medicaid recipients. This problem was exacerbated in California because it has the largest population in the country with at least 750,000 individuals expecting to join Medi-Cal, further straining physicians and clinics while adding $3 to $4 billion dollars in Medicaid Costs to the state budget (Kieber-Emmons, 2011).

To address the financial burdens associated with the ACA, the Covered California board took steps to secure available funding from the federal government. California received almost $910 million dollars in grants from the federal government to fund their state exchange (Kaiser Family Foundation, 2013e). These funds were used to build California's health care infrastructure so it would be ready when the ACA came into full effect in 2014. Additionally, by creating a system that promoted negotiation and competition, California's state exchange incentivized insurance companies to be part of the exchange while making prices affordable for those in need of coverage.

Part of California's ability to overcome financial strains and create a successful health care exchange was due to the political makeup of the state. In many ways, health care reform in California was considered much less controversial than in other states, which was demonstrated by the largely bipartisan approach to health care reform taken by California legislators. Although Republicans and Democrats in the state disagreed on many funding aspects of health care reform, they were able to find common ground, as was the case with the sunset clause on Medicaid funding that would allow for further Medicaid expansion consideration if federal funding fell below a certain point. This cooperation matched with overall citizen support meant legislators and health care advocates could be aggressive in their approach to expanding health care access.

At times the strong approach to policy implementation meant making unpopular decisions as was the case with the decision of the Covered California board not to allow individuals to keep their insurance for one additional year as allowed by the Obama Administration. The decision to keep residents in the ACA resulted in success for the insurance companies, and the three largest insurance companies in California accounted for roughly half of all insurance profits in 2014. This profit opened board members up to criticism, even within the Democratic Party, that they were more concerned with the well-being of the insurance companies than the individuals in need of insurance. Ultimately the decision paid off for the Covered California board as 1.395 million individuals enrolled in the state exchange during the first enrollment period (Seipel & Calefati, 2013; Weinberg & Kallerman, 2017).

Overall, the state was able to overcome budget constraints by utilizing innovation to meet the needs of California's diverse population. Though the state experienced fewer internal barriers to health care reform than other more conservative states, the aggressive nature of policy implementation and bipartisan cooperation was a large part of meeting Dooley's expectations to successfully implement the ACA while becoming a model of how managed competition should work (Weinberg & Kallerman, 2017).

9 The Broader Lessons of State Implementation of the ACA

The ACA stands as a living testament to the tension between national policy goals and state policy preferences. While some states embraced the ACA and its mechanisms for delivering health care, other states obstructed implementation in very direct ways. The result is an ever-changing patchwork of state decisions, all in the face of continued uncertainty about the future of the ACA at the national level. Our focus in this book has been on the initial implementation decisions made by states, and the factors that led to those decisions.

The ACA arguably has the distinction of being the subject of the most concerted and overt effort to oppose implementation of any national legislation passed in recent memory. The U.S. has a long and checkered history of state opposition to national legislation, but the ACA takes the level of opposition to new heights. The efforts to challenge the constitutionality of the law in the courts, coupled with explicit efforts on the part of many states to delay or prevent implementation, is largely unprecedented. Indeed, one might draw parallels between state opposition to the Voting Rights Act of 1965 or the Civil Rights Act of 1964 and state opposition to the ACA. An important difference, however, is that the 1960s' legislation was passed with bipartisan support (and against bipartisan opposition) at a time in our history in which the divisions in our society were drawn along lines other than strict political partisanship.

In this final chapter, we review several themes regarding the state of health care policy and reform that emerge from our case studies. These themes are the result of commonalities and lessons drawn from the individual experiences of the four states under study. Each theme may play out differently in each state, but collectively these themes serve to help us frame some conclusions drawn from our inquiry. Following a discussion of these themes, we offer several broad conclusions about state experiences with implementing the ACA. We then discuss some implications of this work and close with some final thoughts about future scholarly research on the ACA.

Some Emergent Themes

Our examination of initial state implementation of the ACA leads us to five themes that capture the issues in and around the ACA. These themes are largely interdependent and are best considered collectively rather than individually. We present these five themes, in no particular order, as a means to frame our overall conclusions.

Federalism Matters

Since the founding of our nation, people have debated the scope and power of the national government in the context of state governments. In many ways, the ACA is but the latest target for this debate. The architects of the ACA were at least intuitively aware of this debate, and the structure of the ACA reflects an approach to federalism that is very similar to other national legislation enacted over the past quarter-century or so. At its heart is a critical question: *What should the role of the national government be in the health care arena?* Concomitantly, *how much authority and control should states exercise in this arena?* The trend in the U.S. since the Reagan era has been to loosen federal controls and provide greater discretion and decision power to states. Indeed, even the proposition that health care is appropriately within the scope of the national government's power has been questioned.

To the former question, we detail the growth of the national government's role in health care in Chapter 2 of this book. Despite the difficulties in the creation of these programs, they remain very popular in America today, and cuts to these programs have proved politically difficult even to discuss. A majority of Republicans, Democrats, and Independents remain firmly opposed to cuts in these programs (see Altman, 2017). If we are correct in our observation that the ACA is an incremental change in existing policy, and actually expands a program (Medicaid) that Americans support, then one might conclude this question is settled. Our case studies suggest otherwise. In three of the four states, the role of the national government and the states was at the forefront of the debate. Although it played out in different terms, and for different reasons, an interest in preserving states' rights, and a perception of federal overreach, led these states toward a defined set of actions (largely in opposition to the ACA).

To the latter question, state politics and culture appear to be critical elements of this debate. In California, the political question was never about whether the actions of the state were appropriate, but rather, technical questions about how to accomplish the goals were paramount. In Alabama, early interest in the ACA model was eventually replaced with active and complete opposition to the law. Governor Bentley's initial interest was to ensure that Alabama retained control over its health care future, and his early support for a state exchange is indicative of this interest. The end result, however, was a rejection of the ACA as the model of government overreach. Michigan and New Hampshire had political figures in both sides of the question, often working at odds with each other over the actions within those states. In some cases, these positions were tied to party affiliation, but in other cases, party identification does not explain the decisions of state actors.

One critical element of the ACA that is different from some other recent (and similar) debates concerns funding for the policy. The ACA was never designed as an unfunded mandate (see Posner, 1997; Kelly, 1994); the national government was to provide a minimum of 90 percent of the cost of Medicaid expansion, and would begin by providing 100 percent of the cost of expansion. Moreover, the national government made millions of dollars of technical support funds available to help states create state exchanges. Yet in some states, such as Alabama, the potential costs of Medicaid expansion became one of the principal arguments against participation—an argument often tied to the imposition of unwanted and unwarranted national policy requirements on states.

In the context of the nation, the role of the national government and the states, and the ways in which responsibility is apportioned, continues to be a point of debate. The debate over states' rights has many dimensions and raises many questions: Can we have a true national policy if states are free to make significant changes to the policy or to reject some or all of the policy outright? The hidden irony of the federalism question surrounding the ACA is that states that actively opposed the ACA and refused to act to make state decisions ultimately ceded authority back to the national government. By refusing to create and operate a state exchange, states are forced to allow the national government to make all decisions about the options available to citizens in that state. Moreover, several states that initially rejected Medicaid expansion (e.g., Virginia) have since reconsidered their earlier decision and reversed course.

The structure of the ACA is designed to allow states the opportunity to design a state program that fits state needs and capabilities. Although the ACA in its original form required states to expand Medicaid, the net effect of the *Sibelius* case was to provide states the option of whether to expand Medicaid. The issue of state choice is critical to the story of the ACA, and indeed is an underlying tenet of this book in that state choice leads to different choices by states. As noted earlier in this volume, the metapolicy (see Johnson & Heilman, 1987; Dror, 1968) behind the ACA is one of lessened federal control and more state choice. A legacy of the Reagan years, this metapolicy continues to play an important role in the formation, initiation, legitimation, and implementation of public policy. Certainly there are other models that could have been considered in the context of the ACA debate (and some, such as a nationalized health care system, that were), yet the metapolicy in place ultimately served to dictate the kinds of solutions that were acceptable choices. Even so, significant debate about the role of the national government in health care ensued and continues today.

Partisanship Explains Some, but not All, State Decisions

Our next theme addresses the role of partisanship in the ACA debate. Looking at the national level, the ACA was passed along party lines: While 33 Democrats in the House of Representatives voted against the ACA, no Republicans in either the House or the Senate voted in favor of the legislation (How they voted, 2019). The legislation was enacted because Democrats held a majority in the House and, with the inclusion of the two Independent senators in the Senate, held a filibuster-proof majority in the Senate. Even during the national debate, partisan lines were firmly drawn. In many senses, the partisan divide set the tone for the debate in many states. The partisan nature of the debate at the national level could not help but impact debate at the state level. However, while our 50-state analysis affirms the importance of party control at the state level, a more in-depth analysis within our case study states offers a more nuanced understanding of the role of partisanship. A Republican governor expresses early support for the ACA before ultimately becoming firmly entrenched against the idea, even in light of the recommendations of his handpicked commissions. In New Hampshire, gubernatorial power is checked by the Executive Council, an element often overlooked in 50-state comparative studies. New Hampshire had a Democratic governor during the implementation but did not pursue Medicaid expansion since he was certain the Executive Council (5–0 Republican) would veto it. Republican governor Rick Snyder in Michigan moved to expand Medicaid at the same time the Republican attorney general in Michigan was joining other states to mount a court challenge to the ACA. In California, Republican governor Arnold Schwarzenegger was an early supporter of the ACA. In short, partisanship does not tell the full story.

Based on our findings, the moderating factor to partisanship at the state level is state context. Because the context within each state is unique, the important elements of context are also largely unique to each state circumstance. In California, the question of need was an important element of the debate about the ACA. Moreover, Republicans elected to statewide office in California are likely more moderate than their counterparts in other states. If this is the case, then ideology may have a larger influence on the decision process than does partisanship. In Alabama, the Republican physician-governor (ideologically farther to the right than his counterpart in California) expressed early support for the ACA. Governor Bentley's change of position was likely due as much to the opposition created by long-standing political and cultural cleavages within the state, and existing market conditions in the health care industry, as it was to a deeply held partisan position. In New Hampshire, partisanship may have played a larger role than in our other case study states, but even so the effects of partisanship were complicated by the structural complexity of New Hampshire's state government. In Michigan, even a change in the party controlling the governor's mansion did little to change the state's position on the ACA.

The other "takeaway" from this discussion is that the element that replaces partisanship as an explanator differs from state to state and is different in each state. New Hampshire's long-standing aversion to national policy mandates was a critical element in state decision-making, while in California a culture that seeks to extend benefits and care to citizens replaced partisan strife. The lack of a vibrant insurance marketplace, coupled with differences between entrenched political interests (the "Big Mules" vs. rural agricultural interests) is a more effective explanator of state action in Alabama. Likewise, the interplay of interests in Michigan helps explain how a change in party control of the governorship did not result in a shift in policy positions.

The story of the ACA is undeniably tied to political partisanship. Indeed, our case studies suggest that partisanship may be more important (and more stable) in state legislatures than in any other context. Changes in party control can lead to efforts by the new majority party to take actions to repudiate the actions and decisions of the other party, much like the Republican House of Representatives at the national level took nearly three dozen votes to attempt to undo the original ACA passed under Democratic control. In our four cases, legislative party control was generally stable during this period, leaving the political calculus relatively unchanged in the legislature. In none of our cases did the state legislature attempt to drive the state in one direction or another against the wishes of the governor. If partisanship were truly the only explanator in these cases, the stories (and outcomes) in these states would be quite different.

The "Battle" Over the ACA Is About the Proper Role of Government in Society

At its core, the debate surrounding the ACA and its implementation is a debate centered firmly in the rights of citizens and of the proper role of government in society. Although the debate takes many forms, the ACA encapsulates the tension between individual liberties and the interests of society as a whole. Moreover, the terms of the debate are often interchangeable—the same terms are used by both sides in the debate, but the meanings differ (Stone, 1997). The net result is an often-acrimonious dialogue between two sides, each claiming the "moral high ground" in the debate. It is not the values that are different, but rather the way those values are defined and expressed. The debate that occurred at the national level around passage of the ACA was, in effect, the same debate that took place in the states around implementation.

Those who stand in opposition to the ACA see the legislation as a flagrant breach of a long-standing constitutional imperative to protect citizens against government infringement of individual rights and liberties. In particular, the individual mandate and its accompanying tax penalties for noncompliance are seen by many as blatant coercion—an attempt by the government to compel citizens to participate. Our tax code has relied for decades on a series of incentives and penalties to coerce certain behaviors from citizens, but the imposition of a tax penalty for failure to participate in the health care market was seen by many as a "bridge too far." Early opposition to the ACA was often cast in terms of a loss of individual freedoms—from the rhetoric of "death panels" to decide who gets health care to the penalties imposed on those who choose not to participate to (famously) the opposition to the claim that participants could keep their own doctor. The Massachusetts experience tells us that citizens are not necessarily opposed to these kinds of policy solutions, but the national government's role in the ACA has been an important factor.

On the other hand, supporters of the ACA view the legislation as a mechanism for government to take seriously its fundamental duty to protect the health and welfare of its citizens, to end a form of economic discrimination, to improve health outcomes in the U.S., and to bring some sanity to a sector of the economy in which costs have been rising much faster than the rate of inflation (see Claxton, Rae, Leavitt, & Cox, 2018). In this formulation, the legislation is a reasonable and desirable vehicle to achieve these goals, in that the program provides benefits to a large portion of society, and the costs of the program are shared by program enrollees (who purchase insurance in the private market) and a series of subsidies (paid for by tax revenues). Medicaid expansion services are available to a qualifying subset of the population, but the costs are distributed across a much larger group. Moreover, by relieving health care providers of providing health care for free to those who cannot afford services, the costs of health care to all decrease as those with insurance are no longer subsidizing those without insurance.

Is it within the proper scope of the national government to enact such a program? Reasonable people disagree about the answer to this question, which in turn leads to the policy debates surrounding the ACA. In states such as New Hampshire and Alabama, with a rich history of opposition to the power of the national government (and, perhaps, a healthy distrust of all government), the ways in which decision-makers and citizens define the proper role of government differs from those in states like California, which tends toward more proactive stances for government and its functions. It is important to note that in each of our case study states, there are groups representing each side of this fundamental question. Although the debate itself is almost always expressed in different terms, the debate never strays too far from the influence of this fundamental question.

State Decision-Making Is Both Important and Unique

An important assumption of all comparative state policy research is that states are different, and that variation exists across the set of choices available to states. When these criteria are met, scholars are able to focus on the specific factors that lead to state decisions. A further assumption of 50-state comparative work is that patterns exist in these factors; in other words, states with similar characteristics will tend to act in the same manner. The work we present in Chapter 4 is indicative of this approach and is useful for detecting similarities across states. Patterns are useful at a macro level and can tell researchers much about the important factors in state decision-making. Likewise, 50-state comparative work can help eliminate potential explanators that are not common across a set of cases. A variable that fails to achieve statistical significance is dismissed precisely because it fails to contribute to our explanation of variance across our set of cases. Finally, the "cases-variables" problem endemic to implementation research (Goggin, 1986) applies here: A limited number of observations limits the number of variables that can be considered. In cross-sectional studies (such as the initial implementation of a federal program by states), the maximum number of observations available is 50. While such work has undeniable value, its greatest strength is simultaneously its greatest weakness: It necessarily ignores factors that may be critically important in individual, or a small subset of, states. But if Dror (1968) is correct in his observation that states are "policy laboratories," the *differences* between states become more important than the similarities.

Our research highlights some of these differences between states and provides insight into how the decision-making processes in these states led to state policy choices. The Executive Council in New Hampshire (the only one of its kind in the U.S.), coupled with the exceptionally short term of office for the governor, meant that New Hampshire could reverse course on its initial decisions. In Michigan, political pragmatism dictated a pattern of decision outcomes that did not follow the expected partisan explanations. Pragmatism was an important element in Alabama as well, as was process (or, more accurately, the appearance of process). California's well-developed state programs steered a decision process in favor of building on existing institutions within the state. Timing of decision-making is also important. The part-time legislature in Alabama was out of session at the point at which the legislature could have played a role in the decision to create a state exchange, and the governor chose to not call the legislature back for a special session but to make an executive decision about whether the state would create its own insurance exchange. In California, the legislature and the governor worked together to make decisions and create a workable implementation plan. Differences of opinion between constitutional officers in Michigan meant that different decision-makers in the state were simultaneously working against the interests of the other. When viewed as a whole, it appears that Michigan was mildly schizophrenic in its approach to the ACA (both supporting and opposing at the same time), when in fact the actions were taken by very different decision-makers. Much the same was true in Alabama: The attorney general was busy challenging the ACA in federal court at the same time the governor was expressing early support for the law. At a macro level, these important differences are obscured; in sum, the differences matter.

State History and Culture Matter

Finally, we make note of the critical role of state history, culture, and customs in state policy choices. Scholars such as Elazar (1984) have sought to capture and create typologies to express these cultural, with some degree of success. Indeed, the debate surrounding Elazar's typology has been in place for decades (see Savage, 1981; Clynch, 1972; Sharkansky, 1969). While we believe that Elazar's work has great utility, it suffers from the same malady that afflicts other such typologies: It seeks similarities between cases at the expense of (important) differences. Mississippi and Alabama are both strong "traditionalistic" political cultures, but anyone who has studied the politics and culture of the two states understands that the states are very different (see, e.g., Key, 1984 [1949]).

The elements of state history and custom important in a setting such as the ACA are likely more random and dispersed than the factors captured by a coarsely grained typology of political culture. Moreover, it is often the case that history and culture are the result of unique geographical features that themselves set in motion certain events. California, the last state among our cases to achieve statehood (and the geographically farthest west of the group) has a history marked by early Spanish exploration, a gold rush that brought thousands of speculators into the state in the 1840s, and an early reliance on minerals and timber for its economic base. It is also noteworthy that California has seen significant immigration from the Far East as well as Central and South America, all of which have had a unique effect on the state's culture and politics. The political issues in California are very different than those in Alabama or Michigan, and the bases of political power are quite different. While politics in California have been heavily dominated by the coastal regions, Alabama has experienced a more even conflict between rural and urban interests.

Michigan's history of early conflict involving the British, French, and Native American tribes formed an early part of its political culture. Following the Revolutionary War, the territory known as Michigan became part of the Northwest Territories, and settlers from New England began to settle into the area (Dunbar & May, 1995). Michigan saw the birth and rise of a number of competing political parties, which led to an unusually high level of political conflict (Formisano, 1971). This conflict helped shape Michigan politics in the 21st century and helps explain some of the partisanship present in the Michigan case. The same level of partisanship was not seen in Alabama, principally because Alabama has a long history of one-party rule—by the Republicans following the Civil War, then by the Democrats following Reconstruction (Martin, 1975), and then Republicans again in the latter years of the 20th century. The nature of the debate in each state and actions taken by state officials are the product of these unique histories.

Some Conclusions

Viewed in the larger context of the history of health care policy in the American experience, the ACA can be viewed as an incremental step in a long series of steps. Since the dawn of the twentieth century, health care policy has followed a somewhat circuitous route through a series of policy proposals, with more failed proposals than successful ones. The net result is a mixture of national policies that, together, represent the current state of health care policy in the U.S. Throughout this history, however, there are several conclusions that may be drawn.

Health Care Policy Is Highly Conflictual

First, health care policy is hard. By this, we mean that health care policies tend to be conflictual, with deeply entrenched interests on all sides. Political coalitions are hard to build and maintain around specific proposals, and shifting political "winds" coupled with ideological shifts in the electorate mean that a proposal that may be possible at one fleeting moment may not be possible the next. In John Kingdon's (1995) terms, the policy windows available are often of short duration. As detailed in Chapter 2, our history is replete with failed proposals for health care policy, mute testament to the difficulties faced by health care policy entrepreneurs. The reasons for failure rarely have to do with resources or political will, but more often with fundamental disagreements over the identification of perceived winners and losers in the policy space. Shifts in citizen and elite ideology, political coalitions, governmental resources, and competing demands for policy attention (and policy resources) mean that "getting to yes" on a health care proposal is not an easy undertaking. Furthermore, if one subscribes to the notion that policymaking is more straightforward in the face of a clear threat or crisis, the lack of such clarity in this policy arena adds to the difficulty.

The political rancor surrounding the ACA is a clear testament to the issue of "winners and losers." If health care is defined as a right of citizens, then the calculus (and definition) of "winner" and "loser" is fundamentally different than the case in which health care is defined as an entitlement. In the former definition, everyone wins, while in the latter definition, there are clear winners and losers. Coupled with issues of altruism (see Stone, 2008) and questions about the proper role of government, one can perceive the many vectors of conflict possible in this policy arena.

Who Should Provide Health Care?

The role of the national government in the provision, production, and delivery (Savas, 1987) of health care services remains very much an open question. In spite of current-day rhetoric to the contrary, the ACA, along with almost all other successful health care policy proposals, have offered largely market-based solutions to the defined problem. Just as the ACA relies on the private insurance market to provide insurance coverage (and the health services that insurances buy), programs such as Medicaid and Medicare rely on the private sector to deliver health care. Under Medicare, for example, enrollees can purchase supplemental private insurance policies to offset out-of-pocket costs not covered by Medicare. The funds provided by Medicare are thus a subsidy paid to eligible Americans to help offset the costs of health care, and that subsidy is used to purchase health services from private-sector providers. More important, the health services are entirely provided by the private sector. Medicaid service providers are private-sector health professionals who are reimbursed by the Medicaid program for services provided. Indeed, the only large-scale government health care provider at the national level is the Veterans Administration, which provides direct medical services to veterans.[1]

Layered over this argument is the equally important question of federalism: the relationship between the national government and the states. The ACA clearly places requirements on states in pursuit of national policy, and it is no surprise that states respond to these requirements in very different ways. Moreover, attitudes and perceptions about the proper relationship between the national government and the states become a critical part of the story of ACA implementation. In states in which support for the ACA was less than strong, the terms of the debate were often centered around issues of federalism. The issues in the *Sibelius* case were largely enduring matters of federalism, and the power of the national government to impose requirements on states. In that case, although opponents of the ACA had hoped for a clear statement of repudiation of the ACA by the court, the decision ultimately did little to address the underlying question of the balance between the national government and the states. By effectively striking down only the Medicaid expansion mandate, the Supreme Court came down substantially on the side of the power of the national government. In essence, the national government has the constitutional right to engage in national health care policy and to incent citizen participation through the use of tax incentives and penalties.

Values Matter

Successful policies generally reflect a core of common values in American politics. As Deborah Stone (1997) points out, the continuing struggle between the market and the polis is an enduring feature of American politics and underlies much of the rhetoric in the public sphere.[2] While the core values we share as Americans are important to all, the definitions and interpretations of those values vary wildly, in turn, leading to very different interpretations of the role of government. In Stone's terms, the goals of the ACA can be cast as representing the values of equity, security, and liberty. The policy problem is talked about in terms of numbers, causes, and interests; the solutions are cast as issues of inducements, facts, rights, and powers. Because the two sides differ so greatly on the meanings of these core values,[3] the role of the national government is indeterminate. In a sense, however, our common societal values dictate that the national government (and its policies) work to expand market opportunities for the private sector (see Lindblom, 1982) and to protect individual liberties. Like many other policy arenas, the issue in health care is the balance between individual rights and liberties, and the limits on government intervention. In every sense, the issues present in the health care debate in 21st-century America are the very same issues present in the Constitutional Convention in Philadelphia in 1789.

A review of our four cases illustrates these values conflicts. In states in which the debate over the ACA was spirited, questions of equity, for example, became an essential element of the conversation. The value of liberty is another value that was an integral element of the conversation, but the definition of the term varied depending on the point of view of the speaker. States like New Hampshire and Alabama defined liberty in the ACA debate as freedom from the excesses of government, while in California there was little debate about liberty (or the loss thereof). The inducements for the ACA were also portrayed very differently by opposing sides in the debate. For opponents, the inducements took the form of an unreasonable government "taking" by requiring participation in something some people would otherwise fail to choose of their own volition. On the other side, proponents of the ACA saw the ACA as a mechanism to provide a positive inducement: The ACA would provide citizens access to a critical service and would subsidize their participation in the service. Numbers were also portrayed very differently in state debates, particularly in regards to issues of program cost and participation. Much of the public debate regarding Medicaid expansion, for instance, had to do with the number of additional enrollees and the long-term costs to the state. Historically, many federal programs offer significant federal subsidies as a means to incent state participation (e.g., federal highway grants and wastewater treatment plant construction under the Water Quality Act[4]), and such programs have often placed additional requirements on states as a condition of funding. The federally imposed national 55-mile-per-hour speed limit was tied directly to highway funding. Such value conflicts are certainly not new to American policy debates, but they are very much an integral element of the story of the ACA.

Incrementalism in Health Care Is Alive and Well

The ACA is very much an incremental policy choice. The two cornerstones of the ACA are the mandate for individual coverage (provided by private health insurance companies) and Medicaid expansion (private delivery of health services paid for through government reimbursement). The individual coverage element builds on an existing system of health care delivery, and Medicaid expansion simply increases eligibility for existing Medicaid services by altering the income limits for eligibility. Viewed in this light, it would seem that the ACA should not be too controversial; if Lindblom (1959; Lindblom & Woodhouse, 1993) was correct in his observation that incremental policies are less controversial, then the ACA should have been relatively easy to bring to fruition. So, why was it so difficult? Why did some states go to extraordinary lengths to block implementation of the ACA? And, not to forget the question at the heart of this book, why did states make the choices they did under the ACA?

The real story of the ACA at the national level, and often at the state level as well, is the remarkable degree of polarization in our political system at the moment. Rational policy debate has been replaced with ideologically charged rhetoric and a desire to play to 24-hour news cycles, and policy positions are often adopted simply because they are diametrically opposed to the policy positions of the political opposition. As an example, the policy model that became the ACA began life as a program signed into law in Massachusetts by then-governor Mitt Romney, a Republican (Belluck, 2006). In the 2008 presidential primary season, Romney (then a candidate for the Republican nomination) touted the success of the Massachusetts program and suggested its adoption at the national level. By 2012, however, Romney was regularly denouncing "Obamacare" as a dismal failure that represented a government "takeover" of our health care system and promised to repeal the law if he became president (Semuels, 2012). In another example, Senate Majority Leader Mitch McConnell (D-KY) declared in 2010 that his goal was to prevent any Obama-backed policies from consideration in the Senate (Levinson, 2012; see also Skocpol & Jacobs, 2012).[5] McConnell was successful in that effort, to the point that he also refused to schedule a hearing for a Supreme Court nominee (Everett & Thrush, 2016), even though there was nearly a year left in Obama's term—a move unprecedented in American politics (Schier & Eberly, 2017).

The rancor and divisiveness at the national level were felt at the state level as well. When faced with implementing the ACA, many Republican-based states balked, and many actively opposed implementation. However, as detailed in this volume, politics only tells part of the story at the state level. Opposition was offered in some Democratically controlled states, and some solidly Republican states embraced elements of the ACA. Other states appeared to start down one path, only to find themselves at a very different point later in the process. This variation in approach means that politics, as operationalized through party control, does not provide an adequate explanation of state action. Similarly, previous analyses have clearly shown that policy need cannot explain state decisions on the ACA.

Implications for Future Policy and Research

In many senses, the ACA serves as a magnet for debates about the proper role of government in the U.S. Whether the ACA represents a government trying to meet the basic needs of its citizens or the quintessential example of unwarranted government overreach of individual rights, there is no shortage of opinion or position on the ACA. But does the ACA experience change the landscape of national policy or of state implementation of national policy? The short answer is a qualified no. As noted elsewhere in this book, the ACA represents incremental change. Current obstructionism aside, the vast majority of national policy enacted since the ACA has been incremental in nature, as have most policies throughout our history. The structure of American governance—a separation of powers, checks, and balances, and a mix of proportional and equal representation—still makes incremental policy the most palatable outcome (Lindblom & Woodhouse, 1993). The debates about the appropriate role of the national government and the states will certainly continue, and people will continue to differ as to the nature of an appropriate balance between the two.

An interesting element of the ACA is the apparent disconnect between policy positions and public opinion. Indeed, public opinion about the ACA has evolved in the period since its passage. The Kaiser Family Foundation (2018c) has been tracking public opinion[6] on the ACA since its passage, and several interesting trends can be noted from these data. First, throughout the history of the ACA, the country has been more or less evenly divided in terms of opinion (favorable/unfavorable). At its passage, 46 percent of adults rated the ACA as favorable, and 40 percent of respondents had an unfavorable view of the legislation. Opposition to the ACA reached a peak in July 2015, when 53 percent of adults had an unfavorable view of the ACA, and only 37 percent had a favorable view. By and large, however, the differences have been within a few percentage points.

The second interesting trend has been the back-and-forth nature of public opinion: in the 104 monthly data points, the majority opinion has changed 19 times and tied several more. This is no doubt tied to the relatively even division between the groups, but it is notable that in the months immediately preceding national elections (both presidential elections and midterm elections) the percentages favorable and unfavorable tend to be the closest. This suggests that for all the political opposition to the ACA, there is not a clear voter mandate to oppose the ACA. Third, the trend since January 2017 has been one of increasing support for the ACA. The December 2016 poll shows 46 percent unfavorable versus 43 percent unfavorable, but by February 2017 only 42 percent rated the ACA as unfavorable, as opposed to 42 percent who rated it favorably. The gap continues to widen; as of November 2018 (the most recent data available as of this writing), the ACA currently enjoys its strongest support, with 53 percent rating the ACA as favorable compared to 40 percent who rate it as unfavorable. A similar trend is reported by RAND (2019).

Not captured in the Kaiser or RAND data is another interesting element. A poll conducted by CNN in 2013 found that while 46 percent of those polled were opposed to "Obamacare," only 37 percent of those polled were opposed the ACA (CNN, 2013). In this sense political opponents of the ACA were successful in branding the ACA as an extension of a president for whom public opinion was strongly split. But it also suggests that Americans generally support the benefits provided under the ACA. It is important to remember that the ACA was about more than Medicaid expansion, insurance markets, and the individual mandate. A Kaiser Family Foundation poll conducted in 2018 found strong support for both prohibitions against denying coverage for preexisting conditions (75 percent) and against insurance companies charging sick people higher rates (72 percent), both elements of the ACA. Finally, a poll conducted by Gallup (Jones & Reinhart, 2018) reported that 79 percent of Americans remain dissatisfied with the cost of health care; only 34 percent of Americans rate access to health care as "excellent" or "good."

Taken together, the poll data suggests there is a disconnect between public demands for better health care and political responses to these demands. An almost single-minded drive by Republicans in Congress over a period of roughly five years to repeal the ACA was ultimately unsuccessful. The reasons for this are likely many, but we might speculate that the lack of a suitable alternative policy was at least partially responsible. Indeed, following his dramatic "thumbs-down" vote on a repeal vote in the Senate, the late Senator John McCain (R-AZ) cited the lack of an alternative as the reason for his vote (Huetteman, 2018).

In terms of future policy, then, there is evidence of a demand for affordable health care coverage in the U.S. The ACA may (or may not) prove to be a lasting policy instrument to achieve this goal, but opposition to the ACA at either the national or state level will likely not lessen the policy demand. Nor is there reason to suggest that the range of acceptable policy choices will be significantly altered in the short term. The tension between national policy and individual rights is likely too great to bring about a truly nationalized health care system (rhetoric to the contrary notwithstanding). Indeed, the most likely outcome is some version of incremental health care policy based on existing policies and approaches. Private providers and private insurers are too powerful and too ingrained in our society to be made irrelevant—future policy choices must build on these elements. Likewise, there are many questions left unanswered about the ACA and its effects. While our work casts a glance at state dynamics, the variation present in states is too great for us to claim that our cases capture more than a fraction of the story at the state level.

Conclusion

The story of the ACA is still being written. Just as any policy evolves over time, the ACA will also continue to change. The political uncertainty surrounding the Act continues to be an issue as well: Although early attempts to repeal the legislation were unsuccessful, there is little evidence to suggest that such attempts have exhausted themselves. Whether what emerges over time is a strengthened model, a revised model, or a fundamentally different model, remains to be seen. In the interim, however, to understand something about initial state implementation of the ACA tells us much about state policy behavior.

The tension inherent in American politics between the power of the national government and the will of the states is brought clearly into focus in health care. Basic questions about the proper role of government, the relationship between the national government and the states, and how governments at all levels respond to citizen demands are all part of the ACA experience. Moreover, the significant variation in state responses to the ACA, and the reasons states made the decisions they did, is of more than mere academic interest. The ability of government to respond to citizen demands and the debates about the best way to accomplish that response (if at all) are issues central to any study of the ACA. That state governments choose different paths is not a surprising or unexpected finding, but it raises important questions as to *why* states make the choices they do.

The goal of this research has been to move beyond coarse-grained explanations of state behavior and to better understand the nuances within states that drive state decision-making. While the breadth of our analysis is necessarily limited, the issues raised in this analysis can lead scholars toward alternative approaches to understand state behavior. Within that context, however, we must bear in mind that the variation between states is great—the goal should not be to try to reduce this variation into a set of "one-size-fits-all" variables that apply to all states. Instead, our analysis suggests some likely categories of variables and explanators that may be incorporated into similar future studies. Put another way, differences are as important as similarities in terms of understanding state policy behavior.

Notes

1. It should come as no surprise that the Veterans Administration has come under a great deal of scrutiny in recent years for providing a poor level of service. Even less surprising is that the Veterans Administration has attempted to address its lack of capacity by contracting with private health services providers.
2. This was certainly the case in the ACA, where a significant element of the initial debate was whether to include nationalized health care as an element of the ACA. At its heart, the debate was whether the market (the private system if health care) or the polis (government) should control access to health care. The ACA policy theory sidesteps this fundamental debate by offering a government-provided subsidy to allow citizens to purchase services in the private market.
3. For example, the individual mandate is one of the most contentious elements of the ACA. From the standpoint of the backers of the ACA, the program offers a reasonable inducement to eligible individuals to participate: In addition to the availability of health insurance, participants are provided a substantial tax subsidy to help offset the costs of insurance and pay a penalty for refusing to participate. For those opposed to the ACA, the inducement represents an infringement of government on personal liberty, which, in turn, threatens both security and individual rights.
4. The Federal Water Pollution Control Act of 1972 (better known as the Clean Water Act) created the construction grants program (a categorical grant program) to help communities build wastewater treatment facilities. The size of the grant was typically around 60 percent of the planning and construction costs and was used to incent communities to meet national water quality standards. The construction grants program was replaced by the Clean Water State Revolving Load Fund program, a block grant program, under the Water Quality Act of 1987 (see Morris, 1997).
5. McConnell also made clear his strategy was to make Obama a one-term president. Although he said he didn't want the president to fail, his strategy was clearly to make Obama unappealing to voters in 2012 (Kessler, 2012), a strategy that ultimately failed with Obama's election to a second term of office. McConnell has continued his obstructionist behavior in his role as Senate Majority Leader.
6. The poll solicits responses from adults. The poll also gathers data by party identification, income, age, gender, and race. For our purposes, we report only aggregate data, except as noted.

References

Addy, S., & Ijaz, A. (2013). *Economic impact by industry of Medicaid expansion in Alabama under the Affordable Care Act*. Report to the Alabama Hospital Association, Montgomery, AL., September 2013.

Alabama Department of Insurance [ADOI]. (2011, November). *Alabama health insurance exchange study commission recommendations*. Montgomery, AL: Author.

Altman, D. (2017, December 20). Tax cuts could make it harder to change Medicare and Medicaid. *Axios*. Retrieved from www.axios.com/tax-cuts-could-make-it-harder-to-change-medicare-and-medicaid-1515110690-3799fc89-98aa-4d54-914e-1046fb9d7c1d.html

Amadeo, K. (2016, September 15). Obama's health care reform plan: How insurance companies changed Obama's healthcare reform plans. *The Balance*. Retrieved from www.thebalance.com/obama-s-health-care-reform-plan-3305753

American Community Survey. (2017). *United States Census Bureau*. Retrieved from www.census.gov/programs-surveys/acs/

American Health Line. (2016). *CMS Denies NH request to implement work, identification requirements for Medicaid expansion*. American First Line. First Look.

Avalos, G. (2018, February 22). Silicon Valley tech hiring outpaces rivals, but woes worsen. *The Mercury News*. Retrieved from www.mercurynews.com/2018/02/22/silicon-valley-tech-hiring-outpaces-rivals-but-woes-worsen/

Baldas, T. (2013, October 6). How corruption deepened Detroit's crisis. *Detroit Free Press*. Retrieved from www.usatoday.com/story/news/nation/2013/10/06/how-corruption-deepened-detroits-crisis/2929137/

BallotPedia. (2018). *Alabama state legislature*. Retrieved from https://ballotpedia.org/Alabama_State_Legislature

Barks-Hoffman, K. (2010, March 31). State creates council to oversee healthcare. *Crain's Detroit Business*. Retrieved from www.crainsdetroit.com/article/20100331/FREE/100339970/state-creates-council-to-oversee-health-care

Barrilleaux, C. (2013, May). *The state politics of Medicaid expansion*. Paper presented at the 13th State Politics and Policy Conference, Ames, IA.

Barrilleaux, C., & Rainey, C. (2014). The politics of need: Examining governors' decisions to oppose the "Obamacare" Medicaid expansion. *State Politics & Policy Quarterly*, *14*(4), 437–460.

Baulch, V., & Zacharias, P. (1999 February 10). The 1943 Detroit race riots. *The Detroit News*. Retrieved from http://blogs.detroitnews.com/history/1999/02/10/the-1943-detroit-race-riots/

Bazar, E. (2012, June 17). Supreme Court ruling on health care could force Caliornia to "rethink everything". *Monterey Herald News*. Retrieved from www.montereyherald.com/general-news/20120617/supreme-court-ruling-on-health-care-could-force-california-to-rethink-everything

Becker, D. J., & Morrisey, M. A. (2012). *An economic evaluation of Medicaid expansion in Alabama under the Affordable Care Act*. Birmingham, AL: UAB School of Public Health. Retrieved from www.stateforum.org/sites/default/files/becker-morrisey_study_of_alabama_medicaid_expansion_2012.pdf

Bell, D. (1976). The coming of the post-industrial society. *The Educational Forum 40*(4), 574–579.

Bell, D. (2010, March 26). Granholm offers to help defend healthcare legislation. *Detroit Free Press*. Retrieved from https://web.archive.org/web/20100401230531/www.freep.com:80/article/20100326/NEWS15/100326059/Granholm-offers-to-help-defend-health-care-legislation

Belluck, P. (2006, April 6). The nurturing of health care. *The New York Times*, p. A16.

Benen, S. (2010, April 20). ACA gets bipartisan support after all. *Washington Monthly*. Retrieved from https://washingtonmonthly.com/2010/04/30/aca-gets-bipartisan-support-after-all/

Bernick, L. E. (1978). The impact of U.S. Governors on party voting in one-party dominated legislatures. *Legislative Studies Quarterly*, *3*(3), 431–444.

Berry, F. S., & Berry, W. D. (1992). Tax innovation by American states: Capitalizing on political opportunity. *American Journal of Political Science*, *36*(3), 715–742.

Berry, W. D., Ringquist, E. J., Fording, R. C., & Hanson, R. L. (1998). Measuring citizen and government ideology in the American states, 1960–93. *American Journal of Political Science*, *42*(1), 327–348.

Beyerle, D. (2012, November 13). Bentley: No insurance exchange, Medicaid expansion. *Gadsden Times*. Retrieved from www.gadsdentimes.com/article/20121113/NEWS/121119936/1067?Title=Bentley-No-Insurance-exchange-Medicaid-expansion-

Bindman, A. B., & Schneider, A. G. (2011). Catching a wave: Implementing health care reform in California. *The New England Journal of Medicine*, *364*(16), 1487–1489.

Bipartisan Legislation. (2009, July 18). Obama reaches out to Republicans on health care, but bipartisan bill looking unlikely. *Fox News and the Associated Press*. Retrieved from www.foxnews.com/politics/2009/07/18/obama-reaches-republicans-health-care-bipartisan-looking-unlikely.html

Birn, A., Brown, T., Fee, E., & Lear, W. (2003). Struggles for national health reform in the United States. *American Journal of Public Health*, *93*(1), 86–91.

Blavin, F. E., Buettgens, M., & Roth, J. (2012). State progress toward health reform implementation: Slower moving states have much to gain. *Urban Institute*. Retrieved from www.nhchc.org/wp-content/uploads/2011/09/Urban-states-HR-Jan-2012.pdf

Bohn, S., & Danielson, C. (2017, March 21). Just the facts: Poverty in California. *Public Institute of California*. Retrieved from www.ppic.org/publication/poverty-in-california/

Bouffard, K. (2012, November 30). House panel rejects state run health exchange. *The Detroit News*.

Breaux, D. A., Duncan, C. M., Keller, C. D., & Morris, J. C. (2002). Welfare reform-Mississippi style: TANF and the retreat from accountability. *Public Administration Review*, *62*(1), 92–103.

Breaux, D. A., Morris, J. C., & Travis, R. (2007). Explaining welfare benefits in the south: A regional analysis. *The American Review of Politics*, *28*, 1–18.

Brief of the California Endowment. (2011, October 28). On petition for a writ of certiorari to the United States Court of Appeals for the Eleventh Circuit. *Supreme Court of the United States*. Retrieved from www.yumpu.com/en/document/view/27625468/hhs-v-florida-cert-amicus-brief-california-endowment

Brill, S. (2015). *America's bitter pill: Money, politics, backroom deals, and the fight to fix our broken healthcare system*. New York, NY: Random House.

Brown, R. D. (1995). Party cleavages and welfare effort in the American States. *American Political Science Review*, *89*(1), 23–33.

Business Council of Alabama. (2012). *Robert J. Bentley Bio*. Retrieved from www.webcitation.org/69BMnbhqe?url=www.ciclt.net/sn/pol/po_detail.aspx?MemID=

Cable News Network (CNN). (2013, September 27). *Poll: "Obamacare" vs. "Affordable Care Act"*. Retrieved from http://politicalticker.blogs.cnn.com/2013/09/27/poll-obamacare-vs-affordable-care-act/

California 1115 Waiver. (2011, January 12). *Western Center on Law and Poverty*. Retrieved from http://ccrwf.org/wp-content/uploads/2011/01/wclp-fact-sheet-medi-cal-waiver-wfsummit2011-final1.pdf

California Bridge to Reform. (2010). California bridge to reform a section 1115 waiver. *Department of Healthcare Services*. Retrieved from www.dhcs.ca.gov/Documents/1115%20Waiver%20Fact%20Sheet%2011.2.10.pdf

California Endowment. (2012, January 13). *PR Newswire*. Retrieved from www.prnewswire.com/news-releases/the-california-endowment-files-second-brief-in-us-supreme-court-137326058.html

California Health Benefit Exchange. (2012, November 1). Announcement of contract award to Accenture LLC for the California healthcare eligibility, enrollment & Retention System (CalHEERS). *Government of California*. Retrieved from www.hbex.ca.gov/solicitations/archive/HBEX4/library/6-25-12%20Announce%20of%20CalHEERS%20Contract%20Award%20to%20Accenture.pdf

California Health Benefit Exchange. (n.d). Paul E. Fearer. *Covered California*. Retrieved from https://board.coveredca.com/member/fearer/index.shtml

California to expand Medicaid. (2013, June 15). *The New York Times*. Retrieved from www.nytimes.com/2013/06/16/health/california-to-expand-medicaid.html

Callaghan, T., & Jacobs, L. R. (2014). Process learning and the implementation of Medicaid reform. *Publius: The Journal of Federalism*, *44*, 541–563.

Canfield-Davis, K., Jain, S., Wattam, D., McMurtry, J., & Johnson, M. (2010). Factors of influence on legislative decision making: A descriptive study. *Journal of Legal, Ethical & Regulatory Issues*, *13*(2), 55–68.

Cason, M. (2013). Bentley says report of 30,000 new jobs is "bogus": Governor says jobs are already there. *Birmingham News*, p. 10A.

Centers for Medicare & Medicaid Services (CMS). (2014, July 1). *Medicaid*. Retrieved from www.medicaid.gov/medicaid/managed-care/index.html

Chandler, K. (2009). Alabama attorney general Troy King: Supreme Court bingo ruling helps, but questions linger. *Birmingham News*. Retrieved from http://blog.al.com/spotnews/2009/11/post_215.html

Chandler, K. (2011, September 17). Commission begins work on insurance exchange. *Birmingham News*, p. 1D.

Chandler, K. (2012a, May 9). Alabama Senate delays vote on health insurance exchanges. *Birmingham News*, p. 6B.

Chandler, K. (2012b, June 4). State to act after court ruling on Affordable Care Act. *Birmingham News*, p. 2B.

Chandler, K. (2012c, July 20). Bentley waits before acting on insurance coverage. *Birmingham News*, p. 1C.

Chandler, K. (2012d, October 3). Bentley refuses to comply with health care deadline. *Birmingham News*, p. 10A.

Chandler, K. (2012e, November 4). Bentley: No state health care exchange: He stands solidly opposed to Affordable Care Act, including Medicaid expansion. *Birmingham News*, p. 07A.

Chollet, D., Barrett, A., & Bell, T. (2011, September 30). *Current and future sources of health insurance coverage for Alabama residents* (Report No. BMA10T7). Princeton, NJ: Mathematica Policy Research.

Chollet, D., Stewart, K., & Witmer, S. (2011). *Alabama's current insurance Market* (Report No. BMA10T6). Princeton, NJ: Mathematica Policy Research.

Claxton, G., Rae, M., Leavitt, L., & Cox, C. (2018). How have healthcare prices grown in the U.S. over time? *Kaiser Family Foundation*. Retrieved from www.healthsystemtracker.org/chart-collection/how-have-healthcare-prices-grown-in-the-u-s-over-time/#item-prices-for-inpatient-hospital-care-have-grown-rapidly-for-privately-insured-patients

Clay, K., & Jones, R. (2008). Migrating to riches? Evidence from the California gold rush. *The Journal of Economic History*, *68*, 997–1027.

Clynch, E. J. (1972). A critique of Ira Sharkansky's "the utility of Elazar's political culture". *Polity*, *5*, 139–141.

Cohen, J. (2010, May 21). How they did it. *The New Republic*. Retrieved from https://newrepublic.com/article/75077/how-they-did-it

Coleman-Battista, J., & Richman, J. (2011). Party pressure in the U.S. state legislatures. *Legislative Studies Quarterly*, *36*, 397–422.

Conlan, T. (1988). *New federalism: Intergovernmental reform from Nixon to Reagan*. Washington, DC: Brookings.

Covering New Hampshire. (2018). New Hampshire health insurance marketplace. *Covering New Hampshire*. Retrieved from https://coveringnewhampshire.org/

Cox, G. W., Kousser, T., & McCubbins, M. D. (2010). Party power or preferences? Quasi-experimental evidence from the American states. *Journal of Politics*, *72*, 799–811.

Cox, McMillin woo reform foes with legal foolishness. (2010, March 23). *Detroit Free Press*. Retrieved from https://web.archive.org/web/20100327092017/www.freep.com/article/20100323/OPINION01/3230333/1322/Cox-McMillin-woo-reform-foes-with-legal-foolishness

Crotty, P. M. (1987). The New Federalism game: Primacy implementation of environmental policy. *Publius*, *17*, 53–67.

Daniell, J. R. (1981). *Colonial New Hampshire: A history*. Hanover and London: University Press of New England.

Dash, S., Lucia, K. W., Keith, K., & Monahan, C. (2013). Implementing the Affordable Care Act: Key decisions for state-based exchanges. *The Commonwealth Fund*. Retrieved from www.commonwealthfund.org/publications/fund-reports/2013/jul/implementing-affordable-care-act-key-design-decisions-state

Davey, M. (2013 August 27). Medicaid expansion battle in Michigan ends in passage. *The New York Times*, p. A14. Retrieved from www.nytimes.com/2013/08/28/us/medicaid-expansion-battle-in-michigan-ends-in-passage.html

Dawes, D. (2016). *150 years of Obamacare*. Baltimore, MD: JHU Press.

DeWitt, E. (2018, May 7). N.H. Medicaid expansion work requirement approved by Washington. *Concord Monitor*. Retrieved from www.concordmonitor.com/New-Hampshire-

Medicaid-expansion-work-requirement-approved-by-Washington-clearing-major-hurdle-17352811

Diamond, D. (2013, September 2013). California raced to "set the pace" on Obamacare implementation. Did it pay off? *California Healthline*. Retrieved from https://californiahealthline.org/news/california-raced-to-set-the-pace-on-obamacare-implementation-did-it-pay-off/

Dinan, J. (2011). Shaping health reform: State government influence in the Patient Protection and Affordable Care Act. *Publius*, *41*, 395–420.

Dolsen, R. (2009, December 13). U.S. missed a real opportunity for health care reform. *The Herald-Palladium*. Retrieved from www.heraldpalladium.com/features/u-s-missed-a-real-opportunity-for-health-care-reform/article_2dbd043b-03c9-5bb1-98b5-f2e1f5a9d58d.html

Downey, M., & Still, C. (2013). The Affordable Care Act's impact on persons with obesity. *The Downey Obesity Report*, 1–15. Retrieved from www.downeyobesityreport.com/2013/10/the-affordable-care-acts-impact-on-persons-with-obesity-the-full-report/

Dror, Y. (1968). *Policymaking reexamined*. Scranton, PA: Chandler.

Dunbar, W. F., & May, G. F. (1995). *Michigan: A history of the wolverine state* (3rd ed.). Grand Rapids, MI: Wm.B. Eerdmans Publishing.

Easter, M. (2017, May 9). California tourism industry grows for the 7th straight year, report says. *Los Angeles Times*. Retrieved from www.latimes.com/business/la-fi-ca-economic-impact-20170504-story.html

Economic Development Partnership of Alabama (EDPA). (2017). *Alabama transportation overview*. Retrieved from www.edpa.org/wp-content/uploads/Alabama-Transportation-Overview-1.pdf

Eggert, D. (2012a, November 29). "Obamacare vote": Michigan House panel rejects state health insurance exchange; GOP leaders says "we will not have one". *Mlive*. Retrieved from www.mlive.com/news/index.ssf/2012/11/michigan_house_panel_rejects_c.html

Eggert, D. (2012b, June 28). Attorney General Bill Schuette: Healthcare ruling is "body blow" to Constitution. *Mlive*. Retrieved from www.mlive.com/politics/index.ssf/2012/06/attorney_general_bill_schuette_7.html

Eisenberg, J. M., & Power, E. J. (2000). Transforming insurance coverage into quality health care: Voltage drops from potential to delivered quality. *Journal of the American Medical Association*, *284*(16), 2100–2107.

Elazar, D. J. (1984). *American federalism: A view from the states* (3rd ed.). New York, NY: Harper and Row.

Engel, J. (2009, September 3). Saginaw doctors pushing national healthcare reform. *Saginaw News*, p. 4A.

Erikson, R. S., Folke, O., & Snyder, J. M. (2012). A gubernatorial helping hand? How governors affect presidential elections. *Research Institute of Industrial Economics*. Retrieved from http://hdl.handle.net/10419/81485

Everett, B., & Thrush, G. (2016). McConnell throws down the gauntlet: No Scalia replacement under Obama. *Politico*. Retrieved from www.politico.com/story/2016/02/mitch-mcconnell-antonin-scalia-supreme-court-nomination-219248

Fahey, T. (2011, July 14). Health bills become law without Lynch signature. *Union Leader*. Retrieved from www.unionleader.com/news/politics/health-bills-become-law-without-lynch-signature/article_5118abc7-d6ef-5256-8020-ce90fbe399d1.html

Families USA. (2016). *A 50 state look at Medicaid expansion*. Retrieved from http://familiesusa.org/product/50- 35 state-look-medicaid-expansion

Fangmeier, J., Jones, D., & Udow-Phillips, M. (2014, December 1). Michigan baseline report: State-level field network study of the implementation of the Affordable Care Act. *The Nelson A. Rockefeller Institute of Government: The State University of New York*. Retrieved from https://www.chrt.org/publication/michigan-baseline-report-state-level-field-network-study-implementation-affordable-care-act/

Flynt, J. W. (1989). *Poor but proud*. Tuscaloosa, AL: University of Alabama Press.

Formisano, R. P. (1971). *The birth of mass political parties in Michigan, 1827–1861*. Princeton, NJ: Princeton University Press.

Foster, R. S. (2009, December 10). Estimated financial effects of the "Patient Protection and Affordable Care Act of 2009," as proposed by the Senate Majority Leader on November 18, 2009. *Department of Health & Human Services*. Retrieved from www.cms.gov/Research-Statistics-Data-and-Systems/Research/ActuarialStudies/downloads/S_PPACA_2009-12-10.pdf

Gibson, S., & Dominiak, M. (2013). The health insurance providers fee and Medicaid managed care capitation rates. *Health Watch*, *73*, 35–38.

Gilbert, G. (2013, July 13). Obamacare, Medicaid expansion not synonymous. *The Oakland Press*. Retrieved from www.theoaklandpress.com/news/gilbert-obamacare-medicaid-expansion-not-synonymous/article_de41f19c-9bdf-56e1-a1d2-8c2e06a730f1.html

Goberstein, E., Gonzales, G., & Sommers, B. D. (2015). California's early ACA expansion increased coverage and reduced out-of-pocket spending for the state's low-income population. *Health Affairs*, *34*(10), 1688–1694.

Goggin, M. (1986). The "too few cases/too many variables" problem in implementation research. *Western Political Quarterly*, *38*, 328–347.

Gornick, M. E. (2002). Disparities in health care: Methods for studying the effects of race, ethnicity, and SES on access, use, and quality of health care. *The Institute of Medicine*, 1–39.

Gornick, M. E. (2003). A decade of research on disparities in Medicare utilization: Lessons for the health and health care of vulnerable men. *American Journal of Public Health*, *93*(5), 753–759.

Grant II, D. S. (1995). The political economy of business failures across the American states, 1970–1985: The impact of Reagan's New Federalism. *American Sociological Review*, *60*, 851–873.

Gray, A. (2012, March 30). California Endowment supports Affordable Care Act. *NewsBlaze*. Retrieved from https://newsblaze.com/usnews/health/california-endowment-supports-affordable-care-act_25127/

Gray, V., Hanson, R., & Kousser, T. (2007). *Politics in the American states: A comparative analysis* (9th ed.). Thousand Oaks, CA: Sage.

Grogan, C. M. (1994). The political-economic factors influencing state Medicaid policy. *Political Research Quarterly*, *47*(3), 589–622.

Guenther, H. (2012, October 15). Report: Michigan could save nearly $1 billion over 10 years by expanding Medicaid eligibility. *University of Michigan: Michigan Medicine*. Retrieved from www.uofmhealth.org/news/archive/201210/report-michigan-could-save-nearly-1-billion-over-10-years

Guthrie, D. (2010, July 22). Healthcare overhaul battle begins in court. *The Detroit News*.

Hacker, J. S. (1996). *The road to nowhere: The genesis of President Clinton's plan for health security*. Princeton, NJ: Princeton University Press.

Hacker, J. S. (2011). Why reform happened. *Journal of Health Politics, Policy and Law*, *36*(3), 437–441.

Haeder, S., & Weimer, D. (2013). You can't make me do it: State implementation of insurance exchanges under the Affordable Care Act. *Public Administration Review, 73*(Special Issue), 1–14.

Haeder, S., & Weimer, D. (2015). You can't make me do it, but I could be persuaded: A Federalism perspective on the Affordable Care Act. *Journal of Health Politics, Policy and Law, 40*(2), 281–323.

Halpin, H. A., & Harbage, P. (2010). The origins and demise of the public option. *Health Affairs, 29*(6), 1117–1124.

Haveman, J. (2013, July 10). My take: Voting to expand Medicaid while expanding Obamacare. *The Holland Sentinel*. Retrieved from www.hollandsentinel.com/x946749430/MY-TAKE-How-to-vote-for-Medcaid-expansion-while-opposing-Obamacare

Hayes-Clark, J. (2012). Examining parties as procedural cartels: Evidence from the U.S. states. *Legislative Studies Quarterly, 37*(4), 491–507.

Hayes-Clark, J. (2017). Immigrants in California. *Public Policy Institute of California*. Retrieved from www.ppic.org/publication/immigrants-in-california/

Health for California. (2018). The Affordable Care Act for California. *Covered California*. Retrieved from www.healthforcalifornia.com/affordable-care-act

Health Happens Here. (2018). Fact sheet: The California Endowment files amicus brief with U.S. Supreme Court on Affordable Care Act. *The California Endowment*. Retrieved from www.scribd.com/document/84431092/The-California-Endowment-Amicus-Brief-Fact-Sheet

Health Policy Brief: Health insurance exchanges and state decisions. (2013, July 18). *Health Affairs*. Retrieved from www.healthaffairs.org/do/10.1377/hpb20130718.132696/full/

Higuera, V. (2018, Feburary 13). Emergency rooms and urgent care: Costs, treatments, and wait times. *Healthline*. Retrieved from www.healthline.com/health/right-care-right-time/cost-treatment-wait

Hoffman, B. (2008). Health care reform and social movements in the United States. *American Journal of Public Health, 98*(Supplement_1), S69–S79.

Holahan, J., Buettgens, M., Carroll, C., & Dorn, S. (2012). The cost and coverage implications of the ACA Medicaid expansion: National and state by state analysis. *The Henry J. Kaiser Family Foundation: Kaiser Commission on Medicaid and the Uninsured*, 1–61. Retrieved from https://www.kff.org/health-reform/report/the-cost-and-coverage-implications-of-the/

Holahan, J., Buettgens, M., & Dorn, S. (2013). The cost of not expanding Medicaid. *The Henry J. Kaiser Family Foundation: Kaiser Commission on Medicaid and the Uninsured*, 1–24. Retrieved from https://www.kff.org/medicaid/report/the-cost-of-not-expanding-medicaid/

Holtz-Eakin, D. (2004). CBO Testimony: Estimating the cost of the Medicare Modernization Act. *Testimony before the Committee on ways and Means*, U.S. House of Representatives, March 24. Retrieved from www.cbo.gov/sites/default/files/cbofiles/ftpdocs/52xx/doc5252/03-24-medicare.pdf

How they voted: How members of Congress voted on health reform. (2019). *Health Reform Votes*. Retrieved from www.healthreformvotes.org/

Huetteman, E. (2018, August 27). McCain's complicated health care legacy: He hated the ACA. He also saved it. *Kaiser Health News*. Retrieved from https://khn.org/news/mccains-complicated-health-care-legacy-he-hated-the-aca-he-also-saved-it/view/republish/

Hulse, C. (2009, January 20). Obama is sworn in as the 44th President. *The New York Times*. Retrieved from www.nytimes.com/2009/01/21/us/politics/20web-inaug2.html

Izraeli, O., & Folland, S. (2007). State income, employment, infrastructure and well-being: Do party control and political competition matter? *Social Science Research Center*, 1–29. Retrieved from http://dx.doi.org/10.2139/ssrn.899454

Jacobs, L. R., & Callaghan, T. (2013). Why states expand Medicaid: Party, resources, and history. *Journal of Health Politics, Policy, and Law*, *38*, 1023–1050.

Jacobson, G. C. (2011). Legislative success and political failure: The public's reaction to Barack Obama's early presidency. *Presidential Studies Quarterly*, *42*(2). Retrieved from http://onlinelibrary.wiley.com/doi/10.1111/j.1741-5705.2011.03852.x/epdf

Jacobson, L. (2013). What can we learn from New Hampshire politics. *Governing*. Retrieved from www.governing.com/topics/politics/gov-what-we-can-learn-new-hampshire-politics.html

Jeter, A. (2013, November 28). Pay for health insurance, or pay a tax penalty. *The Virginian-Pilot*. Retrieved from: http://hamptonroads.com/2013/11/pay-health-insurance-or-pay-tax-penalty

Johnson, B., & Metzker, B. (2017, February 17). The uncertain affordable care act landscape: What it means for California. *Legislative Analyst's Office*. Retrieved from www.lao.ca.gov/reports/2017/3569/ACA-Landscape-021717.pdf

Johnson, G. W., & Heilman, J. G. (1987). Metapolicy transition and policy implementation: New federalism and privatization. *Public Administration Review*, *47*(5), 468–478.

Johnson, H., & Broder, D. S. (1997). *The system: The American way of politics at the breaking point*. Boston, MA: Little Brown.

Jones, D. K. (2014). *Implementing Obamacare: Intergovernmental battles over the creation of health insurance exchanges*. Ph.D. Dissertation, University of Michigan.

Jones, D. K., Bradley, K. W. V., & Oberlander, J. (2014). Pascal's wager: Health insurance exchanges, Obamacare, and the Republican dilemma. *Journal of Health Politics, Policy and Law*, *39*(1), 97–137.

Jones, J. M., & Reinhart, R. J. (2018). Americans remain dissatisfied with healthcare costs. *Gallup*. Retrieved from https://news.gallup.com/poll/245054/americans-remain-dissatisfied-healthcare-costs.aspx

Jost, T. (2014). Implementing health reform: Four years later. *Health Affairs*, *33*(1), 7–10.

Kaiser Family Foundation. (2009, March). National health insurance: A brief history of reform efforts in the U.S. *The Henry J. Kaiser Family Foundation*. Retrieved from https://kaiserfamilyfoundation.files.wordpress.com/2013/01/7871.pdf

Kaiser Family Foundation. (2011, June 30). Five key questions and answers about section 1115 Medicaid waivers. *Kaiser Family Foundation*. Retrieved from https://kaiserfamilyfoundation.files.wordpress.com/2013/01/8196.pdf

Kaiser Family Foundation. (2012a, July). *A guide to the Supreme Court's Affordable Care Act decision*. Retrieved from https://kaiserfamilyfoundation.files.wordpress.com/2013/01/8332.pdf

Kaiser Family Foundation. (2012b). *Medicaid financing*. Retrieved from https://kaiserfamilyfoundation.files.wordpress.com/2013/01/8352.pdf

Kaiser Family Foundation. (2012c, August). *A guide to the Supreme Court's Affordable Care Act decision*. Retrieved from https://kaiserfamilyfoundation.files.wordpress.com/2013/01/8347.pdf

Kaiser Family Foundation. (2013a). Summary of the Affordable Care Act. *The Henry J. Kaiser Family Foundation: Focus on Health Reform*, 1–13. Retrieved from https://www.kff.org/health-reform/fact-sheet/summary-of-the-affordable-care-act/

Kaiser Family Foundation. (2013b). The impact of the Medicaid expansion for low-income communities of color across states. *The Henry J. Kaiser Family Foundation. Key Facts: Kaiser Commission on Medicaid and the uninsured*, 1–10. Retrieved from https://kaiserfamilyfoundation.files.wordpress.com/2013/04/8435.pdf

Kaiser Family Foundation. (2013c). Analyzing the impact of state Medicaid expansion decisions. *The Henry J. Kaiser Family Foundation: Issue brief: Kaiser Commission on Medicaid and the uninsured*, 1–10. Retrieved from https://kaiserfamilyfoundation.files.wordpress.com/2013/07/8458-analyzing-the-impact-of-state-medicaid-expansion-decisions2.pdf

Kaiser Family Foundation. (2013d). Key facts about the uninsured population. *The Henry J. Kaiser Family Foundation.* Retrieved from https://www.kff.org/uninsured/fact-sheet/key-facts-about-the-uninsured-population/

Kaiser Family Foundation. (2013e). *California's reform efforts.* Retrieved from https://kaiserfamilyfoundation.files.wordpress.com/2013/06/8454-california_s-health-care-environment.pdf

Kaiser Family Foundation. (2013f). *Marketplace profiles.* Retrieved from http://kff.org/health-reform/state-profile/state-exchange-profiles-california/

Kaiser Family Foundation. (2014). How will the uninsured in New Hampshire fare under the Affordable Care Act? *The Henry J. Kaiser Family Foundation.* Retrieved from https://kaiserfamilyfoundation.files.wordpress.com/2013/12/8531-nh.pdf

Kaiser Family Foundation. (2015a). Medicaid expansion in New Hampshire. *The Henry J. Kaiser Family Foundation.* Retrieved from http://files.kff.org/attachment/fact-sheet-medicaid-expansion-in-new-hampshire

Kaiser Family Foundation. (2015b). *California healthcare landscape.* Retrieved from http://kff.org/health-reform/fact-sheet/the-california-health-care-landscape/

Kaiser Family Foundation. (2017, November 8). *State decisions on health insurance marketplaces and the Medicaid expansion.* Retrieved from www.kff.org/health-reform/state-indicator/state-decisions-for-creating-health-insurance-exchanges-and-expanding-medicaid/?currentTimeframe=0&sortModel=%7B%22colId%22:%22Location%22,%22sort%22:%22asc%22%7D

Kaiser Family Foundation. (2018a). *Federal Medical Assistance Percentage (FMAP) for Medicaid and multiplier.* Retrieved from www.kff.org/medicaid/state-indicator/federal-matching-rate-and-multiplier/?currentTimeframe=0&sortModel=%7B%22colId%22:%22Location%22,%22sort%22:%22asc%22%7D

Kaiser Family Foundation. (2018b). The relationship between work and health: Findings from a literature review. *Kaiser Family Foundation.* Retrieved from https://www.kff.org/medicaid/issue-brief/the-relationship-between-work-and-health-findings-from-a-literature-review/

Kaiser Family Foundation. (2018c). *KFF tracking poll: The public's views on the ACA.* Retrieved from www.kff.org/interactive/kaiser-health-tracking-poll-the-publics-views-on-the-aca/#?response=Favorable--Unfavorable&aRange=all

Kaiser Family Foundation. (2019). *Health insurance coverage of the total population: Alabama, 2008–2017.* Retrieved from www.kff.org/other/state-indicator/total-population/?activeTab=graph&currentTimeframe=0&startTimeframe=9&selectedRows=%7B%22states%22:%7B%22alabama%22:%7B%7D%7D%7D&sortModel=%7B%22colId%22:%22Location%22,%22sort%22:%22asc%22%7D

Kardish, C. (2014, December 10). Half of listed Medicaid doctors are unavailable. *Governing: The States and Localities.* Retrieved from www.governing.com/topics/health-human-services/gov-federal-probe-medicaid-doctors.html

Kaufman, J., & Kaliner, M. E. (2011). The re-accomplishment of place in twentieth century Vermont and New Hampshire: History repeats itself, until it doesn't. *Theory and Society*, *40*, 437–460.

Keith, K., & Lucia, K. (2014, January 31). Implementing the Affordable Care Act: The state of the states. *The Commonwealth Fund.* Retrieved from www.commonwealthfund.org/publications/fund-reports/2014/jan/implementing-affordable-care-act-state-states

Kelly, J. (1994). Unfunded mandates: A view from the states. *Public Administration Review*, *54*, 405–408.

Kessler, G. (2012, September 25). When did McConnell say he wanted to make Obama a "one-term president"? *Washington Post.* Retrieved from www.washingtonpost.com/blogs/fact-checker/post/when-did-mcconnell-say-he-wanted-to-make-obama-a-one-term-president/2012/09/24/79fd5cd8–0696–11e2-afff-d6c7f20a83bf_blog.html?utm_term=.0a4fa2a59b18

Key, V. O. (1984 [1949]). *Southern politics in state and nation.* Knoxville, TN: The University of Tennessee Press.

Kieber-Emmons, A. (2011). Medicaid expansion and reform: Hopes and lessons from California. *Health Affairs*. Retrieved from www.healthaffairs.org/do/10.1377/hblog20110714.012160/full/

Kim, H. M., Powell Jr., G. B., & Fording, R. C. (2010). Electoral systems, party systems, and ideological representation: An analysis of distortion in western democracies. *Comparative Politics*, *42*(2), 167–185.

Kingdon, J. (1995). *Agendas, alternatives, and public policies* (2nd ed.). New York, NY: Longman.

Kirby, J. B., & Kaneda, T. (2010). Unhealthy and uninsured: Exploring racial differences in health and health insurance coverage using a life table approach. *Demography*, *47*(4), 1035–1051.

Kizer, G. H., Jr. (n.d.). The road to secession: A detailed chronology of the succession debate in the South, secession of the southern states and beginning of the war between the states, with bibliography. *The Museum of Southern History*. Retrieved from www.museumsouthernhistory.com/

Klemm, J. (2000). Medicaid spending: A brief history. *Health Care Financing Review*, *22*(1), 105–112.

Kousser, T. (2002). The politics of discretionary Medicaid spending, 1980–1993. *Journal of Health Politics, Policy & Law*, *27*(4), 639–671.

Krauthammer, C. (2010, January 15). The fall of Obama. *Real Clear Politics*. Retrieved from www.realclearpolitics.com/articles/2010/01/15/one_year_out_the_fall_99907.html

Kumar, A., & Aizenman, N. C. (2011, September 8). Appeals court dismisses Virginia's health law challenge. *The Washington Post*. Retrieved from www.washingtonpost.com/national/health-science/appeals-court-dismisses-virginias-health-law-challenge/2011/09/08/gIQAB81xCK_story.html?noredirect=on&utm_term=.025504e8631c

Langley, K. (2011, December 15). Spending for healthcare nixed. *Concord Monitor*. Retrieved from www.newhampster.com/2011/12/spending-for-health-exchange-nixed/

Lee, H., & McConville, S. (2011). Expanding Medi-Cal: Profiles of potential new users. *Public Policy Institute of California*. Retrieved from www.ppic.org/content/pubs/report/R_811HLR.pdf

Levin, C. (2011, February 13). Myths behind drive to repeal the Affordable Care Act. *Midland Daily News*. Retrieved from www.ourmidland.com/opinion/editorials/article/Myths-behind-drive-to-repeal-the-Affordable-Care-6947307.php

Levinson, S. (2012). *Framed: America's 51 constitutions and the crisis of governance*. New York, NY: Oxford University Press.

Lindblom, C. E. (1959). The science of muddling through. *Public Administration Review*, *19*(1), 79–88.

Lindblom, C. E. (1982). The market as prison. *Journal of Politics*, *44*, 324–336.

Lindblom, C. E., & Woodhouse, E. J. (1993). *The policy-making process*. Upper Saddle River, NJ: Prentice Hall.

Liptak, A. (2011, November 14). Justices to hear health care case as race heats up. *The New Yorks Times*. Retrieved from www.nytimes.com/2011/11/15/us/supreme-court-to-hear-case-challenging-health-law.html

Litwin, K. (2017, June 8). Top industry in California: Agriculture, tourism, technology are major economic contributors. *Livability*. Retrieved from https://livability.com/ca/business/top-industries-in-california

Long, P., & Gruber, J. (2011). Projecting the impact of the affordable care act on California. *Health Affairs*, *30*(1), 63–70.

Lopez-Sanders, L. (2017). Changing the navigators course: How the increasing rationalization of healthcare influences access for undocumented immigrants under the Affordable Care Act. *Social Science & Medicine*, *178*, 46–54.

Luca, K., Corlette, S., & Williams, A. (2014, November 21). The extended "fix" for canceled health insurance policies: Latest state action. *The Commonwealth Fund Blog*. Retrieved from www.commonwealthfund.org/publications/blog/2014/jun/adoption-of-the-presidents-extended-fix

Lucia, L., Jacobs, K., & Bindman, A. (2017, March 21). Medi-Cal expansion under AHCA: Severe coverage and funding loss unless state backfills billions in federal cuts. *UC Berkeley Labor Center*. Retrieved from http://laborcenter.berkeley.edu/medi-cal-expansion-under-ahca/

Lucia, L., Jacobs, K., Watson, G., Dietz, M., & Roby, D. H. (2013). Medi-Cal expansion under the Affordable Care Act: Significant increase in coverage with minimal cost to the state. *UCLA Center for Health Policy Research*. Retrieved from http://laborcenter.berkeley.edu/pdf/2013/medi-cal_expansion13.pdf

Lynch, J. H. (2012). New Hampshire state of the state address 2012. *Pew Trusts*. Retrieved from www.pewtrusts.org/en/research-and-analysis/blogs/stateline/2012/01/31/new-hampshire-state-of-the-state-address-2012

MacAskill, E. (2010, March 22). Barack Obama's healthcare bill passed by Congress. *The Guardian*. Retrieved from www.theguardian.com/world/2010/mar/22/us-healthcare-bill-passes-congress

MacDonald, C. (2016, May 19). Detroit population rank is the lowest since 1950. *The Detroit News*. Retrieved from www.detroitnews.com/story/news/local/detroit-city/2016/05/19/detroit-population-rank-lowest-since/84574198/

Maetz, M. H. (2013, November 27). A case for elective office term limits. *Birmingham News*, p. 02F. Retrieved from www.al.com/opinion/index.ssf/2013/11/a_case_for_term_limits_opinion_1.html?_wcsid=53A8F7CDC37A0164F9ABE3E5EE14B584FC93B05D27ADEDD9C799B4D811A3D986

Martin, D. L. (1975). *Alabama's state and local governments*. Dubuque, IA: Kendall Hunt.

Mayer, M. K., & Kenter, R. (2014, January). *Southern discomfort: Medicaid expansion in southern states*. Paper presented at the Annual Meetings of the Southern Political Science Association, New Orleans, LA.

Mayer, M. K., Kenter, R., Lucero, L., & Morris, J. C. (2018). State implementation of the Affordable Care Act: Four case studies. *Politics and Policy*, *46*, 1–25.

Mayer, M. K., Kenter, R., & Morris, J. C. (2015). Partisan politics or public health need? An empirical analysis of state choice during initial implementation of the Affordable Care Act. *Politics and the Life Sciences*, *34*(2), 44–51.

Mayer, M. K., Kenter, R., & Morris, J. C. (2016, March). *The evolution of state choices in the Affordable Care Act 2012, 2013, and 2014: An empirical analysis of short-term policy stability*. Paper presented at the biannual Citadel Symposium on Southern Politics, Charleston, SC.

McCluskey, P. D. (2017, December 20). Despite tax bill passing, individual mandate remains in Mass. *Boston Globe*. Retrieved from www.bostonglobe.com/business/2017/12/20/despite-action-congress-mass-individual-mandate-remains/7LuXPvjpQ1VeZMjHCjx5GP/story.html

McGhee, E., & Krimm, D. (2012). California's political geography. *Public Policy Institute of California*. Retrieved from www.ppic.org/publication/californias-political-geography/

McHugh, J. (2013, February 12). Beware of Obamacare gifts—If it sounds too good to be true. You know how it goes. *The Manistee News Advocate*, p. 4A.

Mershon, E. (2018, January 22). Congress delays medical device tax for two years. *STAT*. Retrieved from www.statnews.com/2018/01/22/congress-medical-device-tax/

Michigan State Legislature. (2018). Glossary of legislative terms. *Michigan Legislature*. Retrieved from www.legislature.mi.gov/(S(4z2zfjecdakianepb1x3soyf))/mileg.aspx?page=glossary#T

Michigan Tourism. (2017). *Michigan tourism facts*. Retrieved from https://web.archive.org/web/20161015171535/http://www.michigan.org/michigan-tourism-factsMichigan State Senate. (2018). The first capitol. *Michigan State Senate*. Retrieved from www.senate.michigan.gov/history/capitolhistory.html

Miller, S. (2018, January 23). Health care "Cadillac Tax" delayed until 2022. *Society for Human Resource Management*. Retrieved from www.shrm.org/resourcesandtools/hr-topics/benefits/pages/congress-delays-cadillac-tax-until-2022.aspx

Moody, K. (1997). *Workers in a lean world*. London and New York, NY: Verso Books.

Morris, J. C. (1996). Was Reagan federalism good for business? Privatization and state administrative capacity in the state revolving fund program. *Southeastern Political Review*, *27*(2), 323–340.

Morris, J. C. (1997). The distributional impacts of privatization in national water quality policy. *Journal of Politics*, *59*(1), 56–72.

Mount Washington Observatory. (2018). Mount Washington Observatory: History. *Mount Washington Observatory*. Retrieved from www.mountwashington.org/about-us/history/default.aspx

Murray, S., & Montgomery, L. (2009, December 25). Senate passes health-care bill, now must reconcile it with house. *The Washington Post*. Retrieved from www.washingtonpost.com/wp-dyn/content/article/2009/12/24/AR2009122400662.html?sid=ST2009122400904

Musumeci, M. B., Rudowitz, R., Ubri, P., & Hinton, E. (2017). An early look at Medicaid expansion waiver implementation in Michigan and Indiana. *Kaiser Family Foundation*. Retrieved from www.kff.org/medicaid/issue-brief/an-early-look-at-medicaid-expansion-waiver-implementation-in-michigan-and-indiana/

Nathan, R. P., & Doolittle, F. C. (1984). The untold story of Reagan's "New Federalism". *Public Interest*, *77*, 96–105.

National Conference of State Legislatures. (2015). *State laws and actions challenging certain health reforms*. Retrieved from www.ncsl.org/research/health/state-laws-and-actions-challenging-ppaca.aspx

National Conference of State Legislatures. (2018). *2018 State & legislative partisan composition*. Retrieved from www.ncsl.org/Portals/1/Documents/Elections/Post_Election_Legis_Control_2018_December_10th.pdf

National Conference of State Legislatures. (2017). *State & legislative partisan composition (2016 election)*. Retrieved from www.ncsl.org/portals/1/documents/elections/Legis_Control_2016_Post12_28_2pm.pdf

National Federation of Independent Business v. Sebelius, 567 U.S.__, 132 S. Ct. 2566 (2012).

Neff, D. (2013). Fuzzy set theoretic applications in poverty research. *Policy and Society*, *32*(4), 319–331.

New Hampshire Legislature. (2011). House Bill 601. *New Hampshire Legislature Session 2011*. Retrieved from http://www.gencourt.state.nh.us/legislation/2011/HB0601.html

New Hampshire Department of State. (1977). *A history of the state house, New Hampshire almanac*. Retrieved from www.nh.gov/almanac/state-house.htm

New Hampshire Executive Council. (2018). *The history of the Executive Council. New Hampshire Executive Council*. Retrieved from www.nh.gov/council/history/index.htm

New Hampshire Insurance Department. (2014a). *New Hampshire health insurance marketplace plan information*. Retrieved from http://web.archive.org/web/20140712223130/www.nh.gov/insurance/consumers/anthem_mp_plans.htm

New Hampshire Insurance Department. (2014b). *NHID's revised request for findings of fact and rulings of law in re: Petition of Margaret McCarthy, Docket No. Ins. 13-038-AP*. Retrieved from www.nh.gov/insurance/legal/documents/anth_ph_fof_rol_060414.pdf

New Hampshire Insurance Department. (2018). *About us*. Retrieved from www.nh.gov/insurance/aboutus/index.htm

New Hampshire Legislature. (2012). HB 1297: An act relative to federal health care reform and health care exchanges. *New Hampshire Legislature 2012 Session*. Retrieved from www.gencourt.state.nh.us/legislation/2012/HB1297.html

Notable Representations. (2018). Kathleen M. Sullivan. *Quinn Emanuel Trial Lawyers: Quinn, Emanuel, Urquhardt, & Sullivan*. Retrieved from www.quinnemanuel.com/attorneys/sullivan-kathleen-m

Oberlander, J. (2012). Unfinished journey—a century of health care reform in the United States. *New England Journal of Medicine*, *367*(7), 585–590.

Oberlander, J. (2016). Implementing the Affordable Care Act: The promise and limits of health care reform. *Journal of Health Politics, Policy and Law*, *41*(4), 803–826.

Office of Planning and Evaluation. (2015, March 1). Federal medical assistance percentages or federal financial participation in state assistance expenditures FMAP. *U.S. Department of Health & Human Services*. Retrieved from https://aspe.hhs.gov/federal-medical-assistance-percentages-or-federal-financial-participation-state-assistance-expenditures

Oosting, J. (2013, September 1). Despite vote, GOP still really hates Obamacare. *The Flint Journal*. Retrieved from www.mlive.com/politics/index.ssf/2013/08/michigan_republicans_for_medic.html

Orndorff, M. (2011, January 20). One from state votes against repeal. *Birmingham News*, p. 8A.

Orndorff, M. (2012a, March 28). Alabama opposes Medicaid growth: Strange, others worry about rising costs. *Birmingham News*, p. 1A.

Orndorff, M. (2012b, February 14). Bentley says plan may not work: Says insurance idea too complex. *Birmingham News*, p. 1–C.

Pecquet, J. (2011). President embraces ObamaCare label. *The Hill*. Retrieved from http://thehill.com/policy/healthcare/185877-president-embraces-obamacare-label

Pelofsky, J. (2010, October 7). US judge upholds key part of Obama healthcare law. *Reuters*. Retrieved from www.reuters.com/article/obama-healthcare-michigan/us-judge-upholds-key-part-of-obama-healthcare-law-idUSN0716698320101007

Perrin, M. (2009). AG Troy King, Gov. Bob Riley spar over bingo report. *Birmingham News*. Retrieved from http://blog.al.com/spotnews/2009/06/ag_troy_king_gov_bob_riley_spa.html

Pew Charitable Trust. (2007, March 9). Massachusetts Governor rated most powerful. *Pew Charitable Trusts*. Retrieved from www.pewtrusts.org/en/research-and-analysis/blogs/stateline/2007/03/09/massachusetts-gov-rated-most-powerful

PoliData. (2014). *Party control project*. Retrieved from www.polidata.org/party/default.htm

Posner, P. L. (1997). Unfunded Mandates Reform Act: 1996 and beyond. *Publius: The Journal of Federalism*, *27*(2), 53–71.

Quadagno, J. (2014). Right-wing conspiracy? Socialist plot? The origins of the Patient Protection and Affordable Care Act. *Journal of Health Politics, Policy and Law*, *39*(1), 35–56.

Quaile-Hill, K., Leighley, J. E., & Hinton-Anderson, A. (1995). Lower class mobilization and policy linkage in the United States. *American Journal of Political Science*, *39*(1), 75–86.

Quay, J. (2014). Beyond dreams and disappointment: Defining California through culture. In W. Deverell & D. Igler (Eds.), *A companion to California history* (pp. 3–21). Malden, MA: Wiley Blackwell.

Ramer, H. (2013, September 26). Exchange prices in N.H. a bit higher. *Valley News*. Retrieved from www.vnews.com/Archives/2013/09/NH-HealthOverhaul-vn-092613

Ranaivo, Y. (2013, December 12). Alabama groups come together to back Medicaid enrollment. *Birmingham Business Journal*. Retrieved from www.bizjournals.com/birmingham/news/2013/12/11/alabama-groups-come-together-to-back.html

RAND. (2019). *RAND health reform opinion study*. Retrieved from www.rand.org/health-care/projects/health-reform-opinion.html#changes-in-opinion

Rawls, P. (2013a, September 27). *Alabama governor warns against federal shutdown*. AP Regional State Report. AP Newswires, Accession Number APa4f36d67dc914b7ea5083168371bca92.

Rawls, P. (2013b, December 17). *Ala. Governor says he's not behind pension change*. AP Regional State report, Alabama. Accession Number: APe636eecd10994d7abf13c359525ba6a9.

Reich, D., & Kogan, R. (2016, November 9). Introduction to budget "reconciliation". *Center on Budget and Policy Priorities*. Retrieved from www.cbpp.org/research/federal-budget/introduction-to-budget-reconciliation

Reilly, P. J. (2011, August 17). Key part of Obamacare unconstitutional—Eleventh Circuit rules. *Forbes*. Retrieved from www.forbes.com/sites/peterjreilly/2011/08/17/key-part-of-obamacare-unconstitutional-eleventh-circuit-rules/#329ff4547a15

Richardson, L. E., & Yilmazer, T. (2013). Understanding the impact of health reform on the states: Expansion of coverage through Medicaid and exchanges. *Journal of Consumer Affairs*, *47*(2), 191–218.

Rigby, E. (2012). State resistance to "Obamacare". *The Forum*, *10*(2), 1540–8884.

Rigby, E., & Haselswerdt, J. (2013). Hybrid federalism, partisan politics, and early implementation of state health insurance exchanges. *Publius: The Journal of Federalism*, *43*(3), 368–391.

Roberts, C. (2012). Dynamics of healthcare reform: Bitter pills, old and new. *Vanderbilt Journal of Transnational Law*, *45*, 1341–1380.

Robeznieks, A. (2013). California's give and take. *Modern Healthcare*, *43*(3).

Rockefeller Institute. (2014). *Alabama: Round 1: State-level field network study of the implementation of the Affordable Care Act*. Albany, NY: Author.

Rockefeller Institute. (2015). *New Hampshire baseline report*. Albany, NY: Author.

Rosenbaum, S. (2011). The Patient Protection and Affordable Care Act: Implications for public health policy and practice. *Public Health Reports*, *126*(1), 130–135.

Rosenbaum, S., & Westmoreland, T. M. (2012). The Supreme Court's surprising decision on the Medicaid expansion: How will the federal government and states proceed? *Health Affairs*, *31*(8). Retrieved from www.healthaffairs.org/doi/full/10.1377/hlthaff.2012.0766

Ross, R. K. (2012, February 1). Why a California foundation filed an amicus brief with the U.S. Supreme Court. *Health Affairs Blog*. Retrieved from www.healthaffairs.org/do/10.1377/hblog20120201.016665/full/

Ross, R. K. (2018). Authors. *Governing*. Retrieved from www.governing.com/authors/Robert-K-Ross.html

Roy, A. (2013, October 31). Obama officials in 2010: 93 million Americans will be unable to keep their health plans under Obamacare. *Forbes*. Retrieved from www.forbes.com/sites/theapothecary/2013/10/31/obama-officials-in-2010-93-million-americans-will-be-unable-to-keep-their-health-plans-under-obamacare/#15ed40f823a9

Salam, R. (2013, November 8). Obama's apology (of sorts) for his "keep your plan" promise. *Reuters*. Retrieved from http://blogs.reuters.com/reihan-salam/2013/11/08/obamas-apology-of-sorts-for-his-keep-your-plan-promise/

Sallee, C. M., Rosaen, A. L., & Anderson, P. L. (2007, May 7). The economic impact of Michigan State University. *Anderson Economic Group*. Retrieved from https://www.andersoneconomicgroup.com/Portals/0/upload/Doc2117.pdf

Sanders, B. (2017, March 2). Questions proliferate over health care in NH. *NH Business Review*. Retrieved from www.nhbr.com/March-3-2017/Questions-proliferate-over-health-care-in-NH/

Savage, R. L. (1981). Looking for political subcultures: A critique of the rummage-sale approach. *Western Political Quarterly*, *43*, 331–336.

Savas, E. S. (1987). *Privatization: The key to better government*. Chatham, NJ: Chatham.

Scheffler, R. M., Kessell, E., & Brandt, M. (2015). Covered California: The impact of provider and health plan market power on premiums. *Journal of Health Politics, Policy, and Law*, *40*(6), 1179–1202.

Schier, S. E., & Eberly, T. E. (2017). *The Trump presidency: Outsider in the Oval Office*. Lanham, MD: Rowman & Littlefield.

Schlesinger, J. A. (1965). The politics of the executive. In H. Jacob & K. N. Vines (Eds.), *Politics in the American states*. Boston, MA: Little, Brown.

Schoen, C., Doty, M. M., Robertson, R. H., & Collins, S. R. (2011). Affordable Care Act reforms could reduce the number of underinsured US adults by 70 percent. *Health Affairs*, *30*(9), 1762–1771.

Seipel, T., & Calefati, J. (2013, November 21). California's health exchange spurns Obama directive. *The Mercury News*. Retrieved from www.mercurynews.com/2013/11/21/californias-health-exchange-spurns-obama-directive/

Seipel, T., & Calefati, J. (2015, August 26). Obamacare: Poll shows rising support throughout California. *The Mercury News*. Retrieved from www.mercurynews.com/2015/08/26/obamacare-poll-shows-rising-support-throughout-california/

Sekaran, N. (2012, June 29). Deciding Michigan's Medicaid future. *Michigan Radio Newsroom*. Retrieved from http://michiganradio.org/post/deciding-michigan-medicaids-future

Sellek, J., & Yearout, J. (2010, May 14). Cox joined by NFIB and seven more states in suit challenging national healthcare law. *State of Michigan: Michigan.gov*. Retrieved from www.michigan.gov/som/0,4669,7-192-237032--RSS,00.html

Semuels, A. (2012, March 23). Romney vows to repeal and replace "Obamacare" on law's anniversary. *Los Angeles Times*. Retrieved from http://articles.latimes.com/2012/mar/23/news/la-pn-romney-healthcare-anniversary-20120323

Sharkansky, I. (1969). The utility of Elazar's political culture: A research note. *Polity, 2*, 66–83.

Silicon Valley. (2011, March). About Silicon Valley. *ICANN*. Retrieved from https://archive.icann.org/en/meetings/siliconvalley2011/index.html

Sims, B. (2009, May 13). *U.S. Attorney General seeks records from Alabama attorney General Troy King in wide-ranging subpoena* [Web log post]. Retrieved from http://blog.al.com/spotnews/2009/05/us_attorney_seeks_records_from.html

Skocpol, T. (1996). *Boomerang: Health care reform and the turn against government*. New York, NY: Norton.

Skocpol, T., & Jacobs, L. R. (2012). Accomplished and embattled: Understanding Obama's presidency. *Political Science Quarterly, 127*(1), 1–24.

Smith, D., & Moore, J. (2008). *Medicaid politics and policy: 1965–2007*. New Brunswick and London: Transaction Publishers.

Smith, E. (2012, June 28). Timeline of the health care law. *CNN Politics*. Retrieved from www.cnn.com/2012/06/28/politics/supreme-court-health-timeline/index.html

Snyder, R. (2012, July 3). Governors blog: Why we must act now in healthcare. *State of Michigan*. Retrieved from www.michigan.gov/snyder/0,4668,7-277-57577_60279-281739--,00.html

Snyder, R. (2013, January 22). Michigan's intent to participate in a state partnership exchange for 2014. *Correspondence With HHS Secretary Sebelius*.

Solomon, D. (2018, May 8). Feds OK work requirement for expanded Medicare. *New Hampshire: Union Leader*. Retrieved from www.unionleader.com/health/Feds-OK-work-requirement-for-expanded-Medicaid-05072018

Soss, J., Schram, S. F., Vartanian, T. P., & O'Brien, E. (2001). Setting the terms of relief: Explaining state policy choices in the devolution revolution. *American Journal of Political Science, 42*(2), 378–395.

Spangler, T. (2010, March 25). Police will increase patrols around Stupak's home. *Detroit Free Press*. Retrieved from

Spencer, T. (2011). Health system cost to be $50M: Alabama among 26 states challenging federal mandate. *Birmingham News*, p. 1–C.

Starr, P. (1982). *The social transformation of American medicine*. New York, NY: Basic Books.

Starr, P. (2013). *Remedy and reaction: The peculiar American struggle over health care reform*. New Haven, CT: Yale University Press.

State of California. (2018). *Living in California*. Retrieved from www.ca.gov/Living

Steger, W. P., Dowdle, A. J., & Adkins, R. E. (2004). The New Hampshire effect in presidential nominations. *Political Research Quarterly, 57*(3), 375–390.

Stein, K. (2013). Protest march set for Medicaid expansion. *Birmingham News*, p. 11A.

Stock, K., Udow-Phillips, M., Ogundimu, T., & Ehrlich, E. (2010, June 21). Cover Michigan 2010: The State of Healthcare Coverage in Michigan. *Center for Healthcare*

Research and Transformation. Retrieved from www.chrt.org/publication/cover-michigan-2010-state-health-care-coverage-michigan/

Stolberg, S. G. (2009, June 6). Obama to forge a greater role on health care. *The New York Times*. Retrieved from www.nytimes.com/2009/06/07/us/politics/07policy.html

Stone, D. (1997). *Policy paradox: The art of political decision making*. New York, NY: Norton Publishers.

Stone, D. (2008). *The samaritan's dilemma: Should government help your neighbor?* New York, NY: Nation Books.

Swidwa, J., & Matuszak, J. (2012, June 29). Health ruling: Bitter pill or what the doctor ordered? Area health officials describe pluses, minuses in Obamacare. *The Herald Palladium*. Retrieved from www.heraldpalladium.com/localnews/health-ruling-bitter-pill-or-what-the-doctor-ordered/article_f5a39880-30e0-5d87–854c-a7cdcdac925b.html

Talbot, G. (2010, October 17). Robert Bentley campaign leaned on AEA to defeat Bradley Byrne. *The Birmingham News*. Retrieved from http://blog.al.com/live/2010/10/robert_bentley_campaign_leaned.html

Terhune, C. (2015, December 9). California's 3 largest health insurers among few to show Obamacare profit in 2014. *Los Angeles Times*. Retrieved from www.latimes.com/business/la-fi-obamacare-profits-20151209-story.html

Thomas More Law Center. (2018). Battle ready to defend America. *Thomas More Law Center*. Retrieved from www.thomasmore.org/

Travis, R., Morris, E., & Morris, J. C. (2004). State implementation of federal environmental policy: Explaining leveraging in the Clean Water State Revolving Fund. *Policy Studies Journal*, *32*(3), 461–480.

Travis, R., Morris, J. C., Mayer, M. K., Kenter, R., & Breaux, D. A. (2016). Explaining differences in the implementation of the Affordable Care Act: A South/ non-South comparison. *Social Science Quarterly*, *97*(3), 573–587.

Tu, H. T., Carrier, E., Lechner, A., & Draper, K. (2013). *Alabama's pass on Medicaid expansion leaves Birmingham's uninsured with weak safety net*. Princeton, NJ: Robert Wood Johnson Foundation.

Tumulty, K. (2010, March 23). Making history: House passes health care reform. *Time*. Retrieved from http://content.time.com/time/politics/article/0,8599,1973989,00.html

Tuohy, C. H. (2011). American health reform in comparative perspective: Big bang, blueprint, or mosaic? *Journal of Health Politics, Policy and Law*, *36*(3), 571–576.

United Health Foundation. (2019a). *America's health rankings, annual report 2018*. Retrieved from www.americashealthrankings.org/explore/annual/measure/Overall/state/AL

United Health Foundation. (2019b). *America's health rankings, 2017 annual report: Healthiest states*. Retrieved from www.americashealthrankings.org/learn/reports/2017-annual-report/findings-state-rankings

United Press International (UPI). (2010, October 7). *Lawsuit challenging healthcare law tossed*. Retrieved from www.upi.com/Top_News/US/2010/10/07/Lawsuit-challenging-healthcare-law-tossed/67471286506376/

U.S. Census Bureau. (2010). *Decennial census of population and housing*. Retrieved from www.census.gov/programs-surveys/decennial-census/decade.2010.html

U.S. Census Bureau. (2018). *Quick facts New Hampshire population estimates July 1, 2018*. Retrieved from www.census.gov/quickfacts/fact/table/nh/PST045218#PST045218

U.S. Department of Health and Human Services (HHS). (n.d.). *A brief history of the AFDC program*. Retrieved from https://aspe.hhs.gov/system/files/pdf/167036/1history.pdf

U.S. Department of Health and Human Services (HHS). (2013). *Health insurance marketplace: December enrollment report, for the period October 1–November 30.* Washington, DC: HHS, Office of the Assistant Secretary for Planning and Evaluation.

U.S. Department of Health and Human Services (HHS). (2017). *Health care*. Retrieved from www.hhs.gov/healthcare/about-the-aca/benefit-limits/index.html

Vavreck, L., Spiliotes, C. J., & Fowler, L. L. (2002). The effects of retail politics in the New Hampshire primary. *American Journal of Political Science, 46(3)*, 595–610.

Verma, S. (2018, May 7). Letter to Henry Lipman New Hampshire Medicaid director approving New Hampshire's Section 1115 Medicaid expansion waiver. *Department of Health and Human Services*. Retrieved from www.governor.nh.gov/news-media/press-2018/documents/20180507-work-requirements.pdf

Vlasic, B. (2011). *Once upon a car: The fall and resurrection of America's big three auto makers-GM, Ford, and Chrysler*. New York, NY: William Morrow.

Vollers, A. C. (2017, July 3). Alabama is 6th poorest state in nation; poverty rate at 40 percent in some counties. *AL.com*. Retrieved from www.al.com/news/index.ssf/2017/07/alabama_is_6th_poorest_state_i.html

Walsh, A. (2013). Behind Alabama's big blue: The health insurance giant with the power to tell Obama "no". *The Birmingham News*. Retrieved from http://blog.al.com/wire/2013/12/behind_alabamas_big_blue_the_h.html

Walters, D. (2015, June 25). Census bureau report shows California diversity. *The Sacramento Bee*. Retrieved from www.sacbee.com/news/politics-government/capitol-alert/article25485157.html

Wang, J., & Trivedi, A. N. (2017). Enrollment in California's Medicaid program after the Affordable Care Act expansion. *American Journal of Public Health, 107*(11), 1757–1759.

Weinberg, M., & Kallerman, P. (2017). ACA exchange competitiveness in California. *Risk Management and Insurance Review, 20*(2), 173–188.

Weinberg, M., Kallerman, P., & Carhart, A. (2014). California: State-level field network study of the Implementation of the Affordable Care Act. *The Nelson A. Rockefeller Institute of Government*. Retrieved from www.rockinst.org

White, D. (2011, June 10). State to vote on health care opt-out to be on 2012 ballot. *Birmingham News*, p. 10A.

White, E. (2012). The Anti-Injunction Act: What it is and how it could impact Obamacare. *American Center for Law and Justice*. Retrieved from https://aclj.org/obamacare/anti-injunction-act-could-impact-obamacare

Wilkinson, R. G., & Marmot, M. G. (2003). *Social determinants of health: The solid facts* (2nd ed.). Copenhagen: World Health Organization.

Williamson, D. E. (2013). *Report on the Alabama Medicaid Advisory Commission*. Montgomery, AL: Alabama Medicaid Advisory Commission.

Woodward, J. D. (2013). *The new southern politics* (2nd ed.). Boulder, CO: Lynn Reiner.

Word, R. (2010, March 24). McCollum leads effort to sue over health law. *Gainesville Sun*, p. B1.

WSFA-TV. (2012, May 3). Governor promises veto of insurance exchange bill. *WFSA.com* [Web log post]. Retrieved from www.wsfa.com/story/18075972/governor-promises-veto-of-insurance-exchange-bill/

Yin, R. K. (1994). *Case study research: Design and methods* (2nd ed.). Thousand Oaks, CA: Sage.

York, A. (2010, December 31). Schwarzenegger names Susan Kennedy to top health-care post. *Los Angeles Times*. Retrieved from http://latimesblogs.latimes.com/

california-politics/2010/12/schwarzenegger-names-susan-kennedy-to-top-health-care-post.html

Young, J. (2013, February 7). Snyder backs major Obamacare initiative. *The Huffington Post*. Retrieved from www.huffingtonpost.com/jeffrey-young/michigan-medicaid-expansi_b_2631367.html?utm_hp_ref=detroit&ir=Detroit&ec_carp=4591074409059806745

About the Authors

Robert C. Kenter is an adjunct assistant professor of public administration at the School of Public Service, Old Dominion University and a 30-year veteran of the Norfolk Police Department; he currently works in the Office of Special Projects as a policy and data analyst. He holds a PhD in public administration from Old Dominion University; an MPA from Troy University, Troy, Alabama; and a BA in sociology from East Stroudsburg University, East Stroudsburg, Pennsylvania. His previous work has been published in *Social Science Quarterly*, *Politics and the Life Sciences*, *Politics and Policy*, and *Police Chief*. Additionally, he has coauthored book chapters in *Prison Privatization: The Many Facets of a Controversial Industry*, *Advancing Collaboration Theory: Models, Typologies and Evidence*, and *The Global Encyclopedia of Public Administration and Public Policy*. His current research interests include collaboration, privatization, southern politics, and procedural justice.

Luisa M. Lucero is a lecturer in the College of Health Sciences at Old Dominion University. She holds the PhD from the School of Public Service at Old Dominion University. Luisa has contributed to work that appears in the journal *Politics and Policy*, and her current research interests include obesity policy and health-related policy design. She has worked with the Sentara Foundation as a grant consultant and the City of Norfolk as an administrative analyst. She received her Master's of Arts in Political Science in 2011 from the University of Guelph and an undergraduate degree from Mansfield University in 2009, double majoring in philosophy and political science and minoring in biology.

Martin K. Mayer is a visiting assistant professor of public administration at the University of North Carolina at Pembroke. He holds the PhD in public administration from Old Dominion University in Norfolk, Virginia. Prior to that, he earned degrees in public administration and political science from The University of Akron. His previous work is centered primarily on decision-making and resource scarcity in the domains of health policy, local government, and transportation finance. He has contributed book chapters to several projects and his journal publications appear in *Social Science Quarterly*, *Politics & Policy*, *The Social Science Journal*, and *Politics and the Life*

Sciences, among others. His current research interests include health policy, sustainable development, and collaboration.

John C. Morris is a professor of public administration and public policy in the School of Public Service and holds a joint appointment as a professor of political science in the Department of Political Science and Geography at Old Dominion University in Norfolk, Virginia. He holds a PhD in political science and public policy from Auburn University. He has published widely in the fields of public administration and public policy. He is the lead author (with William A. Gibson, William M. Leavitt, and Shana C. Jones) of *The Case for Grassroots Collaboration: Social Capital and Ecosystem Restoration at the Local Level* (2013). He is the coeditor (with Katrina Miller-Stevens) of *Advancing Collaboration Theory: Models, Typologies, and Evidence* (Routledge Press, 2016); *Speaking Green With a Southern Accent: Environmental Management and Innovation in the South* (2010, with Gerald A. Emison); and *True Green: Executive Effectiveness in the US Environmental Protection Agency* (2012, with Gerald A. Emison). Professor Morris is also the coeditor (with Douglas Watson) of *Building the Local Economy: Cases in Economic Development* (2008) and is the coeditor (with Byron E. Price) of *Prison Privatization: The Many Facets of a Controversial Industry*, a three-volume set published by Praeger (2012). His most recent book is entitled *Organizational Motivation for Collaboration: Theory and Evidence*, written with Luisa Diaz-Kope (forthcoming, 2019). His journal publications appear in the *Journal of Politics*, *Public Administration Review*, *Policy Studies Journal*, *State & Local Government Review*, *Publius*, *Politics & Policy*, and *Public Works Management & Policy*, among others. His current research interests include collaboration, environmental policy, and federalism.

Index

For Product Safety Concerns and Information please contact our EU
representative GPSR@taylorandfrancis.com
Taylor & Francis Verlag GmbH, Kaufingerstraße 24, 80331 München, Germany

www.ingramcontent.com/pod-product-compliance
Ingram Content Group UK Ltd.
Pitfield, Milton Keynes, MK11 3LW, UK
UKHW021300190926
475701UK00009B/92
9781032091969